The colour of summer's gone,
Of golden days when I was young,
Of girls who came but soon moved on.
Is in my summer wine.

The perfumes of earth and vine,
Of meadows when the rain has gone,
Of women with their finery on.
Is in my summer wine.

The memories I can see,
Here in my cup,
Of sweet short days, bitter days,
Now all drunk up.

The taste of the life that slips,
From day to day through fingers blind,
The honey from the woman's lips,
Is in my summer wine.

Lyrics to Last of the Summer Wine
By Roy Clarke

Did I really play Clegg in *Last of the Summer Wine* for thirty-seven years? Goodness me. I wouldn't say that Alan J W Bell was instantly popular with the actors, as he had this obsession for laying tracks everywhere for the camera, and giving us marks on the ground where we had to stand – or else. But we must have got used to him, for I see that we allowed him to stay with the series for two hundred and fifty episodes (so, he's not such a bad chap, really). In truth, I can say that the series would never have run for so long without Alan's tireless energy and enthusiasm in faithfully bringing Roy Clarke's scripts to the screen.

Did we really make two hundred and eighty-four episodes?

Peter Sallis

It was a privilege to work with such a wise and creative director as Alan Bell. He had the gift of lifting Roy Clarke's wonderful writing off the page bringing it to life. He would capture stunning and beautiful backgrounds and place the actors in front where he would bring out the best performances in us all. He knew every scene; he made them warm and he made them funny. His work was a joy to watch - great fun for all ages. Thank you Alan, I would say you were "The *Best* of the Summer Wine".

Russ Abbot

The legendary Alan J W Bell directed two of the *Ripping Yarns*. He will say they were the best two, and few would disagree with him, owing to his powerful muscular build and violently aggressive tendencies. I actually think they were pretty good, and I very much enjoyed working with him – despite his powerful muscular build and violently aggressive tendencies. What I liked about Alan was that he was always prepared to spend as much of the BBC's money as possible. Both Terry and myself felt it very important that *Ripping Yarns* looked like small cinema films and Alan was definitely up for this. Whether footballing in Yorkshire or driving perilously close to the cliff edge in Cornwall, he helped make Light Entertainment look like drama and we are both very much indebted to him for this.

Can I go now please, Alan. You're hurting my arm!

Michael Palin

Alan produced and directed *Last of the Summer Wine* for 29 years, and his account of that time is a MUST READ for all Summer Wine lovers.

Alan's knowledgeable direction and ability to discover so many beautiful locations in Yorkshire created a great atmosphere in which to work. He was, like all of us, surprised and disappointed when some "new blood" at the BBC decided to cancel a show which gave such pleasure to millions of viewers all over the world.

June Whitfield

Foggy, Compo and Clegg in Bicycle Bonanza (1995)

Last of the Summer Wine
From the Director's Chair

by Producer and Director
Alan J W Bell

First published in 2012 by

Tomahawk Press
PO Box 1236
Sheffield S11 7XU
England
www.tomahawkpress.com

© Alan J W Bell 2012

The right of Alan J W Bell to be identified as the author of this work is hereby asserted in accordance with the Copyright, Designs and Patents Act 1988.

All rights reserved. No part of this publication may be reproduced or transmitted in any form or by any means, electronic or mechanical, including photocopy, recording, or other information retrieval system, without permission in writing from the publisher.

ISBN 13: 978-0-9566834-2-7

Proofread by Kenneth Bishton
Edited by Bruce Sachs
Designed by Tree Frog Communication – 01245 445377
Printed in England

All photographs used in this book are © Alan J W Bell with acknowledgement to Malcolm Howarth

LAST OF THE SUMMER WINE is © BBC Television

To my wife Constance and my daughter Cheraine

Introduction

It seemed that I had no sooner completed the first television series of *The Hitchhiker's Guide to the Galaxy* (1981), when that spring I was given the sixth series of *Last of the Summer Wine* to produce and direct. I suppose it was obvious that my treatment of those Galactic adventures was exactly what was needed for a gentle series about three elderly gentlemen wandering around the Yorkshire countryside.

Little did I know then that, 29 years later, I would still be making *Last of the Summer Wine* for the British Broadcasting Corporation, and that, as a career move, it had failed miserably. Well, in truth, not at all miserably – for although I had got myself into a sort of rut, it was a hugely enjoyable rut.

I was the fourth producer to be charged with making what would become a milestone in the history of television comedy. For 38 years, *Last of the Summer Wine* had a large and enthusiastic following, and holds the record as the longest-running situation comedy series in the world. Even the hugely successful Lucille Ball series in America (in three different formats) only ran for 18 years. And besides that formidable record, each and every one of the 284 scripts was written by only one man – Roy Clarke – who, in my opinion, is the finest writer of comedy in the history of television.

In my telling of the background to making some of the 250 episodes of *Last of the Summer Wine* that I personally produced and directed, there are quite a few instances where I took Roy's

Truly, Alvin and Clegg at Yateholme Reservoir

funny ideas and adjusted them to make them visually stronger or, sometimes, just to make them practical to film. It is easy to improve an idea, but the hard bit is writing the scripts initially - which Roy Clarke did with all the confidence and ease of a master craftsman. Roy keenly protected his work from interference, and any of my suggestions (mostly visual) that were used were always with the consent of that master of comedy. However, I have to confess that it gives me a great deal of personal pleasure to hear someone say that they especially liked the episode 'where a mangle demolished a police car' or 'when Compo was in a home-made submarine.'

The fact is that visual comedy is always more memorable than the words, but - without any doubt whatsoever – it is the strength of Roy Clarke's funny scripts that kept the series so popular and fresh for nearly 40 years with young and old alike.

I have always considered it an honour to have produced a comedy series that was described in *The Daily Telegraph* in 1996 as being the favourite programme of none other than Her Majesty the Queen:

'Those who come down for dinner at Sandringham before the titles have rolled are warned not to blunder into the drawing room where she is watching it.'

However, it always puzzled the cast that, shortly after this Royal accolade was published, the Queen made an official visit to the BBC, whereupon she was taken to meet the cast of the ever-popular serial – *EastEnders*. Somehow, I just can't imagine Her Majesty bolting the doors to her drawing room to enjoy the latest squabble at the local Laundromat – as engrossing as it may be. Of course, it is possible that Her Majesty was pleased that *EastEnders* honoured her great ancestor by naming its local public house The Queen Victoria.

It has to be accepted that, in recent years, there was always a faction within the BBC that resented the brilliance of those creative executive producers way back in 1972 (namely Duncan Wood and Bill Cotton) who commissioned Roy Clarke - not yet a comedy writer - to write a series about three older men in their second youth, and their spirited exploits in the countryside. Never before and I doubt if ever again, has there been a comedy series which was so popular for so long.

May I say straight away that I have a story-telling problem here. Quite a few years ago, I had no sooner given a young female Production Manager the opportunity to direct a new Lynn Redgrave series when she asked "Why do all your stories glorify you?" Overlooking the impertinence of the question (she could at least have said 'funny' or 'interesting' stories), I took the criticism very much to heart, and resolved to avoid any trace of self-praise in future. However, when I started to write this book, I soon realised that, if I did, I would only have enough material to fill a small brochure. But I will certainly do my very best not to go too far with the self glorification.

This isn't an autobiography, and because I don't keep a diary, the accuracy of dates isn't guaranteed. Neither is it a compendium of facts and figures - they can be found elsewhere. It is simply my recollections of making a very special television series for 29 of my 52 years working in television.

I began when there were only two television channels in the United Kingdom – BBC and ITV (Independent Television) – and ended in the present digital age, where the airwaves are choked with hundreds of impoverished channels, and the BBC has become simply a commissioning house with no creative craft staff of its own. As Ronnie Hazlehurst, the late musical director of *Last of the Summer Wine* observed not so long ago: "We had the best years."

Because long-running series aren't produced continuously (there are usually gaps of six or seven months between them), my story threads may, sometimes, appear to be anachronistic. And because this isn't going to be an opportunity to wreak revenge on those poor souls at the BBC who didn't recognise the quality of the series – and who, sometimes, actually hindered its success - I shall avoid mentioning some names.

Inevitably, a few recollections may glorify me, but I really am going to try very hard to balance them with those that don't – as near impossible as that is going to be.

CHAPTER 1

The Axe Woman Cometh

Monday, 15th December 2008 wasn't a particularly significant date in the 38-year history of *Last of the Summer Wine* other than the fact that it was the final stage in the production of that year's series. I was in a small dubbing theatre in a remote building at Shepperton Studios where the additional sounds for feature films (footsteps, voices, etc.) are usually recorded. But it was being used this time to add the laughter track to our finished programmes.

This laughter track had been recorded a few weeks earlier at Teddington Studios when a 'house full' audience of 360 had watched the episodes on a large cinema-sized screen. And here I was, now, with Paul Gartrell, the sound mixer, carefully balancing the volume of the laughter with the original soundtrack. Not just adding the recorded laughter, but removing it when it was intrusive. For some reason, the otherwise well-informed *Radio Times* described the results of this quite expensive procedure as 'canned laughter' – it never was.

Also at the dubbing theatre that afternoon was Simone Dawson, our First Assistant Director who, besides being a driving force on the filming, was also in every way enthusiastic and loyal to the series. Much of the success of the filming was due to the organisational skills of Simone. Purely out of interest in her work, she had travelled the hundred or so miles from her home in Wales to attend this final stage of the production, just to see and enjoy the finalised programmes – complete with titles and a good soundtrack.

But there was more interest in the finished programmes than usual, for they marked a significant change in the series: A change that was more fundamental than the death of Bill Owen had been nearly ten years before – when, in mid-series, he played Compo for the very last time. Then, Bill's illness and ultimate death had forced a new era upon the series – an era without Compo, who had been the programme's most popular character. But this time, it was simply a matter of being realistic and accepting that the time had come to rejuvenate the series.

A year earlier, it became obvious that Peter Sallis and Frank Thornton – two immensely popular veterans of the series – and both approaching the astonishing age of 90 – were becoming too fragile to face the rigours and hazards of filming in the Yorkshire countryside. Besides the fact that at that age they were uninsurable, having two vulnerable 90-year-olds playing major parts in the episodes was a risk that we couldn't continue to take. One serious mishap and we would be left with ten unfinished programmes that would, without doubt, bring the series to a sudden and uncomfortable end.

For a part in a recent series, I had considered using the enormously popular and talented comedy actor Russ Abbot, but he wasn't available. Besides having been a top comedy star with his own series on television, Russ had moved into the world of drama as a serious actor, and had been much praised for his acting, particularly in *September Song* (1993-5), a series in which he, a comedian, played the straight man to Michael Williams, a straight classical actor.

Although I was disappointed that I couldn't have Russ on that occasion, he seemed so perfect for *Last of the Summer Wine* that I kept him firmly in mind to use in the future. Consequently, when the idea of rejuvenating the series was beginning to take root, Russ Abbot immediately came to mind.

Roy Clarke said that he would be very happy to write Russ Abbot into the series as the leader of the traditional trio, as long as we didn't lose Peter Sallis and Frank Thornton. There was, of course, no question of them being simply 'dumped' – they had kept the series at the top of the ratings over the years, and deserved all the respect and consideration that they had earned.

At a meeting in his glass-walled office on the fourth floor of the BBC's refurbished Television Centre, I discussed with Mark Freeland, the current Head of Comedy, my plans to liven up the series.

A year ago, Mark had demonstrated his genuine appreciation of the series by visiting the location filming in Yorkshire. As expected, he approved of the idea and gave it his full support.

I had already spoken to Russ Abbot's manager, Mike Hughes, and outlined to him my wish to introduce Russ as a more energetic leader of the Summer Wine trio. However, Mike initially said that he didn't think that Russ would be keen to be cast as an elderly character. He was barely 60, and would, most likely, turn the offer down. Fortunately, Roy Clarke had written a brief description of the new character, which he set as being in his mid-50s – the average age of the original trio way back in 1972 when the series began. Because Mike Hughes was in Los Angeles, it took quite a few late evening calls to convince him that Russ should join the cast of *Last of the Summer Wine*.

To keep Peter Sallis and Frank Thornton in the series, Roy wrote short interior scenes for them, which could be filmed with the minimum of effort over a couple of days at Shepperton Studios. Peter was very pleased that his record of having been in every single episode from the beginning wouldn't be broken. He accepted, as did Frank Thornton, that this was an inevitable and sensible change to the structure of the series.

Filming on location for the rejuvenated 31st series had proceeded very well, and Russ Abbot proved to be a triumph as Luther Hobdyke (Hobbo) the new character.

I have to confess that I wasn't completely happy about Hobbo being a harmless fantasist who asserted that he had been working as a spy for MI5 when he was actually a milkman at Primrose Dairies. However, the absurdity of his imagined secret life was kept in check by the ridicules of Alvin and Entwistle (Brian Murphy and Burt Kwouk). The new trio worked very well together and played Roy Clarke's lines, which had been tailored to match their individual personalities in order to get every bit of comedy out of them.

The established supporting cast loved working with Russ although they were initially a little concerned about his enthusiasm for going through the next day's lines with them after dinner at the unit hotel (The Lodge in Huddersfield). They protested that it was a time for relaxation and rest – not for work. However, realising that it was Russ's sheer enthusiasm to act, they soon began to look forward to their 'homework' in the happy, party atmosphere that Russ created for them nightly in the hotel's private lounge.

I never stay at the unit hotels as I am usually working on the following day's filming, so I was delighted to hear that Russ had taken over as social secretary of our company of players, and even provided carefully selected wines for those who wanted them.

Top Left: The final sound mixing in a Dubbing Theatre at Shepperton Studios. Top Right: Burt Kwouk, Russ Abbot and Robert Fyfe before screenings at Teddington Studios. Bottom: The cast of the previews show take a bow in front of the big screen.

The reaction of the audiences at the Teddington Studios previews in November 2008 proved that Russ Abbot was indeed, very good for *Last of the Summer Wine*. He was far better than anyone could possibly have hoped. His playing of Hobbo livened up the series considerably without spoiling the established premise of the show. We had entered our new era with a winning formula.

Satisfied with the final dubbing of the soundtrack, at the end of the session I collected the two High Definition master tapes from Paul Gartrell and prepared to set off home.

"Will it go again next year?" Simone asked.

"They would have to be mad not to go ahead now," I assured her – but I quickly added "Mind you, they are mad……..but not that mad."

It was early evening and, after saying goodbye to Paul and Simone, I set off into the dark December evening towards the car park at the studio restaurant block. I have to confess

Top Left: Russ Abbot – as Hobbo – sits above the village. Top Right: Would-be MI5 agent Luther Hobdyke (Russ Abbot) is prepared for anything including drafts. Bottom Left: Entwistle and Alvin (Burt Kwouk and Brian Murphy) enjoying the fantasies of Hobbo (Russ Abbot). Bottom Right: The best place for surveillance is the back of Entwistle's pick-up truck.

that, as I walked along the deserted walkways surrounding the studio buildings, I felt very pleased with myself.

I passed Stage 'A' where, only a few weeks ago, the interior sets for *Last of the Summer Wine* had been erected, and where there was always the busy hubbub of production. Now, the studio was deserted, silent, and strangely moving. It was a sensation that I had often experienced in Yorkshire over the years whenever I returned to a location in the hills where, only the day before, it had been a hive of activity with actors, lights and all the paraphernalia of filming. All that was left behind would be the sound of insects and the murmur of the gentle breeze as it combed the long grass. Without the noise of the unit at work, only the occasional strains of a distant lorry or bus climbing a hill somewhere across the valley would disturb the eerie silence. For some reason, it was always a very poignant moment.

But with the master High Definition tapes of *Last of the Summer Wine* in my hands, I had the fruits of all our hard work for that year, and I couldn't wait for the programmes to be transmitted. As I drove out of the Shepperton Studios gateway, I congratulated myself for successfully re-structuring the series and giving it a new lease of life that should last for years.

I returned home and checked my emails. There were the usual unwanted advertisements to be deleted, but there was one from Mark Freeland, our popular Head of Comedy.

I read it. Then I read it again. I couldn't believe my eyes: "was this a joke?" I asked myself. But no, it wasn't a joke. It was an email telling me that *Last of the Summer Wine* was being virtually axed! I say 'virtually' for it was obviously being brought to an end by stealth. The email, couched in apologetic terms, said that there were no 'pre-watershed slots' available to transmit the new series before autumn next year (2009) or the following New Year! It went on to say that the Controller of BBC1 (Jay Hunt) had decided that, before committing to more episodes, she wanted to see how it 'plays out'. After 37 years of success, she didn't know?

Mark Freeland's email then went on to say that the established production routine would be suspended, and that we would have to wait a year until Summer 2010, before going into production with more filming, adding: *"Which means that Roy should not start writing, as we have to be honest and realise that a future positive decision is not guaranteed."*

This was the nearest anyone could get to being mugged – and it hurt just as much.

Why, after I had had produced and directed *Last of the Summer Wine* for 28 years, couldn't their strategy have been discussed with me at a meeting? But by an email? What was the point of all my meetings with Mark Freeland about the future of the series? Why wasn't the possibility of its being dropped even hinted at? This was management at its very worst. It is unimaginable that this would have happened when the BBC was being managed by experienced hands-on producers, and not vastly overpaid executives who play a lucrative version of musical chairs – flitting between broadcasters without any loyalty.

Shocked by the email, I telephoned Roy Clarke to give him the bad news. Roy was even more disappointed than I that his popular series was being cancelled for no good reason whatsoever.

The new Controller of BBC1– Jay Hunt – had recently been Controller of Channel Five, and was welcomed with open arms by the Director General, Mark Thompson, as being a valuable acquisition by the Corporation. But Quentin Letts in the Daily Mail thought otherwise and described her as 'Thin-lipped – the Killer Kitten who is steering Auntie on to the rocks'.

I telephoned members of my crew who were, understandably, very disappointed that the series was being killed off. The future of the series had seemed certain to them, too, and they would inevitably suffer some hardship. This bad news found its way into the ever alert *Huddersfield Examiner*, and then the National press, which provoked uproars of disapproval from all quarters. Maybe the 'New BBC' didn't rate the programme, but it seemed that there was a huge section of the viewing public who did, and who were prepared to complain loudly, that the one comedy series that they found funny was being scrapped.

The whole situation was bizarre. Here was the BBC's most successful comedy series *ever* being cancelled by someone who had dropped-in from an opposition channel, and who, with indecent haste was very soon to vacate her seat at the BBC and move across to Channel Four as its Controller!

There is no question that I was deeply hurt and angry by the news and the clumsy manner in which it had been conveyed to me. But I had to accept that, no matter how wrong everyone may see it to be, it was a decision that the BBC management was entitled to make.

I realised that maybe the time had come for me to take a step back and reflect on my good fortune to have been given *Last of the Summer Wine* to produce in the first place. I asked myself: How could I, having left school at 15, have ended up as the producer and director of a series that is so hugely popular with viewers around the world? The answer was simply: 'passion' – A passion for filming that began when I was still at school and had made amateur movies with a friend along the Fife coast in Scotland. It is a passion that has transported me along the bumpy road of television production, over the fiercely competitive potholes dug out by ambitious competitors, but never running out of the fuel of genuine enthusiasm.

I have no better example of this motivation than the story of my years producing and directing *Last of the Summer Wine*, and how I was able to lavish upon it every possible care.

The ending of the series was a time of reflection. So, let's have a real look at *Last of the Summer Wine* – from the director's chair!

CHAPTER 2
Welcome to Holmfirth

Fate has always played a strong hand in my life, so much so that, whenever anything goes wrong, I always see it as being an indication that something much better is just around the corner. But sometimes fate comes in the form of coincidence when, by just following a natural, unambitious route through life, it proves to be a springboard to new, more exciting, avenues.

And so it was in 1981. I had recently completed the *The Hitchhiker's Guide to the Galaxy* (1980) which, although praised by the press for its imaginative production, didn't do at all well in the ratings. But it had an army of devoted followers, and had won a few awards, which prompted the BBC to commission a second series. However, the author (Douglas Adams) was having trouble coming up with ideas, and it was quite obvious to me that the scripts for a second television series would never materialise – the only idea he revealed to me was that the first episode began with a spacecraft landing on the pitch during a test match in Sydney, Australia. It sounded promising – and I had never been to Australia.

Deadlines were extended and, in desperation, the author even tried to bring in help from his old chums in radio who, having helped him write the original series might pull the trick for him again and allow him the solo writing credit. *The Hitchhiker's Guide to the Galaxy* was very much a series for radio, which is the ideal medium for space fantasy. On radio, mile-high characters on marshmallow planets can be easily and cheaply created.

It was during the period of waiting for the *Hitchhiker* scripts for a second series that Robin Nash, the larger-than-life Head of Variety and certainly my champion over the years, asked me to make some short films for an entertainment programme called *You Must Be Joking* (1981).

My Production Manager, Michael Cager, and I would think up film items in which a statement was made, that teams in the studio would have to decide was either true or false. We soon discovered that the trick was to make the true items appear to be false and the false items undoubtedly true.

A memorable BBC2 documentary film, made a few years ago, suggested a good subject for a *You Must Be Joking* film item. In the *One Pair of Eyes* series ('Programmes offering individuals a platform to discuss issues close to their heart') Barry Took, the popular comedy writer and broadcaster, presented a film about a somewhat bawdy Working Men's Club in Yorkshire. It featured a stripper and an earthy comedian, and was called simply, *The Burnlee Club*.

In the film, Barry pointed out that Burnlee was only a very short distance from the woollen mill town of Holmfirth where once there was, quite unbelievably, a thriving silent film industry. It was an interesting fact that I had held in my memory over the years.

At the start of the century, Bamforths graduated from producing lantern slides for village halls to making silent moving pictures starring a comedian with the unlikely name of Winkey.

These comedies, which were filmed in and around Holmfirth, were so successful that Bamforths even had offices in New York to distribute them. Sadly, the First World War put an end to Holmfirth becoming another Hollywood when the silver nitrate used for film emulsion was requisitioned to make bombs. Bamforths then moved into the production of saucy seaside postcards from their abandoned glasshouse studio that still stands in the middle of the town. Many people would know that the BBC filmed *Last of the Summer Wine* in Holmfirth, but few would know the story of Winkey and the Yorkshire silent movie moguls.

There could be no better subject for a *You Must Be Joking* film item than one about this one-time woollen-mill town that could have become the Hollywood of the North. Because it was completely true, I set about lampooning Holmfirth and its inhabitants to make it appear to be, very obviously, untrue.

The best place to find out who's who in a town is the local public house – there is always someone there who knows someone who knows someone who can help. So it was in the well-worn, nicotine-stained interior of The Shoulder of Mutton public house, in the heart of Holmfirth, that our research began.

The landlord of The Shoulder (as it was generally known) had never quite mastered the technique of mental arithmetic, and when adding-up simple bar bills he would make vague guesses that were always in favour of the customers. "Shall we say.... a pound?" he would suggest. Consequently, there was always a legion of contented drinkers in the bar, and a shortage of small change in the till. He was also worryingly adept at turning his feet around, so that they faced behind him. But, as entertaining as he was, he wasn't the most convivial of landlords. When someone asked him for a gin and tonic with ice and lemon, he said "There's no ice, and if you want lemon, you'll have to go to the greengrocers across the road."

Using this source of local knowledge, I soon began to accumulate a list of likely characters for my *You Must Be Joking* film item about Holmfirth. "Go and see Wilbert Kemp," I was advised. "He knows old Jack up by the laundry." Old Jack, I discovered, was now over 90 and had actually appeared as a child in one of Bamforth's silent movies and, with a bit of prompting, he lamented that he could easily have become a really big star. "Play it again, Sam," he growled to demonstrate his thespian prowess. A less likely film star would be hard to find.

Needless to say, I also used our friendly landlord in the film. He bemoaned the fact that, had the movie industry continued in the town, he might well have been landlord of a Hollywood Hotel and not The Shoulder of Mutton.

Our film ended with a dog that Mike Cager borrowed from the owner of the house used as Nora Batty's home in *Last of the Summer Wine*. It obediently trotted past the town's old cinema leaving its paw marks in some wet cement on the pavement outside – just like the film stars famously did at Mann's Chinese Theatre in Hollywood.

While waiting for the crew to arrive to film the *You Must Be Joking* item, I took the opportunity to become a tourist and visit some of the *Last of the Summer Wine* locations. Mike Cager, who had actually worked on the series in the past, was my tour guide.

The first thing that struck me about Holmfirth was that there was hardly any traffic – even on the main roads that converged in the centre of the town. The stone buildings looked substantial and permanent, but the shops beneath them were well-worn and neglected. Some were in an advanced state of decay because of all the salt that had been sprayed liberally over the pavements to combat the icy conditions of countless winters. In

The centre of Holmfirth today with Clegg's first house seen behind the clock tower.

general, Holmfirth was very much unspoiled by progress, and was, probably, very much as it had been for over a century.

Following the route of the river, I walked with Mike Cager to Nora Batty's house. Situated in the middle of an interwoven row of terraced houses, this location was colourless, stark and immediately attractive. The outside toilets on the first landing were an indication that the town hadn't moved on much since the local mills had spun their last bales of yarn.

Sid's café, painted in depressing brown, sat forlornly in the church square next to some steps. The word CAFÉ had been painted on the window in large white letters for the last bout of Summer Wine filming. Looking through this window, I could see piles of tins neatly laid out on the shelves and on the floor. Mike informed me that, in the distant past, it had been a fish and chip shop, but it was now used as a paint store by Kaye's the Ironmongers on the corner. Every time the BBC filmed there, the entire stock of paint had to be removed and stored elsewhere so that it could be turned into a typical Yorkshire café for all the exterior scenes.

"Don't, whatever you do, go near the building on the other side of the steps," Mike warned. "The fish fryers from the old fish and chip shop were moved there many years ago, and the rancid smell of the decaying fat is overpowering!" It was advice that I took and passed on to others for nearly 20 years. The steps between the café and the house with the rancid fish fryers led to a tidy little alleyway where passers-by were obliged to weave through the whiter-than-white washing, stretched out on a line across the alleyway to dry.

Just around the corner from the Church Square – on the main road – was Joan Bottomley's greengrocery shop. There, she displayed somewhat precariously, her stock of vegetables and fruit on the narrow pavement where, with only inches to spare, the local service buses turned right into the open bus station.

Any thoughts I had that Joan had been sitting in her shop, patiently waiting to supply lemons to disgruntled patrons of The Shoulder, were set aside when, into Mike Cager's hands, she thrust a brown paper bag bulging with a variety of exotic fruits. "Take this back to your hotel room, Mike, you might fancy it later," she said warmly and kindly. Wherever we went in the town, Mike Cager would be greeted as an old friend. There was something about the locals that

Nora Batty (Kathy Staff) deals with Compo (Bill Owen)

Left: Filming activity at Nora Batty's steps.
Right: Sid's Café - spruced up and open for business in 1985.

was immediately engaging: if they liked you, you were a friend for life. If they didn't, well…

Across the main road, on the other side of the river and next to the old cinema, was a sombre building known affectionately by the locals as the Con Club. It emerged later that the Conservative Club was registered as having 'no political affiliations'. Because it always seemed to be extra busy during those hours when the local public houses were obliged by law to close, there was a suspicion that it was being used by non-members as a convenient means of having round the clock access to alcohol. It was a suspicion that was later confirmed when the police raided the premises and according to local legend, didn't find a single *bona fide* member in the crowded bar. The very popular Con Club was subsequently closed down and converted into what is now, the respectable Old Bridge Hotel.

In 1981 there was no hotel in Holmfirth – the nearest was in Huddersfield some six miles away. There were also very few real cafés in the town. There was no need for them as there were no visitors. In fact, there were no signs anywhere of Holmfirth's growing fame as '*The* town where they film *Last of the Summer Wine*'.

Holmfirth was indeed an attractive town, and the locals had been very helpful and genuinely friendly. I wasn't certain that they would remain so, for my *You Must Be Joking* film item had to send-up the town and make any notion that Holmfirth might have become 'the Hollywood of the North' completely unimaginable.

As Mike and I drove out of Holmfirth the next day, I said, "I wouldn't want to be Sydney Lotterby when he returns to film the next series of *Summer Wine*. He'll get lynched."

After the tedious 200-mile drive from Holmfirth in Yorkshire back to the still uncompleted Television Centre at White City in London, I went straight up to my office on the seventh floor. There was a message awaiting me from John Howard-Davies, the Head of Comedy, saying that he wanted to see me.

Although John Howard Davies had produced some of the BBC's greatest comedy successes – *Fawlty Towers, Steptoe and Son, Monty Python's Flying Circus* and *The Good Life* among them, he is probably best known for playing the name part of *Oliver Twist* in David Lean's classic 1948 film. But no-one ever mentions it – especially at meal times. John's father, Jack Davies, wrote the screenplays of many notable British films – including some Norman Wisdom films – so John had more than a dash of comedy in his blood.

I went downstairs to John Howard Davies' office on the fourth floor of the Television Centre. At that time, the offices of the Heads of Variety and Comedy were separated by that of the Head of Light Entertainment Group. These offices were exactly the same as those of the department's producers except for one important and much envied addition – they had green velvet curtains to denote the importance of their occupants. Producers could only dream of, one day, having an office with green velvet curtains.

John Howard Davies didn't invite me to sit down as what he had to say obviously didn't merit any discussion. My eyes widened and my jaw dropped in astonishment as he said in his clipped get-to-the-point manner: "I want you to take over *Last of the Summer Wine*."

I had always been a keen follower of *Last of the Summer Wine* and had watched practically every episode from the very beginning. It had been a breath of fresh air in the stereotyped situation comedy world of semi-detached houses, living rooms, and permutations of couples with either marital problems or awkward neighbours. *Last of the Summer Wine* played its comedy outdoors – in the fields, in the hills and in the gritty alleyways of an old Yorkshire woollen mill town. But, above all, Roy Clarke's scripts were intelligent and witty.

"*Last of the Summer Wine*?" I said to John Howard Davies, in disbelief and hardly able to conceal my joy. "But why isn't Syd doing it?" I asked. Sydney Lotterby, a Senior Comedy Producer with an impressive track record, had produced the previous three series.

"He wants to do other things," John answered.

"Do you know where I have just come from?" I asked.

"No. Where?"

"Holmfirth – and I'm going to be in real trouble there." I told him about the Holmfirth item for *You Must Be Joking*.

"I'm sure you can cope with that," John said with a wry smile.

A few days later, I returned to Holmfirth to see the participants in my *You Must Be Joking* film that was going to be transmitted the following week. I explained to them that I was very pleased with the item, and absolutely delighted that they had such a good sense of humour – which, fortunately for me, they really did have.

CHAPTER 3
On the Level

I'd had a very brief association with *Last of the Summer Wine* seven years earlier when I was a Production Manager. A colleague had been unwell (looking back, I think it was probably Mike Cager) and I filled in for him on an episode called *The New Mobile Trio* (1973).

The location filming had been completed, so all I had to do was attend the rehearsals during the week and the studio recording of the interior scenes on the Sunday when the programme would be performed in front of an audience.

I should point out here that it was the routine at the time and probably still is, that the Production Manager (sometimes called the Production Assistant or Assistant Producer) having attended all the rehearsals would, on the recording day assume the role of a studio floor manager and be the director's voice in the studio, relaying all his instructions to the actors. It was a sensible practice, for who else would know the production better? Certainly not a regular Floor Manager who would only join productions on the studio days.

The Producer/Director of *Last of the Summer Wine*, James Gilbert, cast the series and set its style. Jimmy had a warm and gentlemanly disposition, and was well-liked by everyone for his charm and easy manner.

In the story of *The New Mobile Trio* (1973), a road safety exhibition was taking place in the Town Hall, and Clegg (Peter Sallis) had to sit in a car simulator and pretend to steer it along the road. Jimmy Gilbert asked me to find some library film showing the road ahead – as seen from a moving car. I pointed out to Jimmy Gilbert that it would be cheaper and certainly more satisfactory, if I were to book a film cameraman for a couple of hours and film exactly what was needed for Clegg to watch on the car simulator screen. He agreed to this, and left it to me to organise.

The following day, I went with Tom Ingle, a versatile and reliable film cameraman I knew, to a quiet lane that led to the embankment of the River Thames at Chiswick (near where the Varsity Boat Race ends). I worked out the route that would be seen on the car simulator in the studio. Tom mounted the camera on the bonnet of his voluminous American estate car, and we rehearsed the continuous shot, zigzagging along the roads, across the middle of a little roundabout, and ending up very close to a tree on the bank of the river, just in case it was decided later that Clegg should crash his car simulator.

The route was set and, after a few checks, Tom Ingle was ready. The camera was switched on, and off we went, filming the erratic, bumpy route, up on the pavement, across the roundabout and so on. Unfortunately, during the time it had taken to reset the camera car for the take, a car had arrived and parked in front of the tree. When the driver of the car and his female companion saw our car approaching with a film camera mounted on the bonnet, for some reason, and years before *Top Gear*, they decided to test their car's acceleration capabilities, and quickly screeched off into the distance, leaving much of its tyre treads smouldering on the road.

The scene was successfully re-shot without the mystery car and its terrified occupants. For many years, whenever I saw a car with a white-haired driver, I would think of that morning at the side of the Thames in Chiswick. This filming fitted the scene, and was certainly much better than using library material.

The rehearsals for *The New Mobile Trio* (1973) were held at a church hall near Kensington High Street. As a rehearsal room, it wasn't ideal, but it was very popular because of its nearness to some good department stores.

It was at these rehearsals that I noted Jimmy Gilbert's respect for Roy Clarke's writing. He wouldn't hear of anyone changing a word of what was in the script. In the road safety scene, an additional line was needed for Clegg to get rid of a child hogging the driving simulator. Everyone, including Peter Sallis, suggested a suitable line, but Jimmy wouldn't even consider them. "It's Roy Clarke's script," he said, "and Roy will provide the new line – which is bound to be better than any of our suggestions, as good as they are." And, of course, it was. Clegg says to the boy, "Have you ever heard of 'suffer little children'? Well, be off then."

Because Jimmy Gilbert was promoted to become Head of Comedy, subsequent series of *Last of the Summer Wine* were produced first by Bernard Thompson, and then by Sydney Lotterby. These programmes enjoyed respectable viewing figures, but it wasn't until there was a technicians' strike at the Independent Television network that the viewing figures increased dramatically. The whole of the ITV network had closed down, and the only channels that were an alternative to watching the blue ITV apology card were BBC1 and BBC2. Consequently, the public's thirst for entertainment – any entertainment – forced it to watch the repeats of this unlikely comedy series about three old men in their second youth. Much to its surprise, this new audience found that *Last of the Summer Wine* was both very funny and visually pleasing.

At the same time as the ITV strike, Terry Wogan (the popular presenter and disc-jockey) was immortalising Nora Batty (played by Kathy Staff) on his morning radio show. His humorous observations about her curlers and wrinkled stockings made Nora Batty a household name across the nation and an enduring icon of the series for almost four decades. Together, Terry Wogan and the ITV strike lifted the viewing figures of *Last of the Summer Wine* to new heights.

So, in the spring of 1981, when John Howard Davies gave me the sixth series of my favourite situation comedy to produce and direct, it was like winning the lottery. How lucky can you get?

I still found it hard to believe that Sydney Lotterby had relinquished such a wonderful series to me. So, when I saw him in the Television Centre restaurant soon afterwards, I enquired why.

"You wait until you start filming," he warned. "Besides the terrible weather, you'll find that filming up there will exhaust you – nothing is on level ground – it's all hills."

It was a sentiment later echoed by the programmes most senior actor, Bill Owen (Compo), who said, "If you want anything out of me, mate, don't tire me out on them hills."

The majestic rolling hills of the Holme Valley were an important feature of the series, but they were, indeed, tiring, especially for the crew who had to manhandle heavy equipment up those hills, across rivers, and over the crumbling dry-stone walls for which Yorkshire is rightly famous. It has often been said that the hills and valleys of Yorkshire are equal stars in the series, and I firmly believe that, had the series been set elsewhere, it wouldn't have run for 38 years.

Sydney Lotterby's reason for giving up the series was understandable. He was considerably

*Top: The interwoven terrace of houses where Nora Batty lives.
Left Inset: Filming in Daisy Lane – behind Sid's café in Holmfirth.
Bottom: Discussing the script on a track above Holmfirth.*

older than me, and the physical demands of the filming were considerable. Sydney had graduated into production from the Engineering Department where, as a studio cameraman in live television, detailed planning was mandatory. But the uncertainties of filming on location, mostly due to the weather, could never be accurately anticipated, and were bound to be more of a problem for anyone who doesn't have a flair for single camera filming.

In 1978, I had been given the opportunity to take over *Crackerjack (1955-81)*, a popular children's variety series, by Robin Nash, the then Head of Variety. He must have noted my passion for filming when I wrote and directed the *Don and Pete* silent comedy films that were a popular part of *Crackerjack*. Without saying so, Robin became a sort of mentor to me, and was always evident in the background when there were key advances to my career. He was there when completely out of the blue, the Comedy Department gave me two films in the *Ripping Yarns* series, to make: *Whinfrey's Last Case* (1979) and *Golden Gordon* (1979). When that series received a BAFTA award, Robin said that he was personally delighted that I hadn't let him down. At the time, I didn't realise the significance of the remark, but Robin had obviously played a part in my being assigned to those two gems starring Michael Palin, who also wrote them with Terry Jones.

Robin called me into his office one day to point out that all the Variety producers in Light Entertainment were fairly young, with long careers ahead of them, whereas most of the Comedy producers were getting near retirement age. Robin suggested that I should seriously consider switching to the Comedy Department. It was certainly good long-term advice, but it wouldn't be a simple move to make. But when, after *Ripping Yarns*, I was given *The Hitchhiker's Guide to the Galaxy* (1980), it was clear that I had left Variety behind and had seamlessly moved into Comedy.

Giving me *Last of the Summer Wine* was very good casting, as I was well used to improvising when the weather let me down, or other catastrophes caused schedules to collapse. For me, the business of filming this wondrous series wasn't in any way a challenge, and I am sure that my competitive colleagues in Comedy department saw me as being a bit of an upstart. Why should I be worried? I had a strong cast in Bill Owen (Compo), Peter Sallis (Clegg) and Brian Wilde (Foggy). And, most importantly, Roy Clarke had provided me with some of the best comedy scripts ever written.

In the days before word processors, Roy Clarke's scripts would first go to the two Comedy Department script typists who would set out the pages in television production format with the dialogue and stage directions on the right side of the page, with space on the left for camera instructions. It was, they said, the highlight of their working week when they had to type *Last of the Summer Wine* scripts. They added that the scripts for my first series were the funniest they had ever typed. Well, they should know.

All I needed was some good weather and locations that were level enough for Bill Owen. But first, there was some viewing to do. Although I had always enjoyed *Last of the Summer Wine*, there was something that had subconsciously troubled me about the filming, but I couldn't identify what it was. Then, when I was looking at the tapes of some recent episodes, which were very good, I suddenly I realised what it was: there were too many close shots – so many, in fact, that much of the filming could have been done in Walpole Park (behind the BBC's film studios in Ealing) rather than in the beautiful Yorkshire countryside.

When television began, most viewers had to watch nine-inch screens, and the only way to see an actor's reaction – or even, sometimes, who was speaking – was to have a close-up. Wide angle shots at the time (mostly in feature films) were too wide for these small-screen, low definition televisions, and closer shots were an absolute necessity. However, as domestic television screens began to get larger, there was less need for endless close-ups. In fact, they were downright irritating.

Widening the scope of the filming in *Last of the Summer Wine* proved to be very popular with everyone, except Peter Sallis and Brian Wilde who preferred the filming being weighted in favour of the close shots, and they openly complained about the few close-ups they were now getting. I assured them that they would have close-ups whenever they were appropriate in a scene.

Bill Owen had no such opinions. Bill was a veteran film actor and the only member of the *Summer Wine* trio to have had his name above the titles in feature films, so my style of filming, and it's certainly not unique, suited him down to the ground.

To explain it simply: I see how I am going to film a scene as I read the script, so I know exactly how it will look in the finished film. Therefore,

I only shoot what is going to end up on the screen. Nothing is filmed 'just in case' it might be needed. Experienced film actors prefer this method because they can give their best performance in a shot knowing that it will be used in the finished film. That is not to say that good ideas will be turned down. But they must be better ideas.

Some Directors will shoot a scene from many different angles and work out later how to put it all together. This method is preferred by those actors who want to perform the whole scene as though they are in a stage play. I dislike it, because I am not directing a stage play, and it gives the final construction of the scene to the film editor (or worse, the Executive Producers). But there are no hard and fast rules in filming, and all Directors have their own way of working. It's how it looks ultimately that matters, and certainly not how it gets there.

A few years later, I was heartened by a short, anonymous review of *Last of the Summer Wine* in the TV listings page of *Time Out*, an outspoken publication that pulls no punches. It read:

'Whatever you think of the content, this has got to be one of the best shot series on TV. Not only does it make excellent use of the Yorkshire countryside, but it also assumes that most of its audience have normal eyesight and don't therefore need to be bombarded with close-ups the whole time.'

I didn't think anyone would consciously notice any difference, but it pleased me enormously, even if there was an unfair, implied criticism of the scripts. Oh, and I should mention the fact that as often as possible, I like a scene to develop within the frame of a moving camera. This means that the actors have to wait until a track is laid for the camera. This may consume some time, but it makes the scene more interesting and allows us to sail through pages of the script.

Roy Clarke's scripts for the sixth series were, as the script typists had observed, very good indeed. I arranged a meeting to read-through the scripts with Roy Clarke and the three principals in a conference room at the BBC's Lime Grove Studios.

Lime Grove had, many years ago, been the home of Gainsborough Pictures and was where, on its large film stages, Alfred Hitchcock made *The 39 Steps* (1935). In the early fifties, it became the home of BBC Television, where, in the modified studios, most of its output of drama and entertainment was produced. In the following years, although much of the BBC's production moved up the road to its brand new Television Centre at White City, Lime Grove Studios were kept in pristine condition and constantly refurbished to make maximum use of its facilities. Hence, the conference room we had been allocated, which was below the main studios, had obviously been a crowd dressing room for ambitious productions in its glorious past. It was here that my first meeting with Roy Clarke and the three principal actors took place.

Although I had briefly worked with Bill Owen and Peter Sallis on *The New Mobile Trio* (1973) as a Production Manager, they had forgotten and simply saw me as their new Producer/Director. Roy Clarke, who was tall and agile, welcomed me to the series and hoped that I would enjoy the experience. Bill Owen was dapperly dressed for the occasion and was as far away as he could get from his scruffy Compo character, with whom he was becoming indelibly associated. Peter

Sallis and Brian Wilde were, as expected, smartly dressed and not a million miles away from being the Clegg and Foggy that we all knew.

It was a relaxed and friendly read-through of the first three scripts, with Roy reading, gently, Nora's Batty's fearsome lines, which, strangely enough, made them sound all the more threatening – and funny. The scripts were really excellent, and hearing the actors bringing them to life, cautioned me that there would be no excuse for not making the series one of the best ever – level ground and weather permitting, of course.

Before the meeting ended, our three actors laid down certain ground rules for the filming, which mainly concerned starting times and the size of their caravan, from where they would almost certainly, be spending much of their time looking out at the rain-drenched locations. But we were off to a good start and it promised to be a great series.

Location scenes for a series are usually filmed completely out of order to fit in with cast and location availabilities, so it's impossible to say which episode was the first to go before the camera on my first series. But it probably was *In the Service of Humanity* (1982), which was written as the third episode and was, perhaps, the most memorable for many reasons.

In one of the film sequences, Foggy borrows an apparently abandoned ladder that he finds leaning against an old outhouse. As the men carry it off, they don't notice that there is a man working on the roof of the outhouse. Later, the man shouts to them, "Hey! Fetch that ladder back!" For this very small part, I interviewed three actors in a small windowless conference room in the BBC's Oxford Road studios in Manchester. The actors were all very good, but one of them stood out. He was clearly a natural comedy actor and didn't appear to be acting. He impressed me so much that I reached into my plastic supermarket shopping bag (much lighter than a brief case) and took out the script for *Car and Garter* (1982) – a later episode in the series.

In *Car and Garter*, there was the important part of a would-be mechanical genius, Wesley Pegden, which hadn't yet been cast. I had interviewed one or two leading character actors for the part in London, and had nearly cast the well-known and experienced comedy actor, Gordon Rollings, who would have been very good as Wesley. But it was such a good part that I decided to keep my options open.

So, here I was with Gordon Wharmby who, although he was an actor, was pleased to tell me that he actually earned his living as a full-time painter/decorator and was very proud of the high standard of his workmanship.

Before I handed Gordon Wharmby the script for *Car and Garter*, I told him that I was only interested in his range, to see how good he was, as I wouldn't want to ask him to take on something that would be too much for him. I asked him how he would rate himself. "Oh, although I say it myself, I'm really good, one of the best in the North," he said with enormous confidence. This was re-assuring. However he continued: "I can do a three bedroom semi-detached house in a fortnight – strip off all the old wallpaper, top to bottom, and rub down all the paintwork…" I stopped him and told him that I meant as an actor.

"Oh, as an actor. Well, I'm fine, I do all right," he said more modestly. "I've done bits at Oldham repertory theatre and bits on *Coronation Street*, but nothing much – just one or two lines, like."

I handed Gordon the script of *Car and Garter* and not wanting to build up his hopes, I told him that the part of Wesley Pegden had already been cast, and that I was merely interested to see how he would play him. When Gordon Wharmby read the script, he brought the character to life in a way that made him believably eccentric, real and, more importantly, very funny. He immediately became Wesley Pegden in my eyes.

I wanted to give him the part there and then, but he was a painter/decorator. How could I give a leading role to a painter/decorator?

I decided to put my dilemma to one side. *Car and Garter* was a much later episode and was in the second batch of filming. I had plenty of time to think about it.

It was while we were searching for locations for *In The Service of Humanity* (1981) that Mike Cager and I were caught in a really heavy downpour that lasted all afternoon. It was a salutary reminder of Sydney Lotterby's warnings about the unreliable weather. I could see what he meant, for it certainly wouldn't be conducive to filming comedy scenes. The rain was so heavy that I considered getting some large umbrella-type canopies to shelter the actors in scenes when it rained, but if it was windy they would surely blow away. And anyway, the sound of the rain beating on them would be picked up by the microphones.

I would have to accept that, if it rained, it rained, and cope with whatever happened. I asked Mike Cager to take me to a camping shop in Huddersfield where I bought Wellingtons and extensive rainwear. With all this protective clothing, I felt that I could face any storm. When bad weather came my way, I would be ready for it.

The sun was shining when, in July 1981, the cast and crew congregated in Yorkshire to film the exterior scenes for the first three episodes. And it seemed to shine continuously throughout the following two weeks. I put aside my Wellingtons and the rainwear – for the moment, anyway.

The story of *In the Service of Humanity* (1981) is that Foggy decides that the trio should form a crack First Aid team – ready for any emergency. When Foggy sees some clothes abandoned on a riverbank, he immediately assumes that some poor devil may have drowned. Without a moment's hesitation, he fearlessly sends Compo and Clegg into the water to look for the poor man. As there was no river in the Holme Valley deep enough to have the actors go in up to their waists (or even their knees), I filmed it at the edge of a lake near Brighouse that was used by the local ski club.

The 'rescue' of the missing man at the lakeside was not the easiest of scenes to film, and Bill Owen and Peter Sallis were not at all happy about having to go in up to their waists but there was no alternative. The costume department had concealed chest-high waders under their clothes to keep them dry, but it was with considerable reluctance that they walked out into the lake, through the thick mud underfoot, to a position about ten feet from the bank. I asked Peter to walk a little faster in the water for the shot, to which he replied: "Listen, it would be a lot easier to walk *on* the water than in it."

After a lot of grumbling from the men, when we had finished the scene, I took Peter and Bill to the inn on the other side of the lake to change into dry clothing and warm up. The landlady confided that everyone had been entertained by our filming activities across the lake.

"You do your own stunts then?" she asked with obvious admiration. The actors, now clearly heroes, were pleased to agree that they did do their own stunts.

"Whenever they're not too dangerous," Bill added modestly.

"That was quite dangerous over there, this afternoon," she drooled.

"A drop of water? It was nothing."

"Oh, it's not just the water, it's the thirty foot drop – it's a flooded quarry, you know – I was surprised you didn't go under."

Fortunately, I suddenly remembered a telephone call that I had to make, and hurriedly left. And so began a long relationship of mistrust between the principal actors and their new director.

At the BBC's North Acton rehearsal rooms a few weeks later, the rehearsals for the studio scenes in my first few episodes had progressed very well. These were the interior scenes that would be played before an audience, and were the body of the programme. They consisted of the usual settings of Clegg's living room, a pub and Sid's Café.

I had decided to turn the Café set round by 90 degrees so that the counter, behind which Sid and his wife Ivy would keep their customers in check, was on the right, and the exterior window that looked out on to the church square, was upstage in the centre. Previously, when the entrance was on the left hand side, whenever the characters opened the door, it revealed an unconvincingly painted cloth depicting the church opposite. Having the entrance in the centre of the set, allowed there to be a sizeable gap between the café window and the painted background. Besides that, there was much more room inside the café for the actors to play the scenes.

But not all was well. Long before we had got to the rehearsal stage, Bill Owen, Peter Sallis and Brian Wilde broached the subject of the audience laughter. They firmly believed that the series would be much better without any laughter at all, rather than have something so half-hearted. They urged me to make the series without an audience. I told them that it wasn't my decision, it was Comedy Department policy to have a genuine laughter track, and the answer would be a definite 'No'. Peter persisted: "But they don't laugh, Alan. What's the point of having them there if they don't laugh?" It was true that some of the early episodes were marred by poor audience reaction. Really funny lines received merely a small laugh which damned the comedy rather than enhance it. But here we were, after the ITV strike had introduced a large audience to the series, and Terry Wogan was still giving daily reports of unconfirmed sightings of Nora Batty's wrinkled stockings. There was now a huge demand for tickets to watch the studio recordings – and now, everyone in the audience had seen the show on television and knew what it was about. They had all come along to the studio to laugh and enjoy Roy Clarke's glorious comedy.

When Peter, Bill and Brian heard the volume of laughter at the recordings, they quickly withdrew any motion to do away with the studio audiences and never mentioned it again.

When the filmed 'rescue' scene for *In the Service of Humanity* was eventually shown at the recording of the whole episode in Studio 3 at the Television Centre, we were all very pleased with the appreciative laughter of the audience. However, the following day, when John Howard Davies viewed a VHS videotape of the episode, he wasn't so pleased:

"We don't add fake laughter to our programmes," he said. "I want you to take it off the soundtrack."

I told him that it most definitely was not fake laughter and it couldn't be removed as it had been mixed together with the soundtrack of the film when it was shown to the audience. But John was adamant: "No one will believe that it's genuine. You'll have to show it to an audience again."

On the Tuesday rehearsal for the next episode, I told the cast that we would be showing the sequence again on Sunday, the next recording day. Brian Wilde led the protests. "We have *earned* that laughter," Brian said, emphasising the word 'earned'.

"It is quite unfair that the scene is going to be shown to another audience to get less laughs. It should stay as it is," he said.

We all agreed with him. However, the scene was shown again at the next studio recording the following Sunday. Although the second audience was just as responsive, it wasn't quite as hysterical as the first had been. Everyone was happy, and nobody could accuse the BBC of using canned laughter – except, maybe, *Radio Times*.

There was a traditional formula that producers used in deciding the transmission order of their comedy shows: always start with your best episode (to get the audience to watch the next one). The second episode should be nearly as good (to show that the first episode wasn't a fluke and that the audience should stay with the series). Keep the weakest episode to the penultimate position (the audience by now knows it's a good series), and end with the second best episode, to end with a reminder that it really was a good series and they should want more.

Episode three, *In the Service of Humanity*, was transmitted as the first episode of the series.

In subsequent series, I stopped applying the formula, as I felt that the actors' performances became noticeably better each week as they began to relate together more.

With the first three episodes completed, and generally seen by everyone, particularly James Gilbert and John Howard Davies as being excellent, it was time to prepare for the location filming for the next four episodes and a Christmas special.

CHAPTER 4
Four Episodes and a Christmas Special

I just knew that Gordon Wharmby was right to play Wesley Pegden in *Car and Garter*, but I couldn't avoid the fact that he was still basically a painter/decorator with comparatively little acting experience. Would he be good enough to play the main guest part in an episode alongside actors of the standing of Bill Owen, Peter Sallis and Brian Wilde?

The location filming wouldn't be a problem as I could always re-shoot anything that wasn't quite right. However, for the interior scenes recorded in front of a studio audience of over three hundred people, it would be a disaster if he went to pieces on the night. It was a gamble that could go horribly wrong.

I decided to bring Gordon Wharmby down from Manchester to the Television Centre to read for me again. This time, I confessed that I was seriously considering him for the part of Wesley, and that I needed to be absolutely certain that there was no risk of him letting me down when he was under pressure. Could I rely on him? Would he let me down? Gordon's mouth opened and his eyes widened as he looked at me as though he had been accused of some despicable crime.

"I've never let anyone down in my life," he replied indignantly. Then he added, somewhat intensely, "I'm *known* for being reliable. Last weekend, I did an upstairs flat, took off all the old wallpaper and re-papered the lot. Stripped the paint off and…."

I stopped him and said, "Gordon, I'm talking about your acting." He replied that he was just as confident that he could play Wesley, and that he certainly wouldn't let me down – in any way.

Gordon read the part for me again and, as before, he was really good. But I would be taking a big chance casting someone so inexperienced.

The filming in Yorkshire for *Car and Garter* with the reliable Gordon Wharmby playing the oily mechanic Wesley Pegden, proceeded very well. I had no need to worry for he was word-perfect and played the lines with an instinctive understanding of the comedy.

In the story, Wesley, an inept motor mechanic, has built his own racing car and needs someone to drive it. The racing car was actually made by Chris Lawson, a visual effects genius who took an old Triumph Herald chassis and cleverly built a crudely-made racing body on to it. The result was excellent and a tribute to the BBC's acclaimed (and now disbanded) Visual Effects department.

An old, green-painted corrugated steel garage, that would be Wesley's workshop in the episode, was found in a garden near Jackson Bridge. It satisfied the basic requirements of the script alright, but it wasn't ideal. There was a low wall nearby for our three characters to lean on as they watched Wesley appearing from inside his smoke-filled garage, but I was painfully aware that it wasn't right. It had no scenic background, and looked dull and uninteresting. It was just a rusty garage next to some other more modern garages at the rear of a house, but I would have to make do if it was all that could be found.

When I arrived at the location on the morning of the filming, I was dismayed to see the activity in the field opposite. Bulldozers were levelling the ground, and huge lorries were delivering bricks and drainage pipes. This was, we were told, the first day of work on the construction of a new housing estate! This was a disaster. Our garage location was now totally unusable, and everyone was beginning to assemble there to start filming. There was only one thing to do. I gave the unit an hour off while I searched for another old garage with a nearby low wall.

Without much hope of finding an acceptable substitute garage location – it had taken days of searching to find the one we had – I drove through the lanes of the Holme Valley. About twenty minutes later, just a mile outside of Holmfirth, I happened upon a working mill that had a little lane running up the side of its reservoir. At the end of this lane stood a rusty, green-painted, corrugated steel garage – exactly the same as the one that had just been abandoned – except that it stood there on its own. Its location above the mill's reservoir, amidst the pretty layered houses that were once the mill workers' homes was absolutely perfect and a hundred times better than what we had initially. This picturesque setting, at Hinchliffe Mill, became another iconic location of the series, and was used in subsequent episodes for the following twenty years.

I often drive past the original location – which was so wrong by comparison, and wonder if there is a hidden force somewhere that pointed me in the right direction. It was a good example of fate taking a hand.

A similar example of fate was when I was about to film a scene for '*A Bicycle Made for Three*' (1982), another episode in my first series. The unit had unloaded their equipment and our three main actors were psyching themselves up for their location breakfasts when from somewhere nearby, came the intrusive sound of a pneumatic drill.

I looked out over the valley and saw that on the road below, there were two men with a mobile generator and a pneumatic drill digging a hole in the road. Mike Cager quickly drove down to see if they could be persuaded to defer their digging, but it was emergency work, and they couldn't stop. There was no alternative – if we wanted to film anything that day, we would have to go elsewhere. I told the unit to pack up and get ready to move.

I studied an Ordnance Survey map and saw that a yellow line, denoting a minor road, came to an abrupt end at the top of a hill. Following the map, I drove up the steep winding road to a junction and turned left into 'Intake Lane'. Passing a cottage at the start of this road to nowhere, I saw an elderly woman standing in the garden. She looked at me very suspiciously. I smiled at her and gave a polite reassuring wave of acknowledgement, but she looked as though she thought I was an alien from another planet and just stared back at me.

I followed the road towards where, on the map, it ended. As I drove over the crown of the hill, the continuation of the road ahead came into view.

I saw that it led to a really beautiful junction that couldn't have been more spot-on for my filming.

I parked my car and got out to see if it was as good as it at first appeared to be. It was perfect in every way. It was so quiet and beautiful that it was hard to believe that it wasn't a popular beauty spot. It had no traffic (there was nowhere for it to go) and the road surface was in excellent condition. The end of the road was, in fact, a small crossroads. To the left was a dusty lane that went past a few fields where some sheep were grazing. To the right of this lane over a dry stone wall, were a few windswept trees growing at an angle on a grassy plateau. This plateau dropped down sharply and looked very much like a cliff-edge. In fact, a few years later, I would use it as such for the ending of *Getting Sam Home* (1983).

At the crossroads, ahead of me, was a very rough track that led down the other side of the hill. The heather and the gorse bushes on both sides of this track – which was part of an old

Top Left: *Foggy (Brian Wilde) instructs Clegg (Peter Sallis) and Wally (Joe Gladwin) on how to tow Compo (Bill Owen) on his skis. Top Right: The director shows the water sports enthusiasts what he wants. Centre: A break in the Press day activities (The blonde is Mrs Bell). Bottom Left: Sid (John Comer) Clegg (Peter Sallis) Compo (Bill Owen) and Wally Batty (Joe Gladwin) enjoy a break. Bottom Right: Clegg and Foggy shout at the frogman (Compo) below the water as a very dry Bill Owen speaks his lines out of shot.*

Above: Ronnie Hazlehurst and his orchestra record new music for each episode. Right: Notes to Wally (Joe Gladwin) and Nora (Kathy Staff) in their motor cycle and sidecar.

stone quarry – neatly framed the view beyond of the village of New Mill with its imposing, if somewhat sombre, church.

The script for *A Bicycle Made for Three* required a hill for the three men to coast down on a triple-cycle contraption. It would have been quite difficult to film this at the original location, but here I had been led to the absolutely perfect hill for the scene.

Similarly, for the shot where the three men brake and go sailing over the handlebars of the bicycles, I would have had to improvise quite a bit. Again, here was the perfect wall at the side of the road that was exactly the right height to see the stuntmen clearly, yet mask the cardboard boxes and mattresses where they would land safely. The wall wasn't *almost* the right height – it was *exactly* the right height.

Intake Lane was a perfect location which could be used for an endless variety of scenes. It was a location that I would use in every subsequent series over a period of 28 years. It was as though I was meant to find this obscure filming paradise. It really was fate.

The unit was soon on its way, and must have really confused the lady back at the house when more than twenty unit vehicles passed her heading for the new location.

Gordon Wharmby excelled in his playing of Wesley at the new green garage location for *Car and Garter* (1982), and it was heartening to hear Bill Owen's generous praise of his natural acting style. He certainly didn't let me down in any way.

It was when we were back at the flooded Brighouse quarries again to film scenes for *From Wellies to Wetsuit* (1982) that my assistant, Hilary Bennett, handed me a memo from John Howard Davies, our Head of Comedy. It simply read:

To all Production Departments.
The second series of The Hitch-Hiker's Guide to the Galaxy *has been cancelled because of the author's inability to write it.*

I wasn't at all surprised that the project was scrapped, for it was quite clear that Douglas Adams didn't have an idea in his head for a second television series. Hilary was very impressed by the brevity and directness of John's memo, and said that there should be more bosses like him. I heartily agreed.

There was a press call for *Last of the Summer Wine* at the location that day, and we filmed various scenes with Compo attempting to use a pair of decorated water skis, supposedly made by Wally Batty, played to perfection as always by Joe Gladwin.

The effects team had made a clever mechanism that would dig the skis into the mud of the lake when Compo was dragged off them by Sid on his old motorbike. Unfortunately, they hadn't made a duplicate pair of skis for the rest of the filming, so at least an hour was lost bolting the skis on and off the special rig. This delay on a very sunny day was bad news for me, but good news for the press who had lots of time to photograph my glamorous and efficient assistant Hilary, posing with Bill Owen who was dressed in his rubber wetsuit. It also gave the press the opportunity to interview all the cast. All the cast, that is, except Brian Wilde who refused to speak to any of the journalists.

Brian Wilde had been badly let down when a newspaper printed an off the record remark made over a glass of wine following an interview at his home. Brian had said that he didn't particularly like Bill Owen or his politics, but he liked acting with him. The newspaper headline was something like 'Trouble in Summer Wine Land'. Good relations between Brian Wilde and Bill Owen were never completely restored, but they continued to act well together and had mutual respect for each other's talents. However, Brian never trusted journalists again, and refused to talk to any of them – without exception.

The final scene in *From Wellies to Wetsuit* was also the background for the closing titles. Roy Clarke had written that the three men walk off along the river bed with Compo using his water skis as stilts. I had to veto this idea because – even if there had been a suitable river (and there wasn't), it would have been impossible to get anyone to walk on makeshift stilts along a rocky riverbed. I took the easy option and just had them walking off into the distance down a dusty lane. There was no need to search for somewhere suitable – it was up the hill at our Intake Lane location. After the dialogue, the end titles would be superimposed to Ronnie Hazlehurst's theme tune. I told the three actors not to stop walking until they heard me shout "Cut". So the camera rolled and off they went.

> Compo: *I could murder some fish and chips.*
> Foggy: *You usually do.*
> Clegg: *If ever there's been a neglected subject in poetry, it's vinegar.*

The end title music only lasted about 35 seconds, so when the time was up, I quietly signalled the unit to take down all the equipment and hide behind the gorse bushes that were growing at the side of the lane.

The sound recordist gave me some headphones and, after a minute or two, from the radio mikes, I heard Peter Sallis say, "They must have enough by now." Brian Wilde quickly added, "Don't stop yet – don't stop yet…. or we'll have to do it all again, you know what he's like." Bill Owen then said, "I often walk backwards, I'll have a look." Bill did a Compo slouch turn and started scuffling backwards. He stopped and very grumpily said, "They've gone off and left us – the flaming rotters!" The radio mike actually picked up words that weren't quite 'flaming rotters', but they took it very well. Well, almost.

In later years, Bill Owen would often say that, out of the 150 or so episodes he had been in at the time, *From Wellies to Wetsuit* was his favourite.

In a studio scene, Compo, dressed in his frogman outfit, goes into a newsagent's where two ladies are gossiping. Bill asked me, if rather than just stand there in his frogman outfit, there was anything that he could do to distract the women that was funny. I told him that the women's lines were very funny, and they would be lost if he did anything visually funny during them. But Bill was

Foggy and Clegg during a break in filming From Wellies to Wetsuit (1982).

adamant that he wasn't going to just stand there and be a stooge for two anonymous characters. He wanted some funny business.

This was like being asked to make my silent comedies again. I said that I could have a magazine rack made that would trigger a domino effect: When one of them was turned over, the whole shelf of magazines would then cascade one by one on to the floor. Then, we could make another magazine display that, when Compo leans on it to adjust his wellies, it tips back just enough to send the lot on to the floor and out of sight. Bill loved the idea and worked on this physical business to make it all seem unrehearsed and natural. He really enjoyed playing the visual comedy in the episode which was transmitted as the last in the series, and then again as a tribute to him when he died eighteen years later.

The music for *From Wellies to Wetsuit* was composed, as always, by Ronnie Hazlehurst. The routine was, that we would meet in the film cutting room, and he would carefully make notes of where I wanted the music to be on the film sequences and the feelings it should express (or underline).

In the days of 'Old BBC', programmes were made with few artistic limitations. If an orchestra was required, an orchestra was booked. At that time, music was recorded in the BBC's music studio at Lime Grove. It had formerly been studio H, the home of the old *Tonight* programme – and before that, it was an old silent movie studio.

For the scene in *From Wellies to Wetsuit*, where Nora sees Compo in his frogman suit coming down her basement stairs, I asked Ronnie to write *Jaws*-style shark music. I don't think Ronnie had seen *Jaws*, for although I had asked him to use a double bass, but his music didn't have that ominous feel to it. I'm ashamed to admit that I can't read music, so all I could do was imitate the music that has become synonymous with lurking sharks. Ronnie asked me to come out of the control room and join him on the conductor's podium. "Let the band hear what you want," he said. So I took a deep breath, puffed up my cheeks and blew from within. To me, it sounded like a pretty good imitation of John Williams' famous shark music, but I sensed that I was being sent-up, when the orchestra made a complete hash of improvising what I had just done for them so that I would have to do it again. But after a break, Ron caught the ominous feel of the shark music. But I wasn't at all surprised when some of the musicians said that they much preferred my rendition.

Like Kathy Staff, Ronnie Hazlehurst was born in the village of Dukinfield over the Pennines in Lancashire. Brought up in an atmosphere of mills and brass bands, it was hardly surprising that Ronnie found it easy to write the evocative music for *Last of the Summer Wine*.

In the *25 Years of Last of the Summer Wine* documentary, Ronnie tells of how the theme music, which is basically a waltz, was initially rejected by the BBC because it didn't have the bright feel associated with comedy programmes. In the end, common sense prevailed and his music was recognised as being perfect for a series about three elderly men enjoying their later years in the hills and valleys of Yorkshire.

CHAPTER 5

Car and Garter

Filming in Yorkshire for my first series had been extremely enjoyable. The poor weather that had marred the filming for others in the past just didn't happen for me, although we did have a few bouts of torrential rain which passed very quickly – so quickly that I had only just finished putting on my Wellingtons and rainwear.

One of the best known settings of *Last of the Summer Wine* is the Nora Batty location. But a great deal of work had to be done to make it look like her home. Looking at it from outside, just inside the front door is a staircase that leads up to the real occupants' living quarters. These stairs have to be carefully avoided by our camera whenever the front door is opened in a scene, because in the studio, our set is just a hallway with no stairs.

Outside, to the left of the front door, is the window of Nora's living room – but the window really belongs to the commercial property next door where the occupants kindly allow us to take down their shutters and put up our Nora Batty curtains.

To the right of the front door is Nora's kitchen. This really is a kitchen, but the sink is on the back wall and not at the window – where Nora has to be positioned for her exchanges with Compo. A false sink at the window, with a bucket beneath to collect the water from its drain easily overcomes that problem.

The sink must have looked quite realistic, for when a young design assistant was asked to empty the bucket of water, she very carefully removed it from beneath the sink and promptly poured it back down the sink drain. Much to her embarrassment, the water went everywhere.

Compo's bedroom window has to be positioned where he can open it and verbally harass Nora Batty on the landing beneath. But Compo's home is in the basement, below Nora's kitchen window and there is no bedroom window for Compo, nor is there a logical place for one to be seen. The solution was to use one of the windows belonging to the bookshop on the corner of the block. By never simultaneously seeing Compo at his window and Nora on the landing below, the viewers accept that Compo's basement flat has an upstairs window that is somewhere in the area next to Nora's kitchen window. Visitors to the filming were always confused by seeing Compo at the bookshop window, acting to the bristle end of a broom (to denote the position of Nora's face), or Nora herself, acting to a mark on the wall where Compo would be.

Filming at Nora Batty's steps was tricky, to say the least. Being on several levels, it was well-nigh impossible to position the actors, the camera and the lights on the small, very narrow landings with their uneven paving stones. Sometimes the camera tripod had to be extended to its full height, and the cameraman, in order to be able to look through the viewfinder, would have to balance precariously on boxes next to a fifteen foot drop. It was a situation that would never have passed a Health and Safety risk assessment. It really was very dangerous, but that is how it had been done by my predecessors.

In an attempt to overcome the problem, when we returned for the second block of filming, I had a scaffolding platform built alongside Nora's steps so that there was more room to work with the camera, and it was safe. It was a great success, but initially there was a slight problem. The camera couldn't avoid seeing a short length of scaffold tubing that appeared at the bottom of the frame. "Get some dingle," Fred Hamilton, our film cameraman, called.

Dingle is a technical term for a piece of branch or shrub that can be put in front of the camera to mask unwanted immoveable objects in the frame, or just to add to the artistic composition of a wide shot when there is perhaps too much sky.

While waiting for the dingle to be found, I was introduced to one of Holmfirth's civic dignitaries. He wanted to show me something and took me to the middle of the nearby bridge which had carried the main road into Holmfirth in the distant past. He pointed to a largish plant that was growing out of the river wall.

"The town is very proud of that," he said. "It's a fig tree that grew from a seed that was washed down in the great flood of 1852, when the Bilberry reservoir dam burst." As the councillor went into detail about the odds against that happening to a tiny fig seed, behind him I saw our prop man, saw in hand, go over to the fig tree and start to saw off a branch. I gripped the councillor by the arm and steered him away. "I've heard that story – it's very interesting" I said. "But tell me about that old building over there on the corner." Fortunately, the building on the corner, which was now a book shop, had once been a toll gate for the bridge we were now standing on. I can't say that I took in any of its history, as I was more concerned about the sound of a saw cutting down the historic fig tree behind us. Happily, the acquisition of the dingle went unnoticed and without a diplomatic incident, and filming soon resumed with the historic dingle in place.

Despite the difficulties of filming at Nora Batty's house, it's a location that, like Nora Batty herself, is an icon of the series. Every year, thousands of visitors from around the world visited Nora Batty's steps in the hope that they might be lucky and get a glimpse of some filming taking place, or even see Kathy Staff herself.

Kathy Staff, who played Nora in 255 episodes, was a natural actress and was certainly one of the kindest and most co-operative members of the cast. For a few years, she acted in *Crossroads*, an ATV series, playing Doris Luke. Every year, the producers of that series graciously wrote Doris Luke out of their series for the weeks that she was needed by the BBC to play Nora Batty.

I had the most wonderful weather any director could want for filming – and everything was good. But, nevertheless, there were still minor irritations to overcome. The final scene of *Serenade for Tight Jeans and Metal Detector* (1981) was a wide shot of Compo and Clegg walking along a hillside track above Holmfirth as Foggy uses his ex-army metal detector to scan the area ahead of them. I was with the camera high above the track with my walkie-talkie.

In the scene, Foggy hears the metal detector's screech and searches around the ground in the hope that it might be some Roman artefact. He picks up what turns out to be an old beer can. Clegg says, "Julius Caius Tetley – I like it." Compo then takes the can and tosses it down the hillside. They then walk off for the end titles to be superimposed. The shot was good, but the light had changed in the middle of the take when the sun had gone behind a small cloud. So I told them, via the walkie-talkie, that they would have to do it again. There was much grumbling from the actors as it was the end of a long filming day and to be fair, everyone was getting tired.

Take two, and the same action. Everything was perfect. Then Compo, instead of throwing the beer can away, daintily dropped it on the ground in front of him, before walking off. In disbelief, I shouted, "Cut. Why didn't you throw the can down the hill?"

"Don't get shirty with me, comrade," Bill said in a haughty school-mistress voice. "Your prop man told me not to throw it down the hill because he's the one that has to climb all the way down there to get it back every time."

It was fortunate that there was some distance between the prop man and me or there might well have been a very nasty incident.

Walkie-talkies are a vital part of the filming equipment, especially when there is some distance between the camera and the actors.

The Christmas episode was *Whoops* (1981) and involved some night filming. The very last scene in the episode was at the Church Square next to Sid's café in Holmfirth. We had already filmed our heroes jumping from the rear platform of a bus shouting, "Geronimo!" and to finish the episode, all I needed was a wide shot of the

Top: The Church opposite Sid's café is the final shot of the 1981 Christmas Special. Bottom: A substitute 'tin' shed is found at Hinchliffe Mill.

bus driving away, and Compo, Clegg and Foggy walking off into the square. This was a Christmas episode, so I decided to break with custom and have the church choir singing the lyrics of *Last of the Summer Wine*. To film this one shot, Fred Hamilton and I were 50ft up in the air on a hydraulic hoist, so a walkie-talkie was the only way to communicate with the unit below.

The Christmas lights and decorations had been set up by the designer, Stephan Paczai, and, although it was mid-August, it looked very much like a cold, damp December evening. But there was just one thing that spoiled the whole effect: there was a tree in the middle of the Church Square that had too much foliage for a winter scene.

I asked Stephan to have the prop men standby to prune some of the tree's leaves as soon as Mike Cager had obtained permission from the Church.

Shortly afterwards, the sound of sawing focussed our interest back to the square where I

Top Left: The scaffolding erected at Nora Batty's steps for safety's sake. Top Right: Gordon Wharmby (Wesley) feels at home amidst his mechanical junk. Bottom: A scene from Car and Garter (1982) is filmed in a lane above Holmfirth.

was alarmed to see the whole tree slowly falling over to the ground. "What have you done?" I shouted down the walkie-talkie. The reply from Stephan was, "It's all right, Alan. The vicar gave us permission." Permission or not, this was bad news, for it was a nice tree and I certainly didn't want it felled. It was bad enough when the fig tree was pruned. I felt that our welcome in the town was now seriously at risk.

Just as we were ready to film the bus driving off and the three men walking across the Church Square, it began to rain a little – not a lot, just a few spots. But it didn't really matter; after all, it was supposed to be night-time in December. The bus was ready, the lights were set, and all we needed were the artistes – Bill Owen, Peter Sallis and Brian Wilde. The voice of Alison Selby, our young assistant, came over the walkie-talkie: "I'm afraid they won't come out of their caravan – it's too wet," she reported.

The rain began to get a little heavier, and Fred Hamilton and I, exposed to the elements high up in the cradle of the hoist were beginning to get quite damp. I told Alison to go back into the caravan and explain to the three men that the final shot of them walking across the square would only take a few minutes to film, so if they came on to the set quickly, they could go home earlier, and we wouldn't all get soaked. A few moments later, back came the response: "They refuse to come out while it's raining."

I then told Alison to go back into the caravan and ask them if they would like some refreshments. I carefully watched, from my high vantage point, as Alison went into the actors' caravan. The moment that I saw the caravan door close behind her, I pressed the button on my walkie-talkie:

"Alison, when you're there, would you explain to them, in a very nice way, of course, that the whole crew is getting soaked to the skin out here, and their behaviour is both selfish and unprofessional." A few moments later, Alison came from the caravan and cupped her hand over the mouthpiece of her walkie-talkie. "I'm so sorry, but I had my walkie-talkie open and they heard every word you said."

"Did they?" I said. "Oh dear. Never mind, I didn't say anything I didn't mean."

A few moments later, the caravan door opened and the three men emerged, ready for work. From up in the hoist, I couldn't see if the men were happy or not, but they never ever mentioned my 'broadcast', and the filming was completed successfully. My theory was that they, being very decent chaps at heart, didn't want to get Alison into trouble for having her walkie-talkie open and letting them hear my annoyance, so they pretended not to have heard me. They proved that they were, deep down, true gentlemen.

I ensured that a new tree was planted to replace the one that the local newspaper correctly described as having been 'vandalised by the BBC'. However, the following year, when we returned, the new tree had been snapped in half by some local louts. The newspaper heading said, 'Replacement of BBC vandalised tree is destroyed'. For three more years, our replacement trees were planted, and promptly vandalised.

Then Stephan had a mature, wide-girthed tree planted. There was no way that this one could possibly be snapped in half. And…as a bonus, Stephan proudly showed me a plastic duplicate tree that he had made for the studio scenes. He was very proud of this tree, and would check that the cameras could see it properly through the café window – adjusting its position to suit. This demonstrated an unparalleled devotion to a plastic tree.

It was at the studio recording of *Edie and the Automobile* (1986) a few years later, when I had to record a short scene of Edie (played by Thora Hird) driving along in her little red car. This was played in front of a green screen so that the view of the road behind could be added electronically. The effect was reasonably convincing, but the light was too constant. I asked for something to be passed across the front of the light so that its shadows would give the impression of the car going past trees. This was done quite effectively, and the studio recording ended.

Shortly afterwards, as I was talking to one or two friends in the studio control room, Stephan appeared, almost in tears. I asked him what was wrong. He said that the studio prop men had used his plastic tree to pass in front of the light for my shot, and had snapped it in half! I was very sorry for Stephan, but I couldn't help feeling that it really was poetic justice.

Meanwhile, back in Holmfirth, once again the genuine mature wide girthed tree was chopped down by a person or persons unknown, and the local Council eventually gave up the idea of having a tree outside the café. It opted, instead, for a large stone trough filled with flowers which would be much more difficult to snap in half, and impossible to steal.

With all the location filming completed, we returned to London to record the studio scenes and complete the episodes. In studio 3 at Television Centre it was clear that Gordon Wharmby was a great 'find', but I was still a little concerned that he might let me down.

Before the dress run (the final rehearsal when the camera shots are checked and the actors are in full costume and make-up), it was customary for the actors to sit in the audience seating. There, they would watch for the first time, the edited location film sequences on the overhead television monitors. These sequences would be shown later to the audience in story order to link the live studio scenes being performed before them.

Afterwards, in the BBC Club bar, Peter Sallis came up to me with a long face.

"Alan, I have to tell you; the filming is terrible," he said. "The timing of the lines is all wrong."

I was somewhat taken aback by this, because I had taken care to ensure that, between the lines of dialogue, there were suitable gaps for the laughter of the studio audience. This isn't easy, for you have to guess how big a laugh might be for a funny line, and not let an actor kill the laugh by jumping in with the next line too soon.

Peter instanced the long gap I had left between Compo's two finger gesture and Clegg's line: "He gives remarkably clear hand signals for a non-driver."

I assured Peter that I had left the gap long to allow for the audience laugh. It was a funny line and it would be a pity not to hear it if it was drowned by laughter. "Alan, believe me, after that long gap, my line is no longer funny. You really must re-shoot all the filming." I was surprised, but not unduly concerned as it was a really good episode and very funny. My only concern at that moment was still Gordon Wharmby. Would he be as good in front of the audience when the pressure is on?

I needn't have worried. Gordon was absolutely perfect – and so was the audience, who laughed so much during that damned gap, that their laughter only just finished in time for Peter's line. To his great credit, Peter couldn't wait to apologise after the recording, and say that he had been entirely wrong and that it was one of the best episodes ever. It was a good example of how important audience laughter is in comedy programmes.

Getting the laughter isn't always easy, even on the funniest of shows. Sometimes, for no obvious reason, an audience will turn up that is vocally unresponsive. They will smile at all the funny lines but there are hardly any audible laughs to record. This phenomenon even happened sometimes on the Morecambe and Wise show. Before each recording, they would perform their sure-fire, tried and tested, big-laugh warm-up routine of Ernie showing Eric how to be a ventriloquist. Sometimes, however, although the audience would thoroughly enjoy the very same sketch, they would just sit there with big smiles on their faces and refuse to laugh out loud.

Eric said that it was someone at the front of the queue who writes a note saying: 'Don't laugh tonight –pass it on.'

I have always found that having a family audience is best, as the parents want their children to have a good time and encourage them to enjoy the comedy. But, in the end, it is the indefinable chemistry of every audience that determines if the laughter is going to be rich or sparse.

However, sometimes you can get a pretty good idea of what to expect when the audience is seated and ready for the show to begin. It is the custom at the recording of situation comedies for the Producer to greet the audience, tell them a little about the episode, and introduce the warm-up man. On one show quite a few years later, I walked out in front of the audience and looked at what fate had brought us. I looked at them and couldn't believe what I saw. Everyone in the first three rows was Japanese. This didn't bode well for the desired laughter quotient, but there was another reason for my dismay. There was a sequence in the location filming where Foggy says, "How many can say that they have shot a Japanese sniper out of a tree at 200 yards?"

I was certain that the Japanese party would be deeply offended by this, and I waited with bated breath for this sequence to come up. When it did, there was a good healthy laugh from the audience, and I could see through the production gallery window, that our far-Eastern visitors were rolling about laughing at the line. Afterwards, I asked one of the audience supervisors (who issue the tickets at the BBC and look after the audiences) why they ignored the potentially upsetting line. She said that the Japanese party had come from the Commonwealth Institute in Kensington and that none of them spoke any English. This explained why they weren't offended. But, if they didn't speak any English, how could they laugh at the humour so heartily? The answer was that the Japanese are very polite, and when the rest of the audience laughed, they joined in.

Nora Batty (Kathy Staff) enjoys giving her steps a good brushing.

CHAPTER 6
Sit Down and Read This

For the first block of filming in 1981, I had rented a small terraced house in the middle of Holmfirth, only a hundred yards from The Shoulder of Mutton. It was good to be seen around the town in the evenings as it generated a great deal of goodwill. I wasn't seen as being just one of those anonymous BBC folk that arrive in the morning and go back to their hotels in Huddersfield at the end of the day. I became a friend to whom they could easily relate. Even today, in Holmfirth, vaguely-remembered faces from that period call out to me whenever they see me in town.

For the second block of filming that year, Bill Owen invited me to share a rented farmhouse with him. Bill was pleased to inform me that this would substantially reduce our accommodation costs.

Bill was very happy with the arrangement as he had the large master en-suite bedroom with a superb view over the valley, and I had the small single room along the corridor which I came to call the servants quarters.

I could always tell when Bill was up in the morning because he had an irritating habit of whistling through his teeth (after he had put them in, of course). When it stopped, it meant that he was either eating, gargling or learning his lines for the day's filming. Bill liked to learn his lines first thing in the morning because they would be fresh in his mind when he went on to the set. He always had a pretty good command of his lines with only a touch of paraphrasing which, Bill always insisted was what Compo would say in the various situations. Roy Clarke accepted that Bill was getting on in years and as long as it didn't make nonsense of the speeches, he would reluctantly have to accept Bill's version. Fortunately, it didn't happen often enough to become an issue.

Sharing the farmhouse with Bill for the second block of filming had worked out quite well. It was very relaxing to have a quiet environment in the evenings and on the days off. Being only a walkable mile out of Holmfirth, it wasn't too remote.

One afternoon on one of the days off, I was getting ready to go out when Bill came down the stairs from his bedroom. He asked me if I was busy. I thought that he was going to ask me to take him into Huddersfield again where he would get his favourite frozen fish pie from Marks and Spencer. But no, when I told him that I wasn't doing anything, he handed me a paperback book. "Sit down and read this," he ordered. I looked at the cover and it was simply entitled *Last of the Summer Wine*. Bill added, "This is the best black

The unit at work near Holme Moss.

comedy I have ever read, and the BBC should make a film of it."

"The BBC don't make feature films," I told him.

"I know. I know. That's what they've told your predecessors, but you're the bloke with all the awards, they might listen to you."

'The bloke with all the awards' was a bit of a giveaway as this was how I had been 'sold' to the cast and, possibly, the writer.

I started to read *Last of the Summer Wine*, the novel, and it was so good that I couldn't put it down. Roy Clarke had written a very funny story about old Sam, their heavily married friend, and his desire, before he dies, to have one last fling with Lily Bless Her, his dubious floozy girlfriend in the village. It was a very funny book and I was certain it would make an excellent feature-length film. Regardless of the fact that the BBC don't make TV movies, I decided to try and sell the idea to John Howard Davies.

When I returned to London a week later, I showed John Howard Davies the book and said that I would like to make it as a film – a TV movie. As expected, John said, "We don't make TV movies."

"Why not?" I asked.

"We just don't," he replied.

"But this would be a fantastic move for the department."

"Nobody does TV movies at the BBC," he said.

"Then why don't we break new ground and be the first?"

John thought about it for a moment and then smiled.

"Alright, I'll tell you what. Commission Roy to write a script, and we'll take it from there."

Roy Clarke was very pleased when I told him that there was a strong likelihood of his book being filmed as it really was a very funny story.

The reaction of the studio audiences to my first series indicated that it would do very well in the ratings, but transmission timing is all. Get a poor slot and you're finished. In later years, the series was damned by being shown too early in the evening, and worst of all, in the middle of summer. Who in their right mind would rush back from the beach, or a barbeque, to watch a television show?

About a month before Christmas 1981, I was coming up in the lift from the basement at the Television Centre. The doors opened at the ground floor and Alan Hart, the new Controller of BBC1, entered. He didn't actually know me, but we had been nodding acquaintances along the studio corridors when he was Head of Sport. "What are you working on?" he enquired benignly.

"I've just finished *Last of the Summer Wine*," I replied.

"Ah, my wife's favourite programme."

I quickly replied, "Could you ask your wife if she would get the Controller to put out our Christmas show at seven o'clock on Christmas evening? It's really good, and will be top of the ratings."

He laughed and, as the lift doors opened, said that he would ask her.

When the transmission of *Whoops* was announced, I was astonished – and gratified – to see that it was to be shown on Christmas evening at 7:15! And it really was top of the ratings that Christmas, beating the premiere showing of *Gone with the Wind* (1939) that had cost the BBC millions of pounds. Thank you, Mrs. Hart.

The simple reason for its success was that *Last of the Summer Wine* is a gentle comedy that the whole family can watch together – perfect for Christmas night. Since then, I have often travelled up and down the lifts in the Television Centre lifts near Christmas but to no avail, and *Last of the Summer Wine* has had to suffer from really appalling scheduling at Christmas.

Compo (Bill Owen)

CHAPTER 7
Intrigue

Before 1981 had ended, I was summoned to see James Gilbert, who was now Head of Light Entertainment. Having started *Last of the Summer Wine* off as its first Producer/Director, he understandably had a paternal interest in the series. Jimmy had previously remarked how much he liked the way I made the series – particularly in turning the café set around by 90 degrees which he agreed looked much better on the screen.

But Jimmy had some bad news for me. He got straight to the point: "Brian Wilde says he won't sign his contract if you do the next series."

I was shocked and deeply hurt by this unexpected turn of events. I had certainly been firm with the actors, and avoided the traditional fussing over them. But I had always treated them with respect for their excellent work. We had all worked together well, and I had believed that I had a good relationship with Brian Wilde. Other than refusing his requests to have more close-ups (which I put down to vanity), there were certainly no obvious signs of dissent.

Jimmy asked if I could think of any reason why Brian was taking such an unexpected stand. I told him I had absolutely no idea whatsoever. But when I mentioned that I had shared a large farm house with Bill Owen for the duration of the second block of filming, he immediately reasoned that it must be that. "Brian may well have felt that Bill had some advantage, because he had your ear in the evenings." Jimmy then said, "Brian Wilde will have to be persuaded to change his mind."

When Bill Owen heard that Brian wouldn't sign his contract if I did the next series, he was very angry and formally told Jimmy Gilbert that he wouldn't sign his contract if I *didn't* do the next series. I suspected that Bill's stance was not so much in support of me, but rather that Brian Wilde, who was the newcomer to the series, shouldn't be calling the tune.

Without warning, the machinations to persuade Brian to join us again suddenly fell apart. Sydney Lotterby told Brian Wilde that he would be happy to take back the series. I felt that this was highly unethical because Sydney really should have discussed his desire to take back the series with me, and not one of my artists. He had given up the series, and should not have been interfering.

Brian Wilde later revealed to me that, throughout the production of my first series, Sydney had called him regularly to find out how it was all going. I felt that this was a bit below the belt, as it was bound to undermine my authority and give Brian Wilde a receptive ear for any grumbles he might have. Sydney was clearly looking for embers of discontentment to fan.

Clegg, Foggy and Compo (Peter Sallis, Brian Wilde and Bill Owen)

Sydney Lotterby was considerably senior to me, and it was going to be difficult for the department to tell him that he couldn't have the series back, particularly as Brian Wilde was demanding him. It was a very difficult situation.

Then, out of the blue, I was told that Spike Milligan, who hadn't been happy with the production of his last series (the *Q9* series) had asked for me as his next producer/director. It was well-known that both the producer and the director of his last series weren't at all happy with Spike's undisciplined way of working, which had resulted in over-long recording times.

I was told that Spike had said that he wanted a Producer who was sympathetic to his comedy – namely me. Looking back, I wouldn't mind betting that a bit of horse trading took place to get Spike to want me so badly. Well, that's show business, and I had no complaints. I liked Spike Milligan very much.

So the awkward problem of Bill Owen versus Brian Wilde was diplomatically resolved without any blood being spilled. I was very pleased to receive a personal letter from Roy Clarke expressing his extreme anger at Brian Wilde's unreasonable behaviour. Although it was some comfort to me, I was still very disappointed to lose the BBC's No.1 comedy series, just when it was at its height of popularity.

But, now I had Spike Milligan to work with, and I was going to enjoy every moment of it.

It was when I was halfway through making the Spike Milligan series that I had a telephone call from Bill Owen. He asked me if he could come along to the Television Centre and watch Spike at work. I would never have put Bill down as a Spike Milligan fan, but he arrived in the morning and came into the production gallery to watch the recording. He didn't say anything. He just sat in a seat where he could look down through the production gallery window into the studio. He laughed at Spike's comedy and, after watching for a while, took his leave and went off home.

Bill called me the next day to thank me for letting him visit the Spike Milligan recording. He then remarked that I held Spike down too much. I should give him more latitude to be himself. Bill's interest in coming along and his remarks went completely over my head until recently, when I discovered that, in the early fifties, Spike and Bill had worked together in a hugely successful West End production of *Son of Oblomov*. In this play every single night, Spike would abandon the script and ad lib his way through the rest of the play. Bill Owen had enjoyed this experience of working with Spike, and had come along to see him working again. I can now understand Bill's disappointment and the reason for his comment.

I can only hope that he met Spike that morning. He never said.

On reflection, although Spike's series was trouble-free and well-received, I think that Bill was probably right. I did keep him too tightly in control. Spike really is at his best when he ad libs. But nonetheless, there were still favourable reviews. Herbert Kretzmer (the lyricist of *Les Misérables*) wrote in his review of the series in the *Daily Mail* that Spike had been around so long that we tended to take him for granted, "like a pair of familiar fireside slippers".

He went on to say that *There's a Lot of it About* (1982) demonstrated that Spike was still the most inventive and significant figure in British comedy at the time. Coming from the lyricist of *Les Miserables*, it was praise indeed.

As well as making the Spike Milligan series, I also, at the behest of James Gilbert, reconstructed a Ronnie Barker film silent comedy called *By the Sea* (1982). I had given up being a film editor many years ago but, whenever there was a filmic problem in Light Entertainment, I would inevitably be asked to advise. Film Editor was a tag that I wanted to avoid; it was in my past and I wanted to leave it there. But Jimmy said that Ronnie Barker's film was not transmittable. The department would be eternally grateful if I could 'save' it. I felt that I had a duty to help.

Ronnie Barker, besides being hugely talented, was notorious for interfering in the production of his shows, and it was felt that the major problem of *By the Sea* was probably Ronnie Barker, even though he had written its script. The film's producer apologised for the state of the film, but said that Ronnie had taken over the filming and wouldn't even let the director look through the camera viewfinder.

On the clear understanding that Ronnie Barker would be kept away from the restructuring of the film, I agreed to undertake this unrewarding and onerous task. It took me about a month of sitting with the film editor in a small, unglamorous cutting room in the middle of Soho. Every shot in every scene was painstakingly assessed and adjusted. In the end, with the help of Ronnie Hazlehurst's music (which I insisted upon having), *By the Sea* was a huge critical success, and top of the ratings on BBC1 at Easter that year. As it would be all too easy to dismiss my work as being simply a matter of re-editing the film, I took the precaution of keeping a copy of the original version. Although I didn't want an on-screen credit, I was credited on the video releases as 'Post Production Director' which I think was fair.

While I was working on these programmes, the hijacked 1983 series of *Last of the Summer*

Wine was being made in the wild north by Sydney Lotterby. It would be completely dishonest of me to say that I was sorry to hear that quite a few filming days were lost because of extremely bad weather, but my reaction was that it served him damned well right.

CHAPTER 8
Getting Sam Home

Sydney Lotterby may have successfully succeeded in snatching back the series, but I wasn't going to let him have the feature-length film without a fight. It was mine: it was I who had persuaded the BBC to commission it, and I couldn't see why I should step aside and let another Producer make it, no matter how senior he may be. It was another problem for the front office: how can they tell an Executive Producer that he can't have the coveted *Last of the Summer Wine* film to make? The answer was found quite simply: have both Producers budget the film.

Although the film was quite demanding of time and effort, I said that I could make it in four weeks. Sydney's estimate was considerably longer than that (I wasn't privy to the details, but I heard it was six weeks) So the film, which was ultimately called *Getting Sam Home* (1983), went to me to make in four weeks.

I have to confess here that my estimate was not the result of careful consideration. Like a fairground 'guess your weight' man, I simply looked at the weight of the printed script and thought that four weeks would be long enough. This would, obviously be less costly for the department, but it would also be more challenging for me personally, as I would be working to a very tight filming schedule.

But what of Brian Wilde? Well, I said to John Howard Davies that it was my opinion that artists should never have producer or director approval, and Brian should be told that he either works with me or he will be replaced. He should be reminded that although he was excellent in every way at playing Foggy and was popular with the viewers, he was not the only star of the series: there were three principal actors, and Bill Owen and Peter Sallis had as big a following, if not bigger than Brian Wilde.

John wholeheartedly agreed with me that Brian Wilde would be diplomatically told that, if he wouldn't work with me, we would be forced to recast. This was an option that I didn't want to think about for the novel and the adaptation strongly featured the Foggy character, and he would have been impossible to replace quickly.

Brian's response was unexpectedly friendly and helpful. He asked John if he could clear the air and take me to lunch for a face-to-face meeting. The following week, a rendezvous for the luncheon was set – halfway between the BBC Television Centre and Brian's home. Brian and his actress wife, Eva Stewart, came from their home in the Hertfordshire town of Ware to a pub restaurant opposite Elstree Film Studios in Borehamwood. It was a very relaxed and informal lunch, and there was no feeling of awkwardness whatsoever, which would have been quite understandable, bearing in mind the upset that his actions had caused.

Brian immediately addressed the compatibility issue which had caused him to make the demands that he did. He said that, in past, he had been used to the routine of rehearsing and blocking-out the scenes with Bill, Peter and the director (Sydney Lotterby) who would then break the scene down into shots to 'cover' it. Brian hadn't liked my way of having them work to the camera and only shooting what was needed – particularly when I had the camera on a track with marks on the ground for them to hit. He felt that it interfered with the business of acting.

But, graciously, Brian went on to say that he had watched my series and he had very much liked what he had seen. He said he thought it was very well shot, and that he now understood what I had been doing and why I worked the way I do. He said that he could see the advantages of the director having a firm idea of how the scenes would appear on the screen.

We parted good friends (I'm not sure that we were otherwise) after agreeing that what had passed should be put aside. And it was.

Brian added however, with no hard feelings, that he didn't think he would do any more episodes after the feature-length film, the script of which, he thought was excellent.

Roy Clarke's script for *Getting Sam Home* was a truly marvellous adaptation of his book. It was the story of their ailing friend, Sam, who asks the trio to help him escape from the boredom of life with his humourless wife Sybil for one night of bliss with the local floozy.

I asked Roy to consider having a montage scene at the start to make it a stand-alone film: showing the characters as they were when they were young, I felt, would set-up the film for those who hadn't seen the series. But Roy said that he wanted to keep that as a separate idea for a series.

Roy Clarke did later write *First of the Summer Wine* which showed the cast as teenagers just before the Second World War. This series was also hijacked – this time by Gareth Gwenlan, a new Head of Comedy who overcame the BBC's sensible and firm rule that heads of department can't also produce programmes.

Gareth, who had produced and directed the popular *To The Manor Born* (1979-81) and *'The Fall and Rise of Reginald Perrin* (1976-79) a few years earlier, made sure that the filming dates for *First of the Summer Wine* conflicted with those of *Last of the Summer Wine*. Gareth originally decreed that *First* had to be made for less money than *Last*, which was going to be difficult as period productions are always more expensive. However, when he took it over money was suddenly no object. Our Head of Department was now a competitor.

Although Gareth's pilot episode and the subsequent episodes (in the hands of Michael Stephens) were very good, *First of the Summer Wine* (1988-89) never attained the popularity of the senior series.

I felt that this was mainly because some of the cast were too old to play teenagers and it didn't have Ronnie Hazlehurst's music to create the period atmosphere and be a clear link with *Last of the Summer Wine*. The idea of using gramophone records of the period had, by this time, been done to death.

Local Holmfirth shopkeepers had a different theory. Whereas Bill Owen and his fellow actors had co-operated in letting them sell their photographs and other memorabilia, the new young cast visited the shops and demanded that they remove from their shelves everything featuring their images until they received some payment. Consequently, when tourists walked around the town, there was no lasting publicity for *First of the Summer Wine*, but plenty for *Last of the Summer Wine*.

The script for *Getting Sam Home* ended with Sam's floozy, Lily Bless Her (dressed in black for his funeral), getting a lift in his wife's limousine. Although this was exactly as in the book, I felt that there should be an additional scene to make the ending a little stronger and keep Compo, Clegg and Foggy in the film to the very end. Roy agreed and, a few days later, he sent down the new scene. When I read it, I laughed out loud. The new scene had the three men on a cliff edge about to scatter Sam's ashes. Foggy says that they should give the moment some dignity by scattering the ashes ceremoniously. However, in performing wide sweeping movements, Foggy loses his balance. The final stage direction was:

FOGGY DISAPPEARS OVER THE EDGE WITH A MOURNFUL HOWL – END

When I showed the script of this additional scene to John Howard Davies, he too laughed out loudly at Foggy's demise. This would explain Foggy's absence should there be any problem of Brian refusing to sign for the next series. As I didn't foresee any such problem, I decided that I would film an additional final shot of Foggy, unharmed, struggling to climb back up the cliff face. If the worst came to the worst and Brian declined to appear in any more episodes after *Getting Sam Home*, I would have the explanation in the can.

In May 1983, just before we went off to make *Getting Sam Home*, Bill Owen telephoned to tell me that he'd had lunch with Brian Wilde, Peter Sallis and 'someone else'. He wouldn't say who the 'someone else' was, but what had been discussed over lunch had made him very, very angry, but he would say no more. I told Bill that it might have been better for him not to have said anything rather than leave me mystified. Bill replied, "I just wanted you to know how angry I was."

I was also mystified by the reaction of the unit to one of Mike Cager's remarks. There were no cell phones at the time, and CB Radios (Citizen Band Radios) were beginning to catch on. There was limited range to the transmissions, but I told some of the crew to get themselves one so that we would always be in contact with each other. We would never again lose one of our trucks when moving between revised locations.

To use the CB radios, you had to identify yourself with a name – or 'handle'. Mike Cager gave me the handle of 'Top Producer' (I had been credited so in an embarrassing newspaper article). Mike said that he would like to have 'Scapegoat' as his handle which for some reason, everyone on the unit thought was very funny – and appropriate. I can't think why.

The *Getting Sam Home* script called for Sam to live in a detached bungalow with a low hedge at the front (so that a mobile fish and chip van could be seen from the doorstep) and a gate that squeaked, because Sam was in hospital with heart problems and hadn't been able to oil it. The search for this location was proving to be protracted and fruitless. There were plenty of bungalows in the Holme Valley, but none had all the particular requirements of the script.

Mike Cager, despite the scale of the production, was the Production Manager, First Assistant Director, Production Accountant and Location Manager (we were a very small, efficient, team in those days). Mike had found a bungalow at Jackson Bridge (near Holmfirth) that looked as though it could be adapted to look right for us. However, the owner said that she hated *Last of the Summer Wine* and wouldn't, under any circumstances, allow us to film on her property.

After three weeks of getting nowhere, I said that we should get an Ordnance Survey map again, and look for a crop of housing on the outskirts of Huddersfield where such bungalows were being built before the Second World War.

I pencilled a circle on the map where on a hillside, some houses were shown which might be just such a development. I set off with Mike Cager to find this elusive location.

Following the map, we drove up a hill at Almondbury on the outskirts of Huddersfield. We turned right, and there, quite astonishingly, was the exact bungalow as described in Roy Clarke's script. The name on the white painted gate identified the bungalow as 'Hillcrest' and, quite incredibly, it squeaked! Even more incredibly, the lady owner of the house apologised for the squeaky gate, and said that her husband hadn't been around to oil it because he had been in hospital with a heart problem! This was exactly as in the script and was an unsettling co-incidence.

'Hillcrest' proved to be absolutely perfect for our filming. It was situated at the end of a quiet road, overlooking the rooftops of a tidy part of Huddersfield. Because the bungalow was built on a hillside, the rear windows were about ten feet off the ground, which would be perfect for their struggle to get Sam out of his bedroom window to be spirited away in the night to see Lily Bless Her.

All we had to do was reduce the height of the hedge in the front garden, and put a shed on the lawn at the side. And, best of all, because it was on a quiet road, it wouldn't have any passing traffic to interrupt our filming.

Recently, I called at Hillcrest, and found that, 25 years on, it had changed very little. The gate still squeaked, but the hedge had grown tall again. Sadly, the lady's husband had since passed away. But she had very fond memories of the filming, which had made her a bit of a celebrity with her relatives and neighbours.

Because we had a lot of filming to do in four weeks, on the day before we started, I called Bill Owen, Peter Sallis and Brian Wilde to a rehearsal at the George Hotel in Huddersfield. I had booked a small conference room and wanted to rehearse all the location scenes so that everyone knew exactly what they would have to do. There was a noticeably cold atmosphere as they took out their scripts and put their coats over chairs.

"What's the point of all this?" Bill finally asked, somewhat critically.

"I just think we should rehearse the whole film," I said.

"We don't need to rehearse." Bill declared, as he faced up to me.

"We know our characters inside out, and with a script like that, you'd have to be a complete idiot not to understand how it should be played. You tell us what to do for your camera, and we'll do it." Peter Sallis and Brian Wilde nodded in agreement.

I must say that I was gratified to hear this, as it was, in a way, a testament to my way of working, which had upset Brian so much two years ago.

"So, it's coffees all round, and home?" I suggested.

At this, the three men lightened up and started putting their coats back on.

Of course, Bill Owen was right. I am always disappointed when actors need to 'find' the character or the mood, when they are so clearly drawn in the words of the script. I have found that the best actors can always act on cue with no warm ups or getting psyched-up. Maybe I was spoiled by working with some of the best.

When I audition actors I don't know, I sometimes ask them to play the scene differently – interpreting the role in a slightly different way. This shows if they are capable of taking direction.

I have had some pretty galling experiences – sometimes with quite well-known actors – when a simple line, which calls for an obvious intonation, is delivered in a way that makes a complete nonsense of the speech. Then, of course, there is the old bugbear of the emphasis being wrongly put on the personal pronoun which, again, usually makes the whole speech meaningless. In his autobiography, Sir Alec Guinness complains of the BBC announcers who say "It *is* nine o'clock." As he pointed out, "Who's arguing?"

I was absolutely delighted when I was able to get Fred Hamilton as my Cameraman on *Getting Sam Home*. Fred had worked on some of the episodes in my first series. He was tall and good-looking, and wouldn't have looked out of place in front of the camera. But I had asked for him because of his no-nonsense, pragmatic style of filming. Having said that, he always gave his best and achieved excellent results with very little fuss. Fred expected the same enthusiasm from his assistants and didn't hesitate to keep them in order if he sensed a lack of commitment.

For me, the really great thing about Fred Hamilton was that he didn't over-light set-ups, which helped the filming to be achieved efficiently and smoothly. Had it not been for Fred's enthusiasm and support, we would certainly have been hard-pressed to keep to the very tight schedule.

Fred strongly advised me to accept the first take whenever possible, and re-take only when it was absolutely necessary. Reluctantly, I agreed, and

Top: All our heroes need is some transport. Centre: Ready to film Sid's Mobile Fish and Chip shop in the hills. Left Inset: Sid's bus trundles down into Holmfirth

Top: Peter Sallis and Bill Owen about to film the end of scene of Getting Sam Hom (1983). Bottom Left: Getting Bottom: Filming the final scene of Getting Sam Home (1983).

throughout the filming, nearly always accepted the first take. Looking at the film now, there is hardly a shot that could have been bettered. The old adage that 'Take 1 is always best' proved to be spot-on.

Filming of *Getting Sam Home* progressed rather well – even on the dreaded night filming at Nora Batty's steps. A very drunk Wally Batty (played by Joe Gladwin) had to climb up the winding steps to his front door. This could have taken some time to film on the various landings, but I decided to use a camera crane. I had used camera cranes many times before on other productions, but they were nothing like the Moby Crane that was supplied that night. This was essentially a counterbalanced crane arm mounted on a hydraulically adjustable central column that was built on to the back of a giant American pick-up truck.

The Moby crane was easily reversed into position at the bottom of Nora Batty's steps and, after the operator had pressed a few buttons, quickly levelled. It was then simply a matter of the camera following Wally Batty as he climbed the steps to his front door. It demonstrated that here was the answer to the problem of filming on those difficult steps.

Although the Moby Crane has long-since been consigned to the scrap yard, I have always used a camera crane at Nora Batty's steps. It can safely put the camera and the cameraman into virtually any position on the different landings: no more scaffolding, no more dingle, and no more awkward incidents with Holmfirth councillors.

It was becoming clear that my estimate of completing the film in just four weeks had been a little optimistic. It never crossed my mind for one moment that we might fail to meet the deadline, but it was going to be a struggle all the same.

Then I got lucky. Very lucky! The BBC had instituted a new expenses policy which had the effect of making the crew stay at hotels and not 'Bed and Breakfasts' (where, previously, a small profit could be made on the overnight allowance). Fred had decided that, if he had to stay in a hotel, it might as well be a good one, so he decided to stay at a hotel in Elland, just beyond Huddersfield.

On the morning of the night shooting at Sam's house, Fred found himself having breakfast at the hotel with none other than Brian Wilde. I don't know what they talked about, but later that day, when the unit was assembling for the night filming, Fred arrived and came straight over to me. He asked me if he might address the unit. I wondered what was going on, but I said it was fine with me. Maybe it was somebody's birthday.

Near the mobile catering kitchen, which was parked on the road near Hillcrest, Fred gathered everyone together. The make-up department, the costume department, the effects crew and the whole film unit were in attendance. Fred told the assembled company that the *Last of the Summer Wine* film was very important to me, but it was obvious that the filming schedule was impossibly tight. Fred then told everyone that he'd had breakfast with one of the principal actors earlier, and discovered that there was 'someone' back in London who was waiting for me to fall flat on my face and return to London with an unfinished film. Fred said that he liked me, and he was going to do everything he possibly could to help get the film made in the scheduled four weeks. He then asked everyone in the company if they would pull together to help me get the film finished on time, even if it meant helping out on work they didn't usually do. There was a cheer of support from everyone without exception, and a resolve to follow Fred's example. It was extremely touching. I hadn't realised that anyone liked me that much (if at all).

Unfortunately, my right hand man, Mike Cager, was unwell and couldn't work. However after dinner and just before the night filming began, Dave Mason, the lighting gaffer, asked me to keep showing him the next two set-ups in advance. He said that he would pre-light them and get the camera tracks laid in readiness. It would then be simply a matter of us moving quickly from one set-up, to the next.

I suddenly found that the night filming, where everything that has to appear on the film has to be lit, and which usually progresses at a much slower pace, was moving along very quickly.

My daughter Cheraine became an unpaid runner and efficiently kept up the flow of artists to the various set-ups.

Dave Mason had virtually taken charge of the unit, ensuring that filming proceeded at a quite incredible pace.

I really couldn't think who this 'someone' was, back in London, who had caused this to happen, but I was extremely grateful.

The following evening, as we were driving to the bungalow location again for more night filming, Bill Owen asked me if I felt it was right that the stars have to queue with everyone else for their meals at the location catering truck. I told him that the meal breaks were a time of equality, and I wouldn't like to be the first producer to introduce a class system at meal times. Bill was not at all happy with this response, which was surprising really, as he was usually proud of his strong socialist leanings.

A little later, I was queuing for dinner with Bill at the catering truck. In front of us was Dave Mason, our invaluable and super-efficient lighting gaffer. I knew he had recently worked on the acclaimed television production of *Smiley's People* (1982) so I asked him if Alec Guinness was good to work with. "He was a real gentleman," Dave said. "For example, we all stepped aside to let him get to the front of the queue for his food, but he said 'Thank you, but no. You are just as important to the production as the actors, and I am very happy to take my place in the queue.'"

Bill Owen didn't say a word. Neither did I, because I don't think he would have believed any assurances that Dave's story hadn't been rehearsed – and it really wasn't.

An early scene in *Getting Sam Home* was set on a hillside overlooking a quiet track that ran alongside a river. The location I chose was over the hills from Holmfirth – beyond the BBC's transmitter at Holme Moss, and near the disused Woodhead Tunnel. In the scene, Compo, Clegg and Foggy are discussing the hospitalisation of their friend Sam when on the track below, they see 'Fairburn from Co-op Tailoring' arriving in his car with 'Her from the Bacon Counter' – no doubt in pursuit of a snatched romantic moment.

Getting up the hill to where the men would sit was, to say the least, difficult. The only way was to cross a river and climb up a fairly steep embankment. The crew could easily climb up to the higher level, but to convey our elderly actors (and the equipment), a four-wheel-drive Land Rover was hired. As usual, the actors were in high grumble and complained about the inaccessibility of the location and the extreme discomfort of being bounced about in the Land Rover as it crossed the rocky riverbed.

Unfortunately, it was overcast and damp, and much too dark and gloomy for an opening scene. This was the middle of May, and in Yorkshire the trees weren't yet in leaf, so it wasn't the pretty scene that I had hoped it would be. There was only one thing to do, and that was re-scheduling the scene for another day.

At the next attempt, a couple of days later, the weather had improved only slightly, but it was a bit brighter. We were preparing for the ordeal of getting everyone up the hill again, when I saw that Brian Wilde's son, Andrew, had come to visit us. The Land Rover would have to make two journeys up the hillside. Andrew could travel with his father, me, and Eileen Mair (our make-up designer), on the first trip. Gallantly, so that Eileen could sit at the front next to the driver,

Getting Brian Wilde across the river to the set above.

Brian said that he would sit with Andrew and me on the wheel-arch seats in the rear, which were far from being comfortable. Any grumbles would be understandable.

As the Land Rover went across the river, it rattled over the rocks and tilted alarmingly. There was no danger, but the bumping resulted in Brian being tipped onto the floor at the rear. I braced myself for the usual grumbles. But Brian laughed heartily. "I'm alright," he said and turning to his son as he climbed back onto the seat added, "It's nothing. You get used to putting up with this sort of thing." He laughed heartily again as though he was thoroughly enjoying the adventure. At that point, I wondered if I should persuade Andrew to stay with us for the rest of the filming as his father, obviously, wanted to be seen as a sort of Action Man by his son.

Just before we were about to film the scene of the scattering of Sam's ashes, Peter Sallis and Fred Hamilton were standing together on the hillside at Intake Lane, looking down at a grassy field below that was covered in mole hills. Peter asked Fred, in all seriousness, "Why, do you think, Fred, there aren't any molehills up here?" Fred, believing that this was a joke question, obligingly replied, "That's easy. They don't make molehills out of mountains." Peter fell about laughing at Fred's quick thinking.

In the script, there was only one short scene to be filmed in the café, and it wasn't worth the expense of building the set in the studio. Instead, I decided to film it inside the Ironmonger's paint store. This meant that we would have to make the interior of the paint store look exactly like the well-known café set that was seen in the studio. There wasn't much room for the camera and our lights, but the scene was static and didn't need much room.

During the whole time that I was in the café telling Fred how I was going to shoot the scene, there was a constant flow of people trying to enter. They all thought that Sid's Café was a real working café. With the counter in place, and all the set dressing of buns and tables with their green checked table cloths, it was easy to see how they could be deceived. It was after all, supposed to be a real café.

The following day, Fred came to me and suggested that the ironmonger on the corner should open his paint store as a real café. It would obviously be very successful. I thought it was a good idea, and duly passed Fred's idea on to the ironmonger. But he wasn't interested. He said that his trade was hammers and nails, not teas and buns. Some time later, Fred suggested that, as it was such a good idea, maybe he and I should buy the café and put in a couple of elderly local ladies to sell teas to the tourists.

I was seriously considering the proposition, more for the fun of it than any desire to be a threat to McDonalds, when the ironmonger hurried out of his shop when he saw me and said, "I've talked to my son, and he's all for doing it – running the store as a café."

As there was a promotional aspect to the venture, I said that we would leave our set standing when we were finished filming there. Of course, it wasn't just a matter of plugging in a kettle. There were regulations to consider. But the café opened, and it is still a major tourist attraction over twenty years later. All thanks to Fred Hamilton.

Another venture that began around that time, was a fish and chip restaurant. The owners telephoned me to ask permission to call it 'Compo's Café'.

I checked with Roy, and he said that he had no objection and was pleased that the town could make some money out of the series. I then checked with BBC Enterprises, the commercial arm of the BBC. I explained the request and told them that Roy Clarke had no objections. They said they would call me back, and two days later, they did. The girl explained about Compo's Café and Roy Clarke having given his permission, and asked if I, as the producer of *Summer Wine*, had any objections. I was pleased to tell her that I hadn't. Another two days later, I received a call from BBC Enterprises telling me that they had checked with the producer and he had no objections, so it was alright to use the name.

On a quiet Sunday morning in Holmfirth,

from a 50ft hoist, we filmed the arrival at the café of Sid in his mobile fish and chip shop. As the garishly-painted converted bus made its way down the hill past the grey stone houses, it looked completely out of place. When the old bus had stopped, Fred and his camera moved down to street level for the continuation of the scene. It was the first day of filming for John Comer, who played Sid, and it was a real pleasure to welcome him on to the set. As well as being a very good comedy actor, John was an extremely likeable member of the company.

John had only a few lines to speak, but there was obviously something wrong with the resonance of his voice. It was very croaky, and so quiet that it was quite difficult to hear what he was saying. I suggested that he might have a viral infection, but he said that it was because he had recently had some minor medical attention on his throat. "But I'll soon be back to normal," he cheerfully assured me with a big grin.

Sound is never a big problem in filming, as it can all be replaced, including the dialogue which can be post-synchronised in a dubbing theatre. It can then be treated to make it sound acoustically correct for any location. The pictures, on the other hand, are a different matter. What the cameraman shoots – the lighting and the framing – is usually what you have to the very end, unless they are digitally improved, which is very expensive.

The post-synching of John Comer's lines wouldn't be a problem. When his voice returned, all we would have to do is get him into a dubbing theatre and synchronise his usual voice with what he had recorded on location. It was a very straightforward and everyday procedure.

As well as Sid's Café, quite a few of the other interior scenes for *Getting Sam Home* were filmed on location in Yorkshire: Sam's bedroom and hallway (at Hillcrest), Lily Bless Her's living room, Ivy and Sid's front room and Sam's hospital ward. There was also the grubby, nicotine-stained interior of The Shoulder of Mutton, last seen on that *You Must be Joking* item. It was ideal for the scene where the men and Lily Bless Her lament their predicament of having a dead body on their hands.

To add to the atmosphere, the effects team supplied a fine mist with their smoke machines. At this point the landlord pulled me aside to voice his genuine concern: "I hope all this smoke doesn't spoil me decorations," he told me in all seriousness.

Some of the night scenes were filmed at the BBC's Ealing studios: the broken-down mobile fish and chip shop on a remote road, the interior of Sam's shed and Sid and Ivy's bedroom.

It was while we were shooting this scene at Ealing that it became obvious that John Comer's voice wasn't getting any better. If anything, it was getting worse. I asked John if he thought his voice was likely to recover in time for him to re-voice his speeches, or should I look for someone with a similar voice to impersonate him. Without a moment's hesitation, he replied that, because it looked like his throat was taking some time to recover, he would be quite happy if I were to get someone to impersonate his voice.

On the radio, I had heard Tony Melody, a Northern comedy actor, who had the same accent and much the same vocal characteristics as John Comer. So I booked him to re-voice all of John's speeches. It wasn't a simple job for Tony, as there wasn't much of John's voice to use as a guide, but he took it all in his stride. Watching Sid's lips on a big screen, he acted out the scenes in synchronisation.

Much later, at a preview screening of the film in the Princess Anne Theatre at the BAFTA headquarters in Piccadilly, Jane Freeman, who plays Ivy, was sitting next to me. When the film ended, I asked her what she thought of John's voice. "Very good………what do you mean?"

Jane had completely forgotten that John had croaked his way through their scenes. If it fooled Jane, it would surely fool everybody.

Later, it occurred to me that, if John Comer couldn't dub his own voice for *Getting Sam Home*, how would he be when we were recording the live studio scenes on the next television series? We could certainly get Tony Melody again for the film sequences, but for the studio sequences, if the audience can't hear John speaking his lines, how

Top: It's May – It should be getting warmer. Bottom: Filming outside the small supermarket in Wooldale.

Top: Filming Foggy, Clegg and Compo at their old school. Bottom: Clegg (Peter Sallis) has been pushed over the school wall by Foggy (Brian Wilde) and Compo (Bill Owen).

could they laugh at them? If John's appearances in the series could only be in the filmed location scenes, then I would have to let Roy Clarke know as soon as possible in order to avoid a lot of hasty re-writing later.

John Comer lived in Blackpool. In January 1984, I decided to drive up there to see him. Just before I left London, I received a message telling me that John had returned to the hospital to have some more treatment on his throat. I went along to see him at the hospital instead. John didn't look too good, but he assured me that he was now on the road to a full recovery. However, after about fifteen minutes, John said that he was getting tired, and thought that, perhaps, I should leave to let him get some sleep.

On returning to London, I went to see Dr. John Newman, the BBC doctor. I told him of John Comer's assurances and my concern that his treatment might not bring his voice back soon enough for the next series. The following day, Doctor Newman told me that he had been in touch with the hospital, and learned that John had only a few weeks to live: he had lung and throat cancer.

I was deeply shocked. I had absolutely no idea that John was so ill. All I could think about was sitting with him in the restaurant at the BBC's rehearsal rooms in Acton two years ago. I had questioned his heavy smoking and suggested that maybe he should cut back. "I've been smoking forty a day, full strength, since I was a lad, and look at me. You won't get anyone fitter," he said with a wide grin as he flexed his muscles. He really was a picture of health. And then I thought of that grey figure in a hospital bed in Blackpool with only weeks to live. Why does anyone smoke?

There was going to be a lot of music in *Getting Sam Home*, so Ronnie Hazlehurst said he had an idea that would be a great help to him when he came to write the music.

"Get a cassette recorder, run the VHS of the film and, as it plays, you do the music for it – as you do. I'll then know the sort of music you want for every scene."

It seemed like a good idea, but after an hour of being a full orchestra, I was beginning to run out of steam a bit, especially when it came to the horn sequences, but I carried on to the very end. My solo performance turned out to be Ronnie Hazlehurst's favourite recording: he had hours of pleasure listening to my impressions of an orchestra. Nevertheless, Ron's finished score for *Getting Sam Home* is exactly what I wanted – only much better, of course, with real instruments and in tune.

It wasn't only the music that was added afterwards, there was the sound of a film on Sam's television. Sybil, played by Olive Pendleton, is watching the television in the front room of the bungalow while the three men quietly deal with the problem of helping Sam escape from his rear bedroom. I thought that it would be appropriate if she was watching a horror film. There was no need for us to actually see the television. All we needed was its flickering light and the soundtrack of the horror film.

To record the Svengali-like male voice for this supposed horror film, I used the veteran actor and comedian Michael Howard. He had been a well-known face in post war British films - like *It Always Rains on Sunday* (1947) and *Front Page Story* (1954). Michael had been a popular comedian with his own show on radio in the early fifties, until he was divorced and the disapproving BBC promptly cancelled his series. They were different times.

Although still playing small parts in films and television, it was obvious that Michael, now in his seventies, had seen better times. However, he had become a really good friend and would regularly come into the Television Centre to join Ronnie Hazlehurst, myself and other producers for lunch. He would entertain us with one of his very funny 'shaggy dog' stories, for which, in his heyday, he was famous.

One day in 1985 the receptionist at the Television Centre called my office to say that Michael Howard had arrived. I immediately left my office on the seventh floor and went down to the ground floor reception desk to meet him and take him on to the restaurant. However, by the time I got to the reception desk, there was no sign of Michael. Assuming that he had gone to the restroom to freshen up, I sat down on a sofa and waited – and waited. After a while, I asked the receptionist if she had noticed where Michael Howard had gone. "Oh yes," she said, "your assistant came and took him into the studio."

Well, my assistant had done no such thing. I had left her in the office, and why would Michael be taken into a studio?

Before I could say anything, the doors leading to the studios opened, and I saw a young lady apologising profusely to Michael. What had happened was that there was to be a pre-recording of an interview for the Panorama current affairs programme with……Michael Howard (then a relatively unknown politician who would later become the Home Secretary).

Apparently, no sooner had one of the receptionists called my office to tell me that Michael Howard had arrived, than one of the Panorama researchers arrived and told the receptionist that they were expecting Michael Howard. And there he was.

Michael Howard (my one) said that he was surprised at being taken to the studio, and that it was only when he was asked for his views on the current problems in the Middle East that he felt something wasn't quite right. He said that his reply – that he would put them against a wall and shoot the lot of them – had caused considerable consternation in the Panorama studio.

"You're not going to say that, are you?" they enquired in astonishment.

"If asked, yes." Michael replied.

Fortunately, the mistake was quickly rectified and an international crisis avoided.

I had hoped to relate this story to the other Michael Howard – now Shadow Chancellor of the Exchequer – when he attended Dame Thora Hird's commemorative service at Westminster Abbey in 2003, but sadly, it was a crowded event and we never met.

The atmosphere throughout the filming of *Getting Sam Home* was harmonious and productive. Brian Wilde had accepted that the filming would be achieved my way – with tracks and marks on the ground for the actors to hit their positions. There was no element of competition in the filming, and it pleased me that the BBC had not given any actor 'director approval'.

Thanks to the magnificent support of the unit, the filming of *Getting Sam Home* was completed in 24 filming days and came in on budget. And that mysterious 'someone' at the Television Centre was deprived of the pleasure of seeing me falling flat on my face with an unfinished film.

Getting Sam Home was transmitted on New Year's Eve 1983 and was generally very well received – although there were one or two letters from viewers saying that the film didn't have the usual atmosphere associated with *Last of the Summer Wine*. For 'atmosphere' read 'laughter track'.

In practical terms, it would have been impossible to get an audience to come along and laugh for an hour and a half at a finished film. And, besides, the laughter would almost certainly have been unacceptably intrusive in the atmospheric sequences.

Brian Wilde must have enjoyed the filming of *Getting Sam Home* for he decided that he would stay with us for the next series. Not surprisingly, Sydney Lotterby laid no claim to taking back *Last of the Summer* Wine for its eighth series in 1984. Everyone took it for granted that I would continue to produce and direct the series as I had for the sixth series in 1981. Roy Clarke was commissioned to write the seven episodes and, with Brian Wilde back with us, it promised to be a good year.

CHAPTER 9

The End of the Pier Show

So popular was *Last of the Summer Wine* that a stage version was independently produced. In its third year (in 1984), it was playing at the theatre on the pier in Bournemouth and was drawing large crowds. Brian Wilde had declined to be in the play from the start, so it was only Bill Owen and Peter Sallis heading the bill, along with Jane Freeman, playing Ivy.

I had seen the play previously at Hillingdon where it had opened, and then at Eastbourne. I found it to be entertaining enough, but it wasn't what you would call 'a theatrical triumph' – nobody was going to get any awards. So when I went along to see it again in Bournemouth, it was more as a sense of duty than any genuine desire to see it again.

I was told firmly by Peter and Bill that I should not – under any circumstances – go backstage to their dressing rooms after the show (as is the custom). They said that it would be more comfortable for me to meet them in the theatre bar afterwards. How thoughtful. What I learned later, was that the dressing rooms at the pier theatre were unbelievably small and, at the time, quite basic. Bill and Peter didn't want me to see the conditions in which they were happily prepared to work when they were away from the pampering of television. They knew that any complaints about their location caravan that they might have in the future would fall on deaf ears.

Because some of the original stage cast were unavailable for this year's production at Bournemouth, some essential re-casting had been necessary. The new actors, superbly cast by the director Jan Butlin, the daughter of Billy Butlin, the holiday camp entrepreneur, improved the play immensely. Roy Clarke also saw the play, and he too was very impressed by the new cast and agreed that they should be brought into the series.

There was Jean Fergusson (who played Clegg's love interest, Marina), Robert Fyfe (who played Clegg's next door neighbour, Howard), Juliette Kaplan (who played Howard's wife, Pearl) and Jonathan Linsley (who played Crusher, Ivy's leather-clad biker nephew). They were all outstanding actors who had suddenly brought the play to life and were getting big laughs. The same play, the same action, but with different actors, demonstrated the importance of good casting.

I mentioned to Bill Owen that we were thinking of bringing some of the new stage cast into the series. He said that it was a very good idea, and agreed that they were excellent players – especially Jean Fergusson, who he said was exceptionally gifted at playing comedy. But he strongly advised against having Juliette Kaplan. Juliette's acerbic wit and brutally candid comments can easily be misunderstood, and I suspect that Bill had met with this unfettered facet of her personality. But I was only interested in her strength as an actress, so I ignored Bill's assessment of Juliette, and I'm very glad that I did, for she played Pearl so perfectly. A couple of years later, I was very pleased when Bill Owen agreed and praised Juliette Kaplan for her acting in the series.

Robert Fyfe was brilliant at playing Howard, and prompted the question: 'He is such a good actor, where has he been for the past few decades?' Robert is a good example of how luck plays such a major part in the careers of actors. The stage director, Jan Butlin, had unwittingly introduced us to some wonderful actors who would contribute enormously to the continued success of *Last of the Summer Wine* for the next quarter of a century.

One day in Bournemouth, Peter Sallis asked Bill Owen if he knew the dates for the filming in September. Bill called me, and I gave him the exact dates for him to book his accommodation at the farmhouse we rented in Holmfirth. A few days later, Bill telephoned the owner, only to find that Peter Sallis had passed the dates on to a friend – who had booked the accommodation for the whole period. Bill was livid and demanded that the owner should cancel the booking, but she couldn't do that as a booking is a booking and she wouldn't let anyone down. But she put Bill in touch with some personal friends who were prepared to move out of their bungalow and let Bill have it for the duration of the filming. Fortunately, Bill was delighted with this accommodation which was on a hillside near the centre of Holmfirth. But he was still cross with Peter for giving the dates to his friend.

It was while the stage show was still running in Bournemouth that the scripts for the 1984 television series began to arrive. I always looked forward to receiving the scripts through the post, as they would never fail to brighten up the day. The scripts that arrived this time were no exception, and I agreed with Bill Owen and Peter Sallis that they were very funny. Astonishingly, Brian Wilde telephoned me to say that he had read the scripts and found them to be very weak: "Send them back to Roy and get him to re-write them," he urged. I told Brian that I couldn't possibly send them back because, in my opinion, they were extremely funny scripts, and there was nothing whatsoever wrong with them.

Brian dug his heels in, and said that, unless the scripts were re-written, he wasn't going to sign for the series. Here we go again, I thought. The scripts had all been written to feature Foggy, so Brian had the advantage over us again.

I politely told Brian that the scripts would not be re-written, and if he really meant what he was saying, in view of his importance to the series, he would have to personally tell John Howard Davies, who was now Head of Light Entertainment. Brian said that he would be more than happy to do so.

The next day, Brian Wilde duly came into the Television Centre to see John Howard Davies. When he had gone, John called me into his office, where, with some incredulity, he told me that Brian was quite serious. "He really doesn't like the scripts, and doesn't want to remain in the series if they're not re-written," he said. I assured John that the scripts were excellent in every way, and there was absolutely no justification whatsoever for sending them back to Roy Clarke for re-writes.

It was a very serious situation, as we were only about three weeks away from the start of filming.

"What are you going to do about it?" John asked.

"Nothing," I replied.

"Are you going to recast?"

"No. I think he'll be doing it."

"I'll leave it to you. Good luck," John said with a complicit smile.

As the scripts were so good, it was my opinion that Brian must be bluffing, and that he would, as usual, be open to persuasion.

A few years earlier, Brian was working on the Dick Clement/Ian La Frenais comedy series, *Porridge* (1974-77). Ronnie Barker, the star of the series, had confided to Brian that he had dispensed with his agent. "Why give away ten per cent when the work keeps coming in?" Ronnie advised. Brian immediately gave up his agent and, from then on, he negotiated his own contracts, which he did very well. This may well have saved him money, but it also lost him work, for he had no one to suggest him for other parts (as agents do).

I returned to my office and telephoned the agent representing Fulton Mackay, the popular comedy actor who had also worked on *Porridge*, playing the part of the Scottish warder, Mr Mackay. In that series, Brian Wilde had made quite an impression as Mr Barraclough, a dithering prison warder, and Ronnie Barker played Fletcher, a wily prisoner. I always have, at the back of my mind, other actors who could replace members of our regular cast in an emergency, and I always thought that with very little adjustment to the scripts, Fulton could play Foggy, maybe as 'Scotty'. In *Porridge*, Fulton played his part with flare and a great sense of comedy.

When I asked Fulton Mackay's agent if he was available from mid-September to the middle of November, he asked what it was for. I told him that it was for a major part in *Last of the Summer Wine*.

Less than an hour later, Brian Wilde telephoned me, as though nothing of what had gone before had happened. "Oh, um…er… I've just realised I, er, I don't have a copy of the film schedule. Could you send me one, please?" There was no mention of his meeting with John Howard Davies, the quality of the scripts or his threatened resignation from the series again. Nor, strangely enough, was there any follow-up call from Fulton Mackay's agent. It isn't difficult to imagine the conversations that must have taken place between Fulton Mackay, his agent and Brian Wilde.

I had been so certain that Brian was never likely to leave the series that I never mentioned the problem to Roy Clarke who was still writing episodes.

For the sake of harmony, there is a firm rule that artist's fees are never discussed openly. But sometimes actors get wind of the fact that one of their fellow artistes is being paid a lot more than they are, and that means trouble. And that's what happened with the three stars of *Last of the Summer Wine*. They had performed a song and dance number (Tiptoe Through the Tulips) in a variety show produced by Ernest Maxin. Bill Owen, who considered himself to be the star of our series, picked up that Brian Wilde was getting double what he was being paid to be in Ernest's show. Bill asked me if this was so on *Last of the Summer Wine*.

I, of course, told him that I could not – would not – get involved in contractual matters, as that is why the BBC had its Artists Bookings Department to spare the producer any embarrassment discussing fees.

In fact, Brian Wilde's fee for *Last of the Summer Wine* **was** much higher than those of his two co-stars, which he effortlessly achieved with his 'persuade me' routine. It was no secret that Bill and Peter colluded to agree their fee, but they had no idea that Brian, the newcomer to the trio, was being paid considerably more than they were. It did seem to me that, besides being unfair, it was an additional burden on my relatively tight budget. In my view, it would be fairer if the three principals all received exactly the same fees.

Bill Owen was very angry about the situation, so much so that I gave him some advice: "Bill, if there are three identical houses on a prime site in, say, Mayfair, and a developer wants to build an apartment block on it – if he buys two of the houses for a million pounds each, the owner of the third house can get double for his house

The unit filming for 'From Wellies to Wetsuit' (1982).

because, without it, the developer has two thirds of nothing."

"What's housing in Mayfair got to do with Brian Wilde's fee?"

"Bill, I can say no more."

After he had a chat with Peter Sallis, they both delayed agreeing their contracts. Brian Wilde then telephoned my office several times over the following weeks to find out if everyone was 'on board'. When I suggested to Brian that the series might not go ahead because nobody had signed up, it precipitated a situation where the developer soon obtained all three properties for near equal fees. At this point, there should have been the newspaper headline: 'Happiness in Summer Wine Land'.

At the end of the Bournemouth run of *Last of the Summer Wine*, and with Brian Wilde all signed up, we were ready to go into production of the 8th series. Besides the pleasure of knowing that I had the perfect trio again, I was absolutely delighted that Roy Clarke had liked Gordon Wharmby enough to bring him back to reprise his role as Wesley Pegden.

In *The Loxley Lozenge* (1984), Wesley confides to the men – "under the strictest secrecy" – that he has found a Loxley Lozenge. Foggy theorises that the lozenge must be a cough sweet that was popular in the Middle Ages. But they soon discover that a Loxley Lozenge is definitely not a cough sweet; it is a vintage motor car. Again, Gordon Wharmby was relaxed on the filming and gave another excellent performance.

The episode had some of Brian Wilde's best scenes ever, which completely belied his assertion that the scripts weren't up to standard.

One of the roles of the director is to improve the basic script whenever necessary, but only when it can be done without spoiling the text. In the case of *The Loxley Lozenge*, Roy Clarke's stage directions would have been impossible to film anywhere in the Holme Valley so, with his approval, some adjustments were made.

In the episode, Compo, Clegg and Foggy are enlisted to help Wesley collect the Lozenge, which they find is nothing more than an engine on a rusty car chassis. Wesley wants them to sit on a settee and steer the Lozenge as it is towed along the road behind his Land Rover.

The script called for the settee to slide around on the chassis which makes it difficult for Clegg to reach the steering wheel to steer it. In the end, the settee falls over backwards and the men are tipped out. It would have been funny to see these happenings, but they were very complicated and, besides being time-consuming to set up, there was no way that they could be safely filmed in the narrow country lanes in the area. So I suggested that, instead, the three men should look very relaxed on the comfortable settee, and that the audience should be lulled into believing that this was an idyllic way to travel through the countryside. Ronnie would write some pleasant travelling music to accompany the shots of the Lozenge being towed along the narrow lanes past some pretty scenery. Then, suddenly it happens: as Wesley drives his Land Rover round a corner, the settee unexpectedly slides sideways off the old chassis, and rolls down the hill with the men still seated on it. Roy liked the idea, which was guaranteed to be funny and with only one effect shot, was relatively easy to film. A special rig was built by the Visual Effects Department that would allow the settee to be set on a rail and actually roll sideways off the moving chassis with our three actors comfortably seated on it.

Meanwhile, I was approached by Ashley Jackson, a celebrated Yorkshire artist renowned for his evocative watercolour paintings that accurately capture the seasonal moods of the Holme Valley. He asked if, as he was part of the Holmfirth scene, there was any chance of him making a small appearance in the programme. I explained to Ashley that the actors' union, Equity, won't allow the use of non-members in programmes. There is a sensible exception, however, when a member of the public is filmed doing a job that they always do, and there is a degree of skill involved – a supermarket cashier for example. That exception wouldn't, of course, apply in the case of Ashley Jackson. Or would it?

Chapter 9 – The End of the Pier Show – 69

It occurred to me that if, during the opening title sequence, Ashley, with his easel, is painting a watercolour in an open field, and Compo, Clegg and Foggy stop to admire his work, then that would be within the Equity rules. And then, if the three men, having just rolled sideways off the Loxley Lozenge chassis, should roll down the hill and end up sitting comfortably on their settee watching Ashley painting again, that would also be acceptable and a bonus for the programme. It neatly tied up the story without losing a word of Roy's rich dialogue. And it was also very funny.

An unplanned stunt was when Wesley sets off in his Land Rover with the Lozenge and the three men in tow. The incline from the yard onto the road was quite steep and the Lozenge managed to unhook itself from the Land Rover's hitch. The heavy chassis of the Loxley Lozenge rolled back into the yard and was only stopped from doing any damage by the crew, who managed to bring it safely to a halt. But it looked so good that I kept it in the show. Our three men were unaware that this extra stunt was in fact, an accident, so there were no complaints. *The Loxley Lozenge* – with Ashley Jackson – is one of the most memorable episodes, and certainly one of the funniest.

Another popular episode in the same series that needed adjusting was *The Mysterious Feet of Nora Batty*. It was a simple idea that allowed the cast to have a lot of fun performing the script. Joe Gladwin (playing Nora's husband Wally) showed his brilliance at playing comedy when he tries to sneak looks under the living room table to find out how big Nora's feet are.

Top: The settee (on the rails) slides off the car chassis. Inset: The settee with Clegg, Foggy and Compo, arrives behind Ashley Jackson.

The original ending had Compo painting some liquid on to a piece of hardboard to measure Nora's feet. When she comes to her front door and steps on it, the impressions her feet leave on the liquid could then be measured. But it sticks to Compo's Wellies instead, and mayhem ensues as he escapes down the steps with the hardboard firmly attached. It was a very funny idea, but it would have been impossible to film because of the lack of space at Nora's doorstep, and the danger to Bill Owen – or, more likely, his double – running down Nora's steps with a square of hardboard attached to his Wellies. There would be no better way to break a leg.

My solution was that they borrow a foot-measurer from a local shoe shop. Then, when Nora is up a ladder cleaning her windows, the foot measurer, like a space ship, comes into view to the music of *Also Sprach Zarathustra* – a homage to the film *2001 - A Space Odyssey* (1968). From the top of a large specially made stepladder, the men try to manoeuvre the shoe measurer, now attached to the end of a pole, into position alongside Nora's feet. Unfortunately, when she adjusts her standing position on the ladder, she stands on, and traps, the thing. They tug on the trapped measurer, but when Nora lifts her foot, their released stepladder tips over and drops them into the river.

Bill, Peter and Brian were very happy to let stunt doubles perform the fall into the river, but they were also quite happy to actually walk along the slippery river bed for the closing shot. Well, they weren't actually happy, but in order to get it over with, and get to lunch, they suppressed any grumbles – for the time being, anyway.

It was in September 1984, a month after the stage version of *Last of the Summer Wine* had closed in Bournemouth that the new characters began to appear in the series. The introduction of Howard and Marina and his suspicious wife Pearl (played by Robert Fyfe, Jean Fergusson and Juliette Kaplan) was in *Catching Digby's Donkey* (1985). The sight of Howard and Marina illicitly practising the tango in a hidden corner of a field was enough to make them firm favourites with viewers for the following 25 years. The hopelessness of their relationship and their endless, bizarre assignations were comedy highlights in nearly every subsequent episode. Pearl wasn't visually funny; her strength was in being able to terrify her errant husband (Howard) with an accusing smile or an insinuating snip of her garden secateurs. Nobody could have played Pearl better, or more menacingly than Juliette Kaplan. These three actors provided endless storylines about unrequited love and the suspicious nature of women.

Holmfirth is always associated with *Last of the Summer Wine*, but in 1984 the requirements of the script took us to Marsden some 12 miles away in the Colne Valley. In *Who's Looking After the Café, Then?* (1985) Roy had written that Compo is on the roof of Wesley's Land Rover and, as it passes the rear of Nora Batty's house, he is able to look into her bedroom window and see her in a state of undress.

Anyone who has visited the location of Nora Batty's house in Holmfirth will know that the actual rear of her house is on the main Huddersfield to Manchester road. Besides the constant heavy traffic, which would make any filming out of the question, the rear façade consists mainly of shop fronts, and isn't how anyone would imagine the rear of Nora's house to look like. There was also the problem that the majority of the older Yorkshire houses have rooms with unusually high ceilings. These would make it impossible for Compo to see Nora in a first floor room from the roof of a Land Rover. So the search was on for a slightly smaller terraced house in a reasonably quiet road.

On the unit's day off (a Saturday), I drove over the hills out of Holmfirth, and found myself in Marsden, a mill town in the Colne Valley. There, I found exactly what I was looking for: The upstairs windows of the three terraced houses were a little lower and exactly the right height to allow Compo to stand on the Land Rover roof and look inside.

To make contact with the owner of the house and obtain permission to film there, I left it to

The special ladder that tips the men into the river.

our location manager, Evan King, an energetic and likeable Scot.

Returning to my rented house in the evening, I found a note from Evan that had been pushed through the letter box. It concerned the next day's filming and said simply, 'The White Horse is OK for tomorrow'. But scribbled at the bottom in capital letters was some re-assuring news about the health of Peter Sallis:

'P. SALLIS WELL IN MARSDEN'

I panicked because I had no idea that Peter Sallis was unwell. Nobody had told me. I tracked Evan down at the unit hotel and asked him what was wrong with Peter. "Nothing as far as I know," he replied. I was relieved when Evan revealed that what he actually wrote was

'P.S. ALL IS WELL IN MARSDEN'.

Evan assured me that he didn't intend the message to confuse me, but he had written it in the rain and in the dark.

When an important location is found, it is sensible to try and find other locations nearby to save unnecessary travelling for the unit. Travelling time is loss of filming time. So I looked around Marsden and found that there was an abundance of possible locations. The first thing I noticed was that, because a new motorway had been built over the Pennines a few years ago, the old Huddersfield to Oldham trunk road that passes through the middle of Marsden was now hardly used. Transport cafés that had catered for armies of exhausted truck drivers in the past had closed down for ever. Then there were the shops in the centre of Marsden, most of which looked rather dilapidated and badly in need of some customers. There was a disused canal near the railway station and, further down the hill, a river with some beautiful, unspoiled houses backing on to it. All around were the derelict woollen mills that still stood defiantly in this valley – a constant reminder of prosperous times gone by.

Marsden was going to be good for us.

On a recce to this haven of interesting locations with the cameraman, the set designer and Mike Cager, we found a traditional butchers' shop whose speciality was home made sausages and pork pies.

It was on a corner and was distinguished by having a Victorian ironwork and glass canopy. Seeing that there was a pretty little tea room attached which was entered from inside the butcher's shop, I ushered my colleagues inside and ordered coffees from a woman who looked at us very suspiciously. As well as coffees, I ordered a hot pork pie which was delicious. The service was very good, although I did feel that we were being stared-at rather a lot by the butcher's customers as well as the butcher himself. I reasoned that it was because they were unused to seeing television people in the town. After a while, I thanked the lady and asked for the bill. She replied that there was no charge.

"No charge? Why ever not?" I asked.

"Because this isn't a café; it's the butcher's home and this is his dining room."

It was an easy mistake to make. It looked like a café – and the coffees and the pork pie were very good.

A good relationship was maintained with the butcher for many years, until an over-enthusiastic assistant turned a delivery lorry away, concerned that the noise of the refrigeration plant on its roof would interrupt the filming. Because it was a delivery of vital supplies, the butcher was not at all pleased. Happily, the patronage of our crew for the butcher's scrumptious pork pies eventually restored good relations.

It was when we were back in London to record the multi-camera studio sequences of the 1984 series that news came that *Last of the Summer Wine* had been chosen to be a part of The Royal Command Performance. It was quite an honour and we were all very pleased to have been chosen.

Roy Clarke wrote a short sketch for the trio to play against a simple dry-stone wall setting. The script was very funny and kept faith with the established style of the series.

Not surprisingly, Brian Wilde didn't like the script at all, and suggested that Roy should have another go at it. There was no support from Peter Sallis or Bill Owen, who thought that it played well and were quite satisfied with it. But Brian was adamant that it wasn't a good script and he wouldn't participate if it wasn't rewritten. This time there was no money involved as performers receive no fees. Brian just didn't like the sketch.

I telephoned Roy and asked him if he could at least come down to London and listen to what Brian had to say.

A few days later, Roy arrived at the Acton rehearsal rooms to see what could be done to resolve the problem that Brian had with the script. Without being precise, Brian made a few general remarks about the ordeal of having to go out on to a stage and perform a script in which he had no confidence. Roy said nothing. I asked them to play the scene for Roy, which they did. At the end of the sketch, which was unarguably funny, Roy packed up his note book and said, "Well, there's nothing wrong with that." And there wasn't. Brian was clearly being awkward and Roy was going to have none of such nonsense. Trying not to let the situation worsen, I said, "You did say, Roy, that you would listen to what Brian had to say." Roy replied firmly, "I have listened, and I don't agree." Then, he left the rehearsal room and departed for his home near Doncaster. We all thought that Roy was right. It was a funny sketch, and would surely be appreciated at the Royal Command show.

To be asked to perform at The Royal Command Performance is quite an honour and can be quite a nerve-racking experience. Ernie Wise told me that once when Morecambe and Wise performed at one of these shows, there was a supportive telegram from the comedy actor-writer, Marty Feldman. It read: 'When you have talent you don't need luck. Good luck.'

The Royal Command Performance was held at the Victoria Palace in London that year. When it was time on the bill for the *Last of the Summer Wine* scene, the curtains opened to reveal the three men sitting in front of a small dry stone wall setting, which was in the middle of the stage about twenty feet back from the footlights.

It may have been its contrast to the raucous music that preceded it, or just that it was too gentle for a variety show, but the black tie audience hardly laughed. It was not a success. Brian didn't say "I told you so", but I bet he was thinking it. It certainly wasn't the script that was wrong, or the performances of our cast, it was just that it wasn't a variety show sketch. It was as inappropriate as a string quartet at a rock concert.

It's easy to be wise after the event, but it would have been better if they had just stood at the footlights and performed something simpler that would have given them close contact with the audience.

Brian Wilde left at the end of the series after making it absolutely clear to everyone that he was sorry he wouldn't be with us again the following year. He added that he had really enjoyed working on the series. And I think he had.

74 – *Last of the Summer Wine – From the Director's Chair*

Top: The new boy – Michael Aldridge joins the series.

CHAPTER 10
Uncle of the Bride

It was a new year and 1985 had dawned. Brian Wilde had now formally and amicably left the series. In order to introduce a new character to make up the male trio, it was decided that, instead of a series, there would be another feature-length film.

Replacing Brian Wilde was going to be difficult, for despite his awkwardness, he was a superb actor who had always played Foggy to perfection. He had established a character that was seen by everyone as being crucial to the framework and possibly even to the continuance of the series. The public liked him so much, there was every possibility that, no matter who would take over the role of the 'third man', he would be shot down and unfavourably compared with Foggy.

To try and avoid any such comparisons being made, I would have to find someone who was entirely different in every way from Brian Wilde and Foggy. But, it would have to be someone who was capable of playing whatever eccentricities that Roy Clarke might write for his character.

An early thought – and it was no more than that – was Norman Wisdom, who was hugely popular for his broad, physical style of comedy, and couldn't be further away from the gentle, thoughtful Foggy. But John Howard Davies said that, in order to protect me from a fate worse than death, he wouldn't allow me to even think of using him. He said that Norman Wisdom almost drove his father, Jack Davies, mad when he wrote scripts for his films. It is well-known that Norman Wisdom, knowing that his films were the main source of income for the Rank Organisation, would continually throw his weight around to get his own way.

I didn't check Norman Wisdom's availability but because he appeared to have no leadership qualities, he would have been completely wrong as the 'third man'. Anyway, it was only a passing thought. It would be another ten years before I would be able to use Norman Wisdom on *Last of the Summer Wine* in *The Man who Nearly Knew Pavarotti* (1995), but this was with a script written especially for him and his style of comedy.

Another wild thought that I had for the replacement of Foggy was Charlie Williams, a likeable comedian from Barnsley, who was very popular at the time. This thought was passed up to the Controller of BBC1, Michael Grade, who thought it was a great idea, for it was good that we would be seen to be looking beyond the more predictable and safer casting options.

However, in the meantime, I had gone completely cold on the idea. Charlie Williams was a black stand-up comedian with an infectious warmth that had won him a huge following. But he didn't have any leadership qualities either, and we couldn't have two clowns in the series. And I didn't even know if Charlie Williams could act. What we really needed was a strong actor: an actor who had a compelling personality and who wasn't one of the regular television comedy performers.

Michael Aldridge was brought to my attention by his agent who sent me some video tapes of his appearances in other productions. I had seen and enjoyed his performance in Keith Waterhouse's gentle comedy, *Charters and Caldicott* (1985). Although he was better-known as a stage actor, the videotapes displayed a versatile actor with a very likeable and distinctive personality who had that necessary feeling for comedy.

I met with Michael Aldridge and was delighted to find that he was exactly right to be our 'third man' who would be entirely different from the irreplaceable Foggy Dewhirst. Michael was large, avuncular and instantly likeable.

Michael Simpson, the renowned drama director (and husband of Jane Freeman, who plays Ivy in the Café), said that it was good casting, but warned that Michael was notorious for never giving exactly the same performance twice. He would be good, but what he did would be slightly different every time, and it was. But each time, he was very funny.

Roy Clarke was pleased with the casting of Michael Aldridge and came down to London to meet him. The result was that Michael would play a character called Seymour Utterthwaite in this second *Summer Wine* film – tentatively entitled '*The Wedding*'.

Seymour Utterthwaite is a frustrated amateur inventor and former headmaster of a dubious educational establishment for boys on the North Yorkshire moors. His intentions of running a world-renowned college were frustrated considerably, by the physical state of its halls of learning:

SEYMOUR
'All it wanted were the old pigsties pulling down, a new roof, and a few trenches filling in that the army had left. The rest was cosmetic.'

So Michael Aldridge would be introduced to the series as Seymour Utterthwaite, the uncle in *Uncle of the Bride* (1985), the second *Last of the Summer Wine* films.

The father of the bride would be none other than Wesley Pegden, played by my discovery Gordon Wharmby, who by this time had earned his place as a regular in the series. The big question now was who would play Edie, Wesley's wife, and of course, the mother of the bride. My wife, Constance, immediately had the answer: "Thora Hird," she said. I gave this suggestion all the respect it deserved: 'Don't be silly – and mind your own business."

But Constance had seen Thora in a magazine programme where she had talked about her love for Yorkshire and the joys of filming there. She had quite recently starred in the long-running comedy series *In Loving Memory* (1979-86) and had enjoyed working in the North immensely. Constance was absolutely certain that Thora Hird would want to be our guest star in *Uncle of the Bride* playing Edie Pegden.

I telephoned Felix deWolfe, Thora's agent, and asked him if she might be interested in playing this relatively small part of Edie Pegden. He said that he was pretty sure that she would, and he would ask her. Within minutes, Felix rang back and said that Thora would be delighted to play Edie.

Meanwhile, I had received a letter from a young actress called Sarah Thomas. It was a very jokey communication – copies of which had, obviously been sent to many producers and casting directors. It ended by saying that she was playing Ruby Birtle in J.B. Priestley's '*When we are Married*' at the Leatherhead Theatre. I looked at Sarah's photograph and saw that she looked as if she could really be Thora Hird's daughter. I am always surprised with productions where sons and daughters are cast who have no physical resemblance whatsoever to their natural parents.

Leatherhead was only about twelve miles from my home in Walton on Thames, so I bundled my family into the car and set off for The Leatherhead Theatre. It was a very good production and was well worth the visit, especially as Sarah gave an excellent performance, proving beyond doubt that she would make a perfect bride. It was quite obvious, by her spirited performance, that Sarah Thomas really loved the whole business of theatre and acting.

I never like to tell actors that I am coming to see them work because, if they aren't good, I can slip away at the interval without any embarrassment. If they know I'm there, I'm obliged to stay to the very end, no matter how disappointing they or the production may have been. However, if they don't know I'm there, and the show is good, I can then go back stage at the end of the performance and tell them in all honesty, that I've just seen the show and thoroughly enjoyed it.

It may be apocryphal but it is said that the comedian Les Dawson went to see a show and had unwisely arranged to meet one of the cast afterwards. Unfortunately, the production was terrible and he was well and truly trapped. Afterwards, he was obliged to go back stage and say something about the show. What could he honestly say?

He told his friend: "There's only one thing that can stop this show being the biggest hit this town has ever had: word of mouth."

On this occasion, I didn't want to speak to Sarah Thomas afterwards because Thora Hird hadn't been formally contracted, and I didn't want to build up the girl's hopes if there was no certainty that I could use her.

A few days later however, I arranged for Sarah to come into the BBC and see me anyway. I really wanted her to play the part of Glenda, but I had to have confirmation of Thora Hird's booking. There would be no point matching them should Thora decide not to take the part.

The moment Sarah left my office our booker rang to say that we had Thora Hird. So I was delighted to call Sarah back and offer her the part. It proved to be very good casting as she is one of those professionals who can learn a new scene very quickly and then perform it perfectly, as though it had been rehearsed for weeks.

The important part of the groom was cast on the recommendation of our assistant floor manager, Dee Dragisic. She said she had recently worked with Mike Grady and that, besides being really good to work with, he was an excellent comedy actor who would be perfect to play the uninitiated Barry Wilkinson. I was grateful for this reminder, for I knew Mike's work from John Sullivan's very funny comedy series, *Citizen Smith* (1977-80). There was no doubt whatsoever in my mind that I wanted Mike Grady to play Barry. So it was really only a formality when I arranged to meet him at an inn near Wimbledon Common. I was to find that Mike Grady is, without doubt, a gifted actor with an intuitive feeling for playing comedy. He played the groom, Barry, to perfection and was an excellent partner for Sarah Thomas.

I now had a complete cast. However, there was one thing that I didn't have, and it was as important to the film as the actors. I didn't have a location for Seymour Utterthwaite's cottage. Roy Clarke's script called for it to be isolated on the edge of the moors, and with a ditch nearby, into which Clegg would reverse a car.

It was very much like trying to find Sam's house for *Getting Sam Home*. After a few weeks of searching with Mike Cager, we had found nowhere remotely close to what was needed. It looked very much as though I would have to ask Roy to re-think his specifications and locate Seymour's cottage on the outskirts of one of the local villages.

Late one afternoon, deeply depressed by our failure to find this location, and having criss-crossed the area for the fourth or fifth time that day, we gave up and made our way back to Holmfirth. As we went round a bend on the main road, I saw across a field in the distance what looked like a small, derelict cottage. We pulled off the road and stopped to take a closer look. From afar, it seemed to be exactly what we had been looking for over the past few weeks: It was isolated and positioned on the edge of the moors. With its stone tiled roof, it looked very promising indeed.

Mike and I opened the gate and walked up the rough track to investigate. When we got near, we saw that it was a small cottage in surprisingly good condition. Its windows and doors were boarded up, and it looked tidy and clean as though it had been regularly washed down. Whatever garden it may have had in the distant past was now overgrown with wild grass and weeds. It was clear that the cottage, with its crumbling, roofless barn nearby, hadn't been occupied for many years. It stood there, bleakly, with very little to commend it as a desirable residence.

We had found the perfect cottage for Seymour Utterthwaite, and we asked ourselves how we could possibly have missed it before. Maybe it was because of having to concentrate on the bend of the road. Whatever, Mike and I were delighted that this key location had been found, and we crossed our fingers that the owners didn't dislike *Summer Wine*.

The following day, Mike Cager, wearing his location manager hat again, found out that the cottage actually belonged to the Hepworth Iron Company who produced extruded clay drainage pipes at its plant in Hazlehead about a mile away. The future of the cottage was uncertain, as it was likely to be demolished sometime in the near future to allow the company to excavate clay (its basic raw material) from the surrounding land. In the meantime, the owners were very happy to let us film there and do whatever we liked with the cottage and the surrounding fields.

The potential of this new location was enormous: there would be no problems of inconveniencing nearby neighbours as there weren't any. But we were warned that the cottage was subject to high winds and driving rain that would blow in from the adjoining moors, hence the washed appearance of the cottage. I said that we would face those problems when they arose. We had Seymour's cottage!

After the cottage had been opened up, the window frames and the front door painted, and a low dry-stone wall built around the front garden, it looked like a very lived-in home. A final touch was having a duck pond dug out which I felt would make this location visually pleasing and be a more likely place into which Clegg could reverse his car.

Roger Cann's set dressing caught perfectly the spirit of Seymour's character. He made the cottage look cosy and filled the garden with scientific experiments and inventions that only a barmy former headmaster and part-time inventor would have around him. And of course, there was the duck pond, with real ducks that laid real eggs at a fair rate.

Uncle of the Bride was fully cast, with good locations, and we were ready to send out the script to everyone when I received a strange call from Gordon Wharmby. In a slightly sombre voice, he said "Alan, I've just heard who's going to play my wife."

"Thora Hird. Yes. It's good isn't it?" I replied. But Gordon just said "Thora Hird?"

"She will be marvellous," I said. After a long pause, he gloomily replied

"But, Alan…Thora Hird?"

I began to think that he was being critical of my casting. It certainly sounded critical. "Gordon, if you don't want to be in the film, you only have to say so," I said.

"Oh, I want to be in it….but Thora Hird?"

I telephoned Gordon's agent to ask if Gordon had a problem. I was relieved to hear that Gordon hadn't been too well recently, but he would be alright for the filming.

A few weeks later, on a Sunday, we were filming at Nora Batty's steps in the middle of Holmfirth when I looked across the river and was pleased to see that Gordon was in the midst of a small crowd. He looked very happy and was obviously enjoying every moment of signing autograph books and posing for photographs with the visitors. There was no sign of a critical or disgruntled actor, or his familiar painter-decorator van.

I asked Gordon how he coped with his decorating business when he was becoming so well-known. "It's quite funny really," he replied with a smile. "I'll be painting away, like, in someone's house. Then I'd see them peeping out

*Top: Seymour's cottage complete with new duck pond.
Left: The car with Peter Sallis, Michael Aldridge, Mike Grady and Bill Owen) is sinking.*

from behind doors, trying not to be seen – just looking at me." Gordon laughed at the thought.

"Then they'll say – 'You know you don't half look like that bloke on Summer Wine'. When I tell them it *is* me, they never believe me."

The filming for *Uncle of the Bride* was proceeding rather well and the scenes with Wesley driving the wedding car – a huge, renovated late-fifties Humber Super Snipe, looked very good. The trail of smoke from its exhaust as it travelled along the narrow lanes would surely confuse weather forecasters in several counties.

Michael Aldridge was fitting in to the production very well. His introduction as Seymour Utterthwaite, a man of so many unfulfilled dreams, was working very well indeed. His tall frame and pleading disposition suited the character down to the ground. Off the set he was a team player and was liked by absolutely everyone. He went out of his way to memorise the names of every single member of the company and comfortably related to them as a friend.

On the unit's day off, Michael insisted that Bill Owen got himself into a taxi to bring him from his rented accommodation in Holmfirth to the Huddersfield Hotel. There, along with Peter Sallis, they would have dinner at a nearby Italian restaurant, and Michael wouldn't take no for an answer. Bill had to attend. It was impossible to imagine Brian Wilde being so socially inclined.

I had three happy actors who got on so well with each other that they were actually enjoying the rigours of filming, and the grumbles from Peter and Bill were noticeably less frequent. This may well have been because they were happier, but there was the suspicion that the easy-going

Top: My versatile Production Manager, Mike Cager. Bottom: Roy Clarke (centre) visits Peter Sallis, Michael Aldridge and Bill Owen.

manner of Michael Aldridge was simply showing them up.

Peter Sallis, tired of staying in rented accommodation, had opted to stay at a new hotel in Huddersfield where Michael Aldridge would also be staying.

I rented the cottage in the middle of Holmfirth that Peter Sallis had rented the previous year. It was sparsely furnished with well-worn pieces that could be described as eclectic but more accurately, as junk. It was above a really good fish and chip shop which tempted my dietary resolutions to breaking point. But it was in the heart of Holmfirth, and I didn't have to travel there every day.

At about seven o'clock one evening, I received a telephone call from Mike Cager to say that we had a huge problem: Gordon Wharmby had gone haywire at the White Horse Inn at Jackson Bridge and thrown a plant pot through a window. Why on earth would he do that? I asked myself. If he wanted to throw something through a window, he should come round to my place, it was made for wrecking.

Worryingly, Gordon Wharmby had been walking up and down the bar at the White Horse, pretending to be me, and shouting 'Action' and 'Cut' and 'No, that's no good, do it again', which I didn't immediately recognise as being part of my repertoire. Mike said that Gordon had been sedated by a doctor and taken off for treatment. This was no laughing matter, it was very serious. Poor Gordon.

At this point, we were nearly two weeks into the six week schedule, and Gordon had been in a lot of the filming. I realised that without him, it would be impossible to finish the film. It was therefore vital that he would be able to complete the location scenes still to be filmed, and the interior scenes that were to be done later in the film studios at Ealing.

Mike Cager then reported that Gordon would definitely not be able to film anymore, and the doctor felt that I shouldn't go and see him in the hospital, as it seemed that in some way, I had brought on his condition. This was a very sad setback to Gordon's career as an actor, but there was nothing that anyone could do to help him.

I telephoned Roy Clarke to give him the bad news. Roy was very sorry for Gordon and asked what I was going to do. I said that there were three options:

We close the production down and start again later in the year. This would be a costly option.

We close the production down for a few days so that I can recast the Wesley role and have the script re-written. This wouldn't be quite so expensive.

I reconstruct the story to use as much of what had already been shot as possible, and carry on filming. This wouldn't be expensive, but would inevitably, spoil a good script.

Roy said, "Just do whatever you need to do."

At this time, Roy Clarke was writing two other comedy series, and it is doubtful if he could have physically coped with the burden of having to quickly re-write a full-length film script as well.

I took option number 3 and decided to carry on and use as much of what had been filmed as possible. It's a well-known fact that one thinks more clearly in the morning (well, I do, anyway), so I got up very early the next day and went through the script page by page, to delete Wesley from the scenes still to be filmed. In some scenes, I would use a double for Wesley and film him from behind. It was all possible, but it was going to spoil what had promised to be a really good film.

Thora Hird was already on her way up from London to join us for the filming, and it was going to be difficult to tell her that her screen partner, whom she hadn't yet met, was unwell and couldn't work any more.

I decided that it would be better if I invited her to join Michael Aldridge, Bill Owen, Peter Sallis, Mike Cager and myself for dinner in Huddersfield. During the dinner, I told Thora what had happened, and that I would completely understand if she didn't want to have to act with a Wesley double. Thora's only concern was for Gordon, and she said, "The poor soul. Of course I'll carry on. I'll do whatever you want to get the film finished." Then she added, in true *Songs of Praise* style, "I'll say a prayer for him tonight."

Over the next few days, I re-shot some scenes with a double standing in for Gordon. A scene where Wesley brings our trio home to his house in the wedding car was changed so that the men get out of the car, and Wesley (a double) drives off to his garage – and so losing Wesley from the rest of the scene.

Kitchen scenes with Thora were altered so that Wesley (a double) would be fixing a leak under the sink, and all we would see of him would be his oily Wellies. This was desperation time, and I had to do whatever was possible to get the film finished.

In a short scene where Edie calls from her bedroom window to Wesley, who is cleaning his car below, it is quite obvious that it is not Gordon Wharmby cleaning the car. It is the versatile Mike Cager. I am pleased to say that no one has ever noticed this.

The revised structure of the script without Gordon was working, but there were two important shots that I needed to have, but we would have to see Gordon's face in them, so they couldn't be filmed with a double. I put this problem to the side, in the hope that a solution would present itself.

Filming at this time was around Seymour's cottage and the duck pond. In the scene where Clegg is a bit heavy on the accelerator and reverses the car into the pond, I only wanted the back wheels of the car to drop into the water. Unfortunately, Peter got carried away, for he reversed at such a speed that the whole car, with Michael Aldridge, Bill Owen and Mike Grady as passengers, went into the middle of the pond and began to sink. Although they had been told that the pond was only two feet deep, when they saw the water coming through the open windows, they quite understandably, panicked. So did I, for the film camera, which was mounted on the car's bonnet, looked as if it was going to get soaked as the car slowly sank. I shouted to Chris Lawson and the effects crew, "Save the camera! Save the camera!" I must say that I was a little disappointed by Bill Owen's expletive-laden reply which showed no concern whatsoever for the well-being of our very expensive film camera.

The sight of the car unexpectedly splashing into the middle of the pond had really impressed the onlookers, but I had only wanted to see the actors reacting to Clegg's bad driving as the water poured in through the open windows.

During the editing, I was persuaded by our film editor, John Wilkinson, to return to Yorkshire and film a wide shot of the big splash using doubles. I must admit that it was well worth the expense, and John was right. Seeing the splash of the car going into the pond did look very good.

It happens sometimes that doing someone a good turn proves to be unexpectedly rewarding. We were preparing to film a night scene at the White Horse at Jackson Bridge where the men come out and get into Wesley's car. Mike Cager told me that Albert Welch, an elderly bit-part player that he knew well, was visiting the area. Could I, perhaps, give him something to do in the film, as the money would come in very useful to him? I said that he could come out of the pub with the men, and Seymour could say, "Albert, you've been on orange juice, you drive." Someone had to drive Wesley's car, as Gordon Wharmby was now no longer available to us, so it might as well be Albert. Having Albert in the scene was politically useful too, as it meant that we wouldn't upset those who are rightly concerned about the dangers of drinking and driving. Albert was drinking orange juice.

A few weeks later, on the film stages at Ealing, where the interior of the White Horse had been recreated, another problem arose. Joe Gladwin (Wally Batty) was struck down with shingles and couldn't do any more filming. Gordon Wharmby's lines in the scene had been given to Joe Gladwin, and now he, too, was unable to play them. This would have been a major calamity, but fortuitously, because I had filmed Albert coming out of the inn on location, I was able to give him Wesley's lines in the preceding scene. It all tied in so perfectly with the location shooting that it looked as if it had all been carefully planned to happen that way. But it was all down to Mike Cager being kind-hearted to old Albert.

CHAPTER 11
Just Two Vital Shots

The end of the location filming for *Uncle of the Bride* was fast approaching, and I was managing to cope with not having Gordon Wharmby available to us. But the solution of how to work around those two vital shots of Wesley, where we really had to see his face, hadn't yet presented itself.

I was talking to a friend who had been a psychiatric nurse and she said that I should have a word with the hospital where Gordon Wharmby had been taken. They would most probably allow him out for a couple of hours. It seemed unlikely that this would be possible, but I had nothing to lose, and I badly needed those two shots.

On the following Sunday, at the end of the day's filming, I went to the hospital where Gordon was recovering. It was in an isolated area of the Huddersfield countryside, and was very old and foreboding. It was the last place in the world where patients should be sent to recover from the stresses of life.

I asked a senior nurse if I could visit Gordon, and I was delighted that her answer was 'Yes', but only when his wife Muriel had finished visiting him.

It wasn't long before Muriel emerged from her visit. She said to me that she was very sorry that Gordon wouldn't be able to work for us any more, adding that the psychiatrists thought that he might be in hospital for some time.

I felt uneasy as a nurse unlocked and relocked the doors of outer rooms as we made our way to a large lounge where Gordon was resting with other patients. When he saw me, he leapt up from his chair and rushed over. With an enormous smile, he shook my hand vigorously. He didn't look at all unwell. In fact, he was very bright and cheerful.

"Oh, it's great to see you. I knew you would come," he said excitedly as he indicated that I should take a seat at a table that looked as if it had been borrowed from my own eclectically-furnished accommodation. After a few more pleasantries, he beckoned a woman patient, who was sitting nearby, to join us.

"Come over. What did I tell you? I knew he'd come," he said proudly. With great reverence he continued, "This is the producer of *Last of the Summer Wine* I was telling you about." The woman, who looked very pale and drained of life, smiled faintly and nodded. Gordon sat down and smiled at her. "Well, go on then, what are you waiting for?" he instructed her, encouragingly.

The woman looked at me for a moment, and then said, "They want to take my baby away."

I wasn't expecting this, and I didn't know quite what to say.

"It's my baby. I'm not going to let them take it away," she continued.

I felt that I had to say something: "Look, I'd love to help, but I really can't do…"

"Leave her," Gordon said – as he gestured her to continue.

"I'd rather die than lose my baby," the woman said as she wiped away a tear. I really was beginning to feel that I should get the poor woman some help when Gordon said, "She's good, isn't she?" Gordon had a wide smile on his face as he waited for my response. I paused for a moment as I assessed the situation.

"How do you mean…..good…., Gordon?"

"She'd be great in *Summer Wine*," he said enthusiastically.

I suddenly realised that Gordon had been rehearsing his fellow patient, and that I had just auditioned her! Gordon then dismissed the woman and called over a male patient, sitting nearby. On a cue from Gordon, he went into a dramatic rendition that suited his somewhat swarthy appearance. I wasn't sure, but it sounded a lot like a speech from an old Humphrey Bogart film I had once seen. The man's performance was certainly convincing, if not memorable.

"There's a lot of great talent here," Gordon proclaimed, emphasising and relishing the word 'great'. I looked around to make sure that there was no piano – at least nobody was going to sing.

I don't know how many of the fifteen or so patients in the lounge were likely to be lined up for audition, but I decided to quickly change the subject. My mission to the hospital had been entirely to try and get Gordon out to film those two vital shots, and I was painfully aware that I was being very selfish in putting my film before his welfare.

"Gordon, you're looking very well," I said. And other than the fact that his eyes were red rimmed, he really did.

"I was thinking that… well… to help you get back to work again, maybe, if I can get you out of here for an afternoon… probably even film a couple of shots, who knows…?" Before I had finished, Gordon leapt up again and went over to a small room in the middle of the lounge where the male charge nurse was sitting at a desk looking at some notes. Gordon introduced me to him. "Tell him what you just said to me," he said to me excitedly.

Gordon had jumped the gun somewhat, as I intended to choose a more appropriate moment to approach the doctors and broach the possibility of borrowing him. But this was the moment of truth.

"Well, I was just thinking that it might be good for Gordon if he could do a teeny bit of work for me, which might help him get back to…. normal."

Unexpectedly, the charge nurse simply said that he would pass on my request to the senior psychiatrist. He wrote down a telephone number on a piece of paper. "Call this number tomorrow morning after ten," he said.

I was surprised and heartened that my audacious request was actually being seriously considered.

The next morning, Mike Cager rang the senior psychiatrist, and was told that Gordon could be allowed out, at my risk, providing he was given the necessary medication. This was very good news indeed.

At lunchtime the following day, Mike and I went to the hospital and after I was given a large box of suppressants for Gordon, with strict instructions on what dosages to administer, Gordon was placed in our care for 24 hours. I was elated that getting those two vital shots was in sight.

Everybody on our film unit was superb and treated Gordon as though nothing had happened, and that he just hadn't been around for a few days. Nobody mentioned the problems he was having.

From the very beginning of Gordon's trouble, the landlord of the White Horse, Ron Backhouse, had strenuously assured curious locals and an inquisitive journalist that nothing had happened.

The problem for me was that Gordon was in my charge, and he would have to stay with me overnight in my rented accommodation.

That night, taking precautions, I locked away all the knives and any sharp implements. And an aspidistra in a pot was moved well out of sight, just in case. But still, throughout the night, I would leap out of bed at the slightest sound. There are lots of clumsy cats in Holmfirth.

The next day, at the church location in Hepworth (where the wedding took place), Gordon completed the two shots. One was of Wesley looking at his daughter Glenda, and saying, "She's right, you look lovely." And the other was where he accidentally wipes some black grease over his face during the wedding ceremony. Gordon was excellent and was as reliable as ever. In the finished film, because it would have been expensive to re-shoot, it is still Mike Cager who actually takes the bride down the path towards the church. It wasn't a good performance, but it was passable.

When lunchtime came, I telephoned the psychiatrist to thank him for his trust. I reported that Gordon had been very good, and that the filming had been completed successfully. The psychiatrist was delighted to hear this, and said that, if this was so, he would get in touch with Gordon's wife to tell her that she can have him back at home. I didn't know if this would be good news or bad news for Muriel. I could only hope that she would want him back.

Gordon, showing no signs of being any different from the Gordon that we all knew – then did some more filming on location for me, and I was soon able to revert to the original script and re-shoot some of the scenes with Wesley that had been deleted in my re-structuring. But the really happy ending is still to come.

Gordon had improved so much that I brought him down to London to film his re-instated interior scenes on the film stages at Ealing. On location, Thora Hird had spent a great deal of time with Gordon, trying to get him to relax, but he was still noticeably uncomfortable in her presence. Then came a scene in the bedroom of their home, where Edie is brushing down Wesley in his hardly-used suit. As can happen with any actor, Thora simply had a mental blockage with one line: 'a decent social occasion'. We did several takes, but the phrase 'a decent social occasion' eluded her. Eventually, I asked her to split the whole speech in two: "Say the first part of the line, 'Just checking for Diesel', then brush Wesley's sleeve while I say 'decent social occasion'. As soon as I've said it, you say, "Look, you're going out on a decent social occasion…." Of course, with my voice removed from the track, it worked perfectly, and no one would ever notice. But what we all did notice was that something had happened to Gordon. He was suddenly much more relaxed and confident.

It soon became clear that Gordon, the painter-decorator turned part-time actor, had simply been terrified of working alongside Thora Hird, the grand lady of film and television. As a result, he had started to drink heavily to calm his nerves and, not being a regular drinker, he had gone too far. Hence the flower pot through the White Horse window. When Thora had trouble with that line on the stages at Ealing, Gordon saw that she was just as fallible as anyone else.

Gordon brightened up after that, and it wasn't long before he was giving Thora notes on how she should play her lines, which didn't go down too well, although she took them in her stride. It was just wonderful to have Gordon back with us.

I knew that Gordon had fully recovered when, later on location, he won a case of wines in a competition. He told everyone that he wanted me to have them, which I thought was really touching. Well, I suppose after all, I was responsible for giving him a new career. But he then said, "Shall we say £5 a bottle?" Everyone was shocked by this. Everyone but me – I was very pleased to buy them – if only to acknowledge that the old Gordon Wharmby had indeed returned.

Thora's visit to the BBC's Ealing studios was very nostalgic for her. Still reliant on a walking stick following a recent operation, Thora asked me one lunchtime to walk with her to the white house at the studio's main gate. It was there, she was pleased to recall, that Michael Balcon, the Head of Production at the old 'Ealing Studios', interviewed her and gave her a contract that would pay her £10 a week. In 1939, that was a great deal of money.

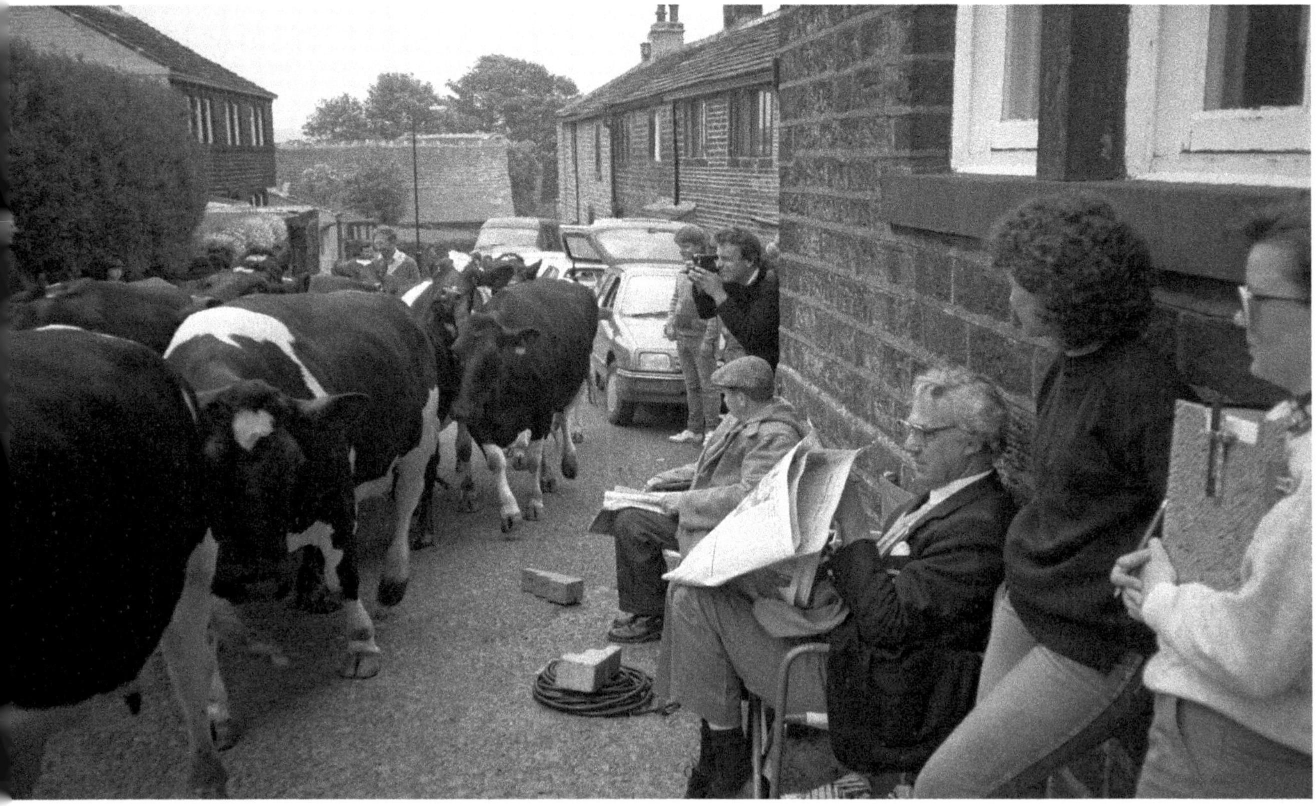

Top: Just when Michael Aldridge is comfortable, along comes a herd of cattle. Bottom: Thora Hird shows Alan the front office of the old Ealing Studios where she was given her first contract.

Despite all the problems, *Uncle of the Bride* was completed without any major delays and was shown on the 1st of January 1986 at 8 p.m.

I had personally gone to the presentation office at Television Centre to warn them not to let the continuity announcer speak over the end credits about the following programmes, as they usually did. In the end title sequence of *Uncle of the Bride*, besides the shots of Barry dropping the wedding ring, and one of those two vital shots with Gordon, a bomb squad is seen arriving at the church to deal with Seymour's motorised wheelbarrow which had exploded. "Stand back, there may be more," a fireman shouted. But when the first credit came up on the screen, the announcer happily chirped away over the whole ending – completely spoiling it. They have better ways of spoiling programmes nowadays: As well as talking over the endings, they shrink the picture so that the credits are unreadable – a real insult to those that work in our industry.

Uncle of the Bride was a big success, as was Thora Hird, who made Edie Pegden another likeable and tough Northern housewife. However, as expected, the press and a sizeable section of the viewing public felt that Michael Aldridge didn't fit in as well as his predecessors had. Even Jimmy Gilbert, who had by now moved to Thames Television, was fiercely critical, and said that casting Michael Aldridge was a huge mistake. Nonetheless, I was certain that the expected criticisms of Seymour Utterthwaite were due entirely to him being unfairly compared to the established and hugely popular Foggy Dewhirst. I said at the time that it was like the head of a family passing away – no replacement father would ever be fully accepted, even if he was a better man.

To overcome the comparison problem, we decided to make a double series the following year in the hope that after about six or seven episodes, Seymour would be well and truly established and liked every bit as much as Foggy had been.

CHAPTER 12
The Extended Series

Roy Clarke had no trouble writing the extended series and because they had been so good in *Uncle of the Bride*, Thora Hird, Mike Grady and Sarah Thomas became regular actors in our company of players. It was Michael Grade, the then Controller of BBC1, who recognised Thora Hird's value to the series and said that he wanted her to be a regular in the cast. Because Thora had been a guest star in *Uncle of the Bride*, I afforded her the same 'guest star' credit in the series even though she would actually be in every episode. There can be no doubt that Thora brought with her a huge following that enjoyed the likeable Edie and her futile attempts to win her war against Wesley's oily fingerprints.

The following series featuring Michael Aldridge, our new 'third man', made extensive use of Seymour's cottage and of course, the duck pond. It was an attractive setting which provided an excellent background for Seymour's wild inventions.

Drilling tests by the Hepworth Iron Company indicated that there was insufficient clay on the land to merit it being excavated. This was good news for us as the location would continue to available for our use. The cottage and the land were then offered to us for five thousand pounds. This was in 1987. It was a bargain, but it would be difficult to convince the BBC that it should move into the property market. As pretty as it was, it would have needed a lot of restoration work to get it to look permanently as it appeared to be in the series. The cottage was just a façade and the pond was only temporary with its water captured by a large plastic sheet.

The pond suggested a slightly altered ending to *Why Does Norman Clegg Wear Ladies Elastic Stockings?* (1987). This episode concerned Seymour's invention of a mobile drilling contraption which was built on a large tricycle. As always, Roy's script was very funny but I felt that the ending would be visually stronger if Seymour were to see a film of oil on top of the pond and immediately deduce that there is oil on his land. What he doesn't see is an empty discarded sardine tin and that the oil from it is leaking on to the surface of the pond. Seymour instructs his reluctant helper Compo to pedal into position and drill through the ground in search of the oil. There is a rumbling sound and we see for the first time a water hydrant sign. A gusher of water then spouts 25 feet into the air soaking them all to the skin.

The effects team successfully achieved this gusher with a fire engine pump and hidden pipes. To add the finishing touch, I had Ronnie Hazlehurst write a pastiche of the *Dallas* signature tune, using his *Last of the Summer Wine* theme. *Dallas*, a series about Texas oilmen, was at the top of the ratings at the time and its production company telephoned to complain that we had used their music without permission! I told them that they were wrong. It was the *Last of the Summer Wine* theme played in the style of the Dallas music. To be fair, the use of trumpets at the same tempo made it sound very much like an exact copy, but it wasn't. It was another tribute to Ronnie's musical virtuosity. I suggested that they play their tape again to a musician who would be able to satisfy them that the tunes in the two versions were entirely different. After a few more insistent calls they were finally convinced, or rather they stopped ringing.

Bill Owen would always complain if he had only a couple of lines in a scene and ask me to take him out of the scene altogether rather than have him just standing there. Then along came *Dried Dates and Codfanglers* (1987). Here was a script with some long speeches for Compo that was beautifully written and touching. Now Bill was worried that he would have trouble with them. He said he would do his best but he might have to stop and ask me to pick-up the scene with a close-up if he should stop in the middle. I agreed to this but in the event he was word perfect and performed them perfectly. Any thoughts that Bill's memory might be failing were swept aside when, a few years later at the age of 75, he played the lead in *The March on Russia*, a David Storey play at the National Theatre in London where he received glowing reviews.

Dried Dates and Codfanglers (1987) revolved around Seymour having devised a secure means of getting into his cottage, or rather <u>not</u> getting into it. The idea for the story was that Seymour had invented a voice recognition lock for his front door. It had some very funny scenes of Seymour demonstrating how his voice – and only *his* voice – would open the door whenever it heard him speaking the secret password, 'Codfanglers'. Needless to say, despite Seymour's confident build-up, it just wouldn't work, and the door obstinately refused to open.

We had nearly finished filming all the scenes at Seymour's for the day when I saw some sheep in the field behind his cottage.

I thought that it would be funny if at the very end of the episode, a sheep was seen passing by the front door. It bleats and the door obediently spring open! Maybe it was a funny idea, but it was easier said than done.

Over the period of an hour countless sheep were cajoled with food and anything else that might tempt one to pass Seymour's front door or even go near it, but they were resolute in their obstinacy. They just weren't interested. In that time, we had used 30 minutes' worth of film and had achieved only one barely acceptable take. Then Evan King, our energetic Scottish production manager, said, "Do you mind if I try something?"

"Go ahead," I said and rolled the camera.

I needed 35 seconds for titles before the sheep was required so Evan, standing some distance from the sheep, awaited his cue. On cue, suddenly there was an almighty roar from Evan that sounded like a hysterical dog being strangled. I'm sorry to say that Evan's virtuoso performance was so vocally and visually funny that I fell over the dry stone wall laughing. The sheep hadn't moved an inch. It just blinked and returned to the business of grazing. In the only take that was useable the sheep doesn't actually bleat, but when the sound was added later, and the door springs open, the effect was nearly perfect, or rather nearly acceptable.

It isn't unusual to return to a particular location for a different production. So when I needed a hillside with a tarmac path overlooking a stream I knew just where to look. The location for *The Ice Cream Man Cometh* (1987) was Dovestone reservoir, exactly where I had filmed the Prehistoric Earth scenes for *The Hitchhiker's Guide to the Galaxy* some six years earlier. It is a well-kept secret that Dovestone is not in Yorkshire but actually in Lancashire even though it is just over the hills from Holmfirth. For *Hitchhiker*, I had chosen the location because it was the nearest place to London that I could find without walls or fences as these certainly weren't around in prehistoric times. For *Summer Wine*, it was the only hillside I could find that had winding tarmac paths ideal for filming a runaway 'Stop Me and Buy One' ice cream bicycle.

I was standing at the top of the hill next to the camera when one of the assistants made her way up the hill to tell me that because Bill Owen was going to see an osteopath, he wouldn't be on set until after ten o'clock the next day. Bill enjoyed his visits to a particular osteopath that he had found in the centre of Huddersfield, but these visits were not for any urgent medical reasons. I told the assistant to go back down to Bill and tell him that he must see the osteopath in his own time as we had a lot to do the next day. The assistant then reported this to Bill, who was in the trio's caravan. Bill came out of the caravan and furiously shouted to me up the hill: "If I'm unable to finish the series, it'll be down to you." He went back inside and angrily slammed the door behind him.

To play picnickers in the scene we were filming, we brought in a dozen or so supporting artists, formerly known as extras. One of them must have tipped off the newspapers that Bill

Top: Seymour has struck water on his land. Bottom: Prehistoric Earth for Hitchhiker, now a picnic area for Summer Wine.

Owen was very ill for the next day a reporter duly turned up with a photographer looking for a scoop. Michael Aldridge and I were walking back to the caravan when the reporter introduced himself and asked if Bill Owen was ill. Michael replied, in his bluff way, "You can never tell with Bill – he never looks terribly well." The reporter was insistent, so Michael said, "Why don't you pop inside the caravan and see for yourself?"

This was not a good move, for the interior of the artists' caravan was strictly out of bounds to everyone except me, and that was only by special invitation. I followed the men inside where Michael offered them a glass of wine, which they were pleased to accept.

"Come along, Bill, chop, chop. These chaps have come a long way to see if you're still alive. Don't let me down now."

Bill was not at all amused, but Michael's humorous handling of the newspapermen was an object lesson in how to deal with awkward situations. After a while, I intervened and said that I had to talk privately to my actors about the filming. The pressmen left, disappointed that there was no story but pleased by Michael's convivial hospitality.

It was around this time, when I was giving Bill a lift in my car, that I told him it was my sixth year on the series and I was thinking of giving

Left: Howard is under Pearl's thumb.
Bottom: Compo (Bill Owen) encourages Barry (Mike Grady) to stand up for himself.

it up and doing other programmes. Bill looked at me in surprise and said, "Don't do that. We've only just got used to you." I wasn't sure how to take that but in the end I reasoned that it was a valid criticism. Little did I think then that I would stay with the series for another twenty plus years.

While shooting an interior scene at Shepperton Studios with Thora Hird we were waiting for a light to be adjusted when she said, "Excuse me asking, Alan, but were you ever a cutter (film editor)?"

I was surprised by the question. "Yes, I was – but how did you know?"

Thora said, "You can always tell by the way you direct. Ex-cutters always know how all the shots will go together. They know the beginning and end of the shots, and there's none of the nonsense of shooting it so many different ways before they make up their minds which one they want."

In Thora's days at Ealing Studios scenes were filmed on relatively expensive 35mm film so it was extravagant to shoot any more than what was actually needed and most actors, especially older ones, get physically tired of playing a scene over and over again. In the world of television, as 16mm colour film became cheaper, directors could afford to shoot more and more material for a scene and make up their minds later.

My shooting ratio on *Last of the Summer Wine* (the amount of film exposed to the amount actually used) was usually less than 5 to 1. The average is about 8 to 1. A film laboratory representative recently told me that a certain director had budgeted to film at a ratio of 27 to 1. It didn't sound to me that the director had any idea of what he wanted.

Ultimately, who cares how the director works? But, in truth, sometimes the actors do. In the break between series my principal actors would often accept small guest parts in long-running drama series. Without exception, they all said that the time taken to shoot a scene from every possible angle exhausted them. Of course, it has to be admitted that our actors were getting older – much older than when they started filming our series.

The very premise of *Last of the Summer Wine* means that most of its actors are elderly. One of the advantages of that is that they bring a great deal of invaluable experience with them. A good example of this came when I was looking for an actor to play the short-sighted Eli, an old friend of Wally Batty. It was in a small conference room at the BBC in Leeds that I auditioned some character actors for the part. The main requirement was that he should be able to play the short-sighted character in a way that wouldn't be getting laughs from his disability. Eli is a robust character who sails through life undaunted by his short-sightedness and the chaos he causes along the way.

I saw five older actors for the part and, although they were all good, none had the ebullient personality necessary to show that Eli, although he was short-sighted, was having a good time. Then along came Danny O'Dea, an actor who had achieved much fame in the North of England playing Dames in pantomimes – and he had made a brief appearance in *Golden Gordon* (1980) some nine years earlier. Danny O'Dea was upright and resilient with a music hall style of delivery. I knew instantly that I had found the right actor. He was absolutely right to play Eli.

As expected, when we filmed for *Jaws* (1987) outside The White Horse at Jackson Bridge, Danny played the short-sighted Eli superbly well. He had to walk over with his hand outstretched to greet Wally Batty and miss him. This Danny performed effortlessly but, as good as he was vocally and physically, I was soon to discover that mime comedy wasn't his forte.

In *Jaws* (1987), Eli had to enter The White Horse and go to the darts board. The script called for him to reach for the darts and, because of his eyesight, have difficulty picking them up. Then, disorientated, he has trouble identifying the darts board. Seeing this, Seymour, Clegg and Compo make a hurried exit before Eli spikes them.

It took an extremely long time to get this simple scene completed and, although the end results were good, I have to confess that I said that I never wanted to work with Danny again if there was any mime comedy involved.

Back in London, Ronnie Hazlehurst wrote a 'music hall' knockabout score for the scene which improved it considerably. When it was shown to the studio audience at the recording of the whole episode, Danny's darts sequence brought the house down. He was sensational. Peter Sallis, never slow to voice an opinion, said, "He's got to be a regular, Alan; he's much funnier than us." Roy Clarke felt the same about Danny and wrote Eli into the series on a semi-regular basis.

Sadly, as Danny got older, his memory for lines began to fade and it wasn't unusual to go for over twenty takes before getting anything usable. However, Danny was so funny that it was worthwhile persevering. Then one morning in Marsden, after spending an hour trying to get a simple line out of him, I had an idea: I would pre-record his speeches. Why not? We do it for singers. So Danny recorded his lines, and on his signal, usually a pointing gesture, the playback would start and Danny would just move his lips. John Wilkinson, our film editor back in London who had sat through the umpteen takes, telephoned me on location to ask what I had given to Danny to suddenly improve his performance so spectacularly. I told John that I had given him a large dose of playback.

Danny O'Dea's scenes were always very funny, and they certainly wouldn't have been as good played by anyone else, but actually getting them on film was a nightmare. He was a kind and loveable man, and his death in April 2003 proved that he really was irreplaceable. There was only one Danny O'Dea.

There can be no doubt that without Ronnie Hazlehurst's music, the Eli darts scene in *Jaws* wouldn't have been nearly as enjoyable. It instantly set the mood and fitted the action perfectly. Ronnie was an admirer of the work of Scott Bradley who wrote the music for the MGM Tom and Jerry cartoons. Bradley's music always fitted the action perfectly without losing the stature of his compositions. Whenever the opportunity arose, it gave Ronnie great pleasure to musically 'point' the visual humour of *Last of the Summer Wine* in much the same way that Scott Bradley's music did with Tom and Jerry.

Ronnie was also a really big fan of Laurel and Hardy and was even a fully paid-up member of their appreciation society, 'The Sons of the Desert'.

As a result of going out to Hollywood with the society, Ronnie had met Stan Laurel's daughter Lois and Laurel and Hardy's producer, the legendary Hal Roach. When Hal came over to London in 1986, Ronnie and I took him to lunch at the Park Lane Hilton. Much to Ronnie's disappointment, Hal wasn't interested in talking about Laurel and Hardy or anything else in his past. He only wanted to persuade me to join with him in making two feature films and three television series a year at Pinewood Studios. His idea was to get together a company of comedy actors who would appear in the productions as required. I asked where the money was coming from and he said that the president of Twentieth Century Fox had guaranteed him 16 million dollars to set the project up. Hal Roach was at the time 96 years old and the project wasn't in any way practical. He was going back to the old days when his studio signed-up comedy actors and produced films pretty much like they were on a conveyor belt.

Accompanying Hal Roach to our lunch was Frances Hilton, a very elegant bejewelled lady who said that she knew a Mrs. Bell whose husband was in real estate. "Have you heard of Bel-Air?" she asked. Well, I had, but it only went to underline the vast canyon that existed between us. Frances, it turned out, was the multi-millionairess widow of Conrad Hilton of Hilton Hotels fame.

A few years later, when Lois Laurel married Tony Hawes, a comedy writer that Ronnie Hazlehurst and I knew very well, we all became very good friends. I was filming a café scene for *Bicycle Bonanza* (1995) at Shepperton Studios when Tony and Lois made a surprise visit to the set. It would have been a pity to lose the opportunity of having Stan Laurel's daughter make a cameo appearance in the episode, so I adjusted the end of a scene where Ivy is ribbing

Top Left: Stan Laurel's daughter Lois, and Alan. Top Right: Lois Laurel visits the set to be in 'Bicycle Bonanza' (1995) Centre Left: The legendary Hal Roach with Frances Hilton and Ronnie Hazlehurst. Bottom: Filming Compo and his 'Sail Skates' at Huddersfield airfield.

Me, Danny O'Dea (Eli) and Jean Fergusson (Marina).

Nora again about her unattractive hat. As Nora is about to leave the café, she says, "You won't find many people with a hat like that." As the café door opens, Nora comes face to face with a woman, Lois Laurel, wearing an identical hat. Ronnie was delighted to have the opportunity to play the Laurel and Hardy signature tune over this link with the past. However, I don't think many viewers would realise its significance, but Ronnie and I did.

A few years later Lois Laurel was thrilled when *Bicycle Bonanza* (1995) was shown in the Los Angeles area. She telephoned me to say that she was inundated with calls from her friends and acquaintances that had seen her brief appearance. For a few days, she said, she was almost as famous as her father.

Joe Gladwin had recovered enough from having shingles to be in most of the episodes filmed in 1986. His final filming for *Last of the Summer Wine* was in September of that year for *Windpower* (1987). It was a damp, icy-cold morning and we were filming on the runway of Huddersfield airfield. Here on the wide runway, we could film a shot that couldn't possibly be accomplished on any of the narrow roads in the Holme Valley.

The camera, the lights and the rest of the equipment were secured to a low load trailer. Wally's motorcycle and sidecar were fixed to the floor, as was a specially made trolley on a rail for Compo. As the convoy moves along the 'road', Compo, on his roller skates and holding a sail, arrives alongside Nora and Wally. He then raises his sail to harness the power of the wind and overtake them. It has to be admitted that a lot of time and money was consumed for one 15 second shot, but it had to be done properly – and safely.

The weather conditions at the airfield were not improving and the grumbles of Bill Owen were entirely forgivable, but the frail Joe Gladwin never once complained. He was, in every way, a trouper.

Joe died in March 1987.

CHAPTER 13

Donkey Business

The third feature-length *Last of the Summer Wine* film was *Big Day at Dream Acres* (1987). It was the tale of a wily tramp who wanders into the middle of the preparations for a garden fete. When the tramp learns that there is to be a donkey derby at the fete he immediately sees an opportunity to make some money for himself by switching donkeys. I have to confess that, even now, I still have trouble working out which donkey is which, but it's a lot of fun and has some memorably funny scenes.

The film was shot at a large stone-built house in its own quite extensive grounds near New Mill, a couple of miles out of Holmfirth. The house, with its large imposing windows, had been built by the owner of one of the many woollen mills in the area.

To create the fete, we erected marquees and stalls in the garden of this house which, for the film, was called 'Dream Acres', and the services of the Holme Brass Band were booked to provide atmosphere.

To play the tramp, I cast Ray McAnally, an Irish actor with a tremendous track record and numerous prestigious awards to his credit. However, I always worry a bit when actors tell me that they know all about the technicalities of filming and that they will do anything asked of them to get the best results for the camera. Would he be able to cope with my positive style of directing? It wasn't long before my hopes were dashed and the usual happy atmosphere of our filming was put in jeopardy.

Early on, a slight ill-feeling arose when I was with Ray McAnally and our trio in their Winnebago caravan, sheltering from the rain. I said that it was my firm opinion that you can't *teach* acting, it has to come from within. I didn't know then that Ray ran acting classes, and I'm afraid that he took it rather personally.

Throughout the filming, Ray became more and more difficult and one day inside The Butcher's Arms in Hepworth, he asked if we could rehearse the scene that we were about to film outside when the rain stopped. I had no objection to this as long as it was just a word rehearsal, as I prefer to direct the actors on the set.

The rain stopped and outside the pub, I carefully placed Seymour, Clegg, Compo and the tramp around a table in the forecourt. Now we could rehearse the scene properly. "Why have you put me here when I was sitting over there when we rehearsed it?" Ray asked.

"That was only a word rehearsal, it wasn't a proper rehearsal and it took place where you had just randomly sat down – and at a table that was half the size."

"But the scene played well inside, why can't we film it that way?"

"I don't want to shoot it that way because I need Compo, Clegg and Seymour to be left in a tight group facing the camera when you go off to get some drinks in the background."

This was a good example of why I prefer to rehearse on the set and how some actors think that a director should simply point a camera at whatever they do in a scene and 'cover it'.

Then, on the last day of filming, we had a scene where Clegg and Seymour are pushing the intoxicated tramp on his bicycle. There came a point where the tramp is boasting about the high social standing of his family and Compo has to interject with some sarcastic remarks. I asked Ray, who was being filmed in a closer shot, to glance at the out-of-shot Compo at the end of each interjection. Not a definite look, just a brief reaction to connect the two shots.

"Why would I do that?" he asked.

"Because Compo is openly mocking what you are saying about your wealthy family."

"I would ignore it, wouldn't I?"

"He is being very critical. If you ignore it, it will appear that you haven't heard Compo or that the directing is inept. All I want is a very brief glance at Compo to connect the two shots."

But Ray persisted. "If I am on the screen, you don't want me to break up my speech with glances to someone off screen."

I said, "OK, just do what you flaming-well want, and let's all get home!" There was a numbed silence from the actors and the crew. Alright, maybe it wasn't exactly what I said, but I had had enough of his nonsense. So much for doing anything to get the best results for the camera.

Had Ray asked if he could play the line differently, I would have been very happy to agree. But it was an antagonistic refusal to do what I wanted. I was really saddened that this happened, as Ray McAnally was actually a very nice man. Years later, I learned from one of my lady actors that a junior member of our company of players spent much of his time actively breeding discontentment. It was the price I paid for not staying at the unit hotel where any dissent can be thwarted before it gets out of hand. I always say that, if it isn't stopped, it spreads throughout the company like cancer.

A year later, I was at the BAFTA Awards at The Grosvenor House Hotel in London when Ray McAnally won an award for his performance in *A Very British Coup* (1988). I made a mental note of where he was sitting and, in order to avoid meeting him when I went to the wash rooms; I carefully took a circuitous route behind the temporarily blocked-off area where the orchestra was sited. Just as I was on the home run, Ray suddenly appeared in front of me. "Alan!" he said as he embraced me warmly. "How are you?"

I immediately thought that he must have mistaken me for someone else. But no, he went on to say how much he had enjoyed our *Big Day at Dream Acres* film. I complimented him on his award and, unlike that last day in Yorkshire, we parted the best of friends.

I had to review my position: first of all, Brian Wilde didn't like my way of working, and he ended up enjoying the finished results of the filming. Then Ray McAnally goes through the very same routine. I had to accept that maybe I'm not a very good director.

Any loss of confidence was set aside when afterwards, completely by chance, I read two books which revealed that Alfred Hitchcock had exactly the same directing style and problems, but I hasten to add that I do not in any way put myself in his category. Then one day, Peter Sallis came into the rehearsal room and said, "Good morning, David" to me. He explained that a documentary programme about David Lean, the previous evening, had revealed that he worked in exactly the same way that I do. And guess what? David Lean had initially been a film editor.

Awkward actors weren't the only problem on *Big Day at Dream Acres*: there were the animals. I'd had some bad experiences in the past of using animal agencies that simply 'borrowed' domestic dogs and cats from their owners and charged the production high fees for 'trained' animals. Consequently, I was keen to personally recruit the two donkeys required for *Big Day at Dream Acres* from local farms. However, it was pointed out to

Top: Crusher (Jonathan Linsley) and Nora (Kathy Staff) deliver food for the Gala. Bottom: The Tramp (Ray McAnally), Clegg (Peter Sallis), Compo (Bill Owen) and Seymour (Michael Aldridge) about to have a drink.

Left: Ivy (Jane Freeman) and Nora (Kathy Staff) at the Gala VIP tent.
Bottom: The Tramp (Ray McAnally) gets Compo, Clegg and Seymour to hide a donkey.

me that there was the matter of insurance if we didn't go through an animal agency. And besides, we would have the advantage of having trained animals which would save us time. I checked with the animal hire company, and they assured me that their donkeys would be trained to do anything required of them.

When it came to the filming amidst the stalls and marquees of the fete there was a scene where Compo had to chase the donkey. But there was no way that the animal was going to go anywhere: it was very happy where it was, thank you very much. So much for the professionally trained donkeys! Then, exasperated, I smacked the donkey's backside – and off it ran. I must assure everyone that there was no pain to the animal but, nonetheless, it hadn't liked the experience of being smacked. The consequence of this was that, whenever I wanted it to run off, all I had to do was walk towards it and off it would run.

A double for Compo had to run off after the donkey, but there was something wrong with his appearance. The costume seemed to have shrunk and was straining under the stresses of containing the generous build of our double. A quick check revealed that we had booked a double for Compo who was much taller than Bill Owen. In their defence, my assistants showed me Bill's published measurements which were identical to those of the double they had booked. Another check revealed that Bill was actually three inches shorter than what was listed. When I asked Bill how the measurements came to be so wrong, he said that he always gave himself a few inches so that he wouldn't lose a good part in a film by being too short. Good old Bill.

Nearly twenty years later, Johnnie Casson, certainly my favourite comedian, revealed that it was he who had doubled for Compo that day when the costume didn't fit.

When the location filming ended on *Big Day at Dream Acres* (1987), the animal agency asked if they could have a screen credit. The answer was 'no' because hire companies don't get credits, and in any case, as trainers, they had failed miserably. However, I said that I could credit the donkey who they said was called 'Shakespeare'.

Shortly after the film was shown on BBC1 at Christmas in 1987, I received a letter from an angry gentleman in Denby Dale which is about five miles from Holmfirth. He said that his daughter was inconsolable when she saw that her much-loved donkey had been credited as being 'Shakespeare' as this was not its name. It emerged that the animal hire company had seen the donkey grazing in a field and had simply knocked on the door and asked the gentleman's young daughter if she would like to see her donkey on television. It was the same old story.

The girl was, of course, delighted, but very disappointed to be told that the BBC wouldn't allow her to attend the filming when, in fact, visitors were always welcome. The hire company had simply collected the donkey every morning from the field and didn't pay the girl a penny, but she would have the pleasure of seeing her pet donkey featured on *Last of the Summer Wine*.

I was very angry about the dishonesty of the agency, especially for stopping the young girl from visiting the set to watch her donkey being filmed. The animal agency strenuously denied that the donkey we used belonged to the young girl, but she knew what her donkey looked like. It was definitely her donkey, and 'Shakespeare' was definitely not its name. Ultimately, the *Daily Mirror* newspaper took Bill Owen back to Denby Dale where, on behalf of the production, he formally apologised to the young girl for her distress.

The cost to our production for the donkey and two handlers was a fair amount of money. In the end, the agency paid a small amount to the donkey's true owner, but it didn't make amends for the lasting hurt to the child. All I had wanted to do in the first place was hire a donkey locally.

Telling donkeys apart might be quite difficult, but sometimes actors can be unrecognisable too. It doesn't happen often, but actors have been known to return to a series looking so different that they are unsuitable to play a particular part. Hairstyles can be a problem and sometimes weight increases.

A typical scene in Ivy's Café with 'Our three' Ivy (Jane Freeman) and, behind the counter, Crusher (Jonathan Linsley).

Jonathan Linsley's size had worked to his advantage over the four years that he had been in the series. He played Ivy's nephew Milburn, a gentle giant known to everyone as Crusher. He had ably filled the gap left by the sad demise of John Comer in 1983, taking his place in the café scenes. Jonathan was very popular, especially with younger viewers, and played the scenes that capitalised on his size and strength very well, but a problem was brewing.

It was clear that, although Jonathan's build was very good for his character in the series, it wasn't good for him personally. He was worryingly overweight which looked medically dangerous. During the period between the *Dream Acres* film and the following series somebody mentioned that they had bumped into Jonathan Linsley and that he had lost so much weight that that he was unrecognisable. I thought that I ought to see him for myself as his build was an important part of his appeal and crucial for playing Crusher.

I was sitting in my office which was opposite the BBC Club on the fourth floor of the Television Centre, a prized position envied almost as much as for having green velvet curtains. I was waiting for Jonathan Linsley who was on his way up from reception to see me. The knock came to the door and this tall, slim gaunt man came in. Had it not been that I was expecting him, I most certainly wouldn't have known that it was Jonathan. I was pleased to see that he had addressed his weight problem, but he had rather overdone it.

I invited Jonathan over to the BBC Club where other members of the *Summer Wine* production team were gathered. Not one of them recognised the new Jonathan Linsley and there was considerable disbelief when I re-introduced him to them.

A newspaper article demonstrated how much weight he had lost by having Jonathan and his girlfriend standing together inside a pair of his jeans.

My immediate thought was to have some padding made for him, but Jonathan had lost so much weight that his face was drawn and unrecognisable. In fact, he looked very unfit. I asked Jonathan if he could put a few pounds back on so that he would, at least, have some flesh on his face, but he refused. It had been such an ordeal losing the weight that he didn't want to put any back on, for *any* reason.

As Jonathan's new appearance would have required considerable explanation to the viewers, and the unavoidable fact that he would no longer fit in with the series, it was with much regret that I had to let him go. It was a pity but he had dieted himself out of the part of Crusher.

Howard (Robert Fyfe) attempts to escape.

CHAPTER 14
Old Friends

The much-loved Joe Gladwin was devoutly religious and had been honoured by the Catholic Church for the good work he did in organising places of worship for touring actors. At a memorial celebration of his life, the church was packed with stars from yesteryear and others who had simply had the good fortune to know him.

Among the many well-known faces that came out of the church after the very touching ceremony was Brian Wilde. Brian had always attended the funerals of fellow cast members and had never once looked for an excuse not to go. It had been two years since he left the series and I asked him how everything was going for him. He replied that he had done one or two bits and pieces, but he was mainly just enjoying working away in his garden at home in Ware, a leafy town in Hertfordshire. Surprisingly, he then said that he had thought of going to Australia to work but, somehow, I just couldn't see Brian Wilde embracing the challenges of a new world down under.

I told Brian that it had always been my hope that he would come back and make a guest appearance as Foggy in an episode. The idea amused him, but no more than that. We shook hands before we went our separate ways. As always, Brian Wilde was polite and sincere.

A couple of evenings later, Brian telephoned me at home, and asked if I had meant what I said about his making a guest appearance in *Last of the Summer Wine*. I said that I did mean it, and it would be a great pleasure to have him back for an episode. I should add here that I had previously considered this possibility, and I asked Michael Aldridge if he would feel uncomfortable if Brian were to return to make a one-off guest appearance. Michael said he wouldn't mind at all. Likewise, Roy Clarke said that he would be very pleased to write a story involving Foggy. First, however, there was another series to make.

Before we started work on the 1988 series, Michael Aldridge came to me and pointed out that the three main characters – Compo, Clegg and Seymour – were in front of the camera much more than anyone else and that it was quite tiring for elderly actors like himself. He suggested that it could prove to be economic if I were to hire three lookalike doubles and rehearse with them on the set until I was completely satisfied. All that the three principals would then have to do is copy what the doubles have rehearsed.

This seemed to be a good idea for me personally as getting the actors on to the set to rehearse was quite a task. But the down side of rehearsing with the doubles was that it removed, almost entirely, any input from the actors in the playing of the scenes. How would Bill and Peter like it?

Well, I put the idea to them. Bill Owen was totally in favour, and Peter Sallis was willing to try it although I sensed that he would have resisted the idea if it had been mine. So, for the 1988 series, most of the location scenes were rehearsed using doubles. Their positions, as the scene was blocked, were marked on the ground with a different colour marker for each character.

When I was satisfied with a set-up, the three principals came out of their nice, warm Winnebago motor home to watch the doubles going through all the rehearsed moves. As they did so, either I read the script or the actors spoke their lines.

Michael's idea worked surprisingly well and sometimes quite complicated scenes with a lot of moves were plotted using the doubles. This resulted in a mass of coloured marks on the ground to denote the varying positions of the different characters. As one of the doubles observed, "There are more marks on the ground here than there are in the Bundesbank."

Only once was there a slight problem. During the time that it took to rehearse a set-up with the doubles, which involved laying a track and lighting the scene, Bill Owen, in an uncharacteristic burst of energy, had been creative. He asked me to look at the same scene performed in a different way. Most scenes can be played a dozen different ways, so I said to Bill, "That's OK with me – let's do it, but are you absolutely sure? Because, re-blocking the scene and re-lighting it will delay lunch by at least an hour."

Without a moment's hesitation, Bill replied, "Forget it. It was just an idea."

There was no doubt that setting up the scenes using the doubles eased the workload for the actors, but I was quite surprised that they liked it quite as much as they did. The real advantage, as Michael Aldridge had correctly forecast, was that the actors could relax between set-ups and could then play the scenes with more energy and enthusiasm.

As the doubles were chosen for their physical likeness to the actors they also performed in the shots where the trio were small figures up in the hills or just in the distance. I would read the lines, which were relayed over loud speakers, so that the doubles could act out what was being said. The principals would then record their lines later to replace my reading of them.

The lookalike doubles would sometimes appear as themselves in pub scenes and quite often they would play small parts. Once, when the scene at The White Horse was too male-orientated, I asked Denis Mawn, one of the doubles, to go to the costume and make up trucks and come back looking like a woman. When he returned wearing a dress and a wig he looked every bit like a woman: an unattractive woman, but a woman nonetheless. Bill Owen came on to the set and smiled at 'the woman' as he sat down near her. The crew soon picked up that Bill didn't realise that it was Denis and they enjoyed watching the scene being played out before them. During the hour that it took to film the scene Bill constantly smiled at 'the woman'. Whenever he walked past the alluring Denis, Bill would say, "Excuse me, love. Sorry to bother you." And when we stopped for lunch, Bill stood back politely so that 'the woman' could pass through the doorway first. We were going to pay-off the joke at the catering truck, but one of the dressers gave the game away. But full marks to Denis for carrying off the ruse so well. Unconvinced, Bill came over to me later and quietly asked, "Was that really Denis?"

A few weeks before Bill Owen would become Compo again for the tenth series, he came into the Television Centre to have lunch with me. It had become the practice over the years that he would collect his expenses and, over lunch, talk to me about anything he had read in the scripts that worried him. I could then explain how I was going to achieve what Roy had written and put his mind at rest.

On this occasion we were joined by Simone Dawson, who would take notes. Simone was an assistant floor manager at the time and later would become a superb first assistant director on the series. Bill had written out a list of things he wanted to discuss and one of them was 'No

Chapter 14 – Old Friends – 107

Top: Clegg (Peter Sallis) and Compo (Bill Owen) help their leader Seymour (Michael Aldridge) to move an unexpected obstacle. Bottom: Eli Wood and James Casey with the late Roy Castle's daughter, Antonia (who just happened to be our Stage Manager).

The classic brow-beaten Yorkshire husband

uneven ground'. I asked Bill what that meant, but he wasn't sure.

"Do you mean no hills?"

"Yes, that's it, no hills. I don't want to have to act and climb hills at the same time," he said. I was very happy to agree to this.

Then Bill said that he thought that the scene in *The Treasure of the Deep* (1988) where Compo has to be held over a bridge by his legs so that he can look under the water was illogical, and besides, holding him over a bridge by his legs had been done three or four times before in the series. I agreed that it wasn't good to repeat situations and that it was an odd way to look under water. Everyone knows that the only way to see under water is by using a glass-bottomed bucket. The thought of having a glass-bottomed boat crossed my mind, then suddenly the 'boat' prompted an idea: suppose Seymour made Compo a submarine out of two old oil drums complete with pedals and a porthole? The submarine could then appear to come alongside Howard and Marina who are in a small rowing boat pretending to fish. Then the submarine's periscope comes into shot and appears to watch them as they speak to each other. Bill loved the idea, mainly, I think, because he knew he wouldn't be involved so much in the actual filming. All I needed was Roy's approval and some new words.

A month or so later, we filmed Compo and Seymour's homemade submarine at Tunnel End near Marsden which is where the longest canal tunnel in the world begins – or ends, if you come the other way. The canal water was like thick oxtail soup and wasn't where anyone would want to dunk valuable actors, but for the sequence where Howard and Marina panic when they see the submarine's periscope and capsize their boat, it was unavoidable that they would get soaked in the brown, slimy water. For health reasons, both Robert Fyfe and Jean Fergusson (Howard and Marina) were whisked off after the scene for a medical check-up.

What I didn't know was that Robert Fyfe couldn't swim – he never said. Valiantly, he went into and under the water where he was immediately rescued by the effects team. Nothing was ever too much for Robert and Jean.

The only shot of Compo looking out through the porthole of the submarine was filmed in the garage of The Foxhouse Inn, about 200 yards from Seymour's cottage. A borrowed fish tank, complete with fish, was simply placed in front of Bill who, from the comfort of a chair, gave the impression that he was inside the submarine pedalling the propellers.

The sure sign of a successful programme is when the studio audience gives a disappointed "Ah" as the closing titles appear. It is a clear indication that they want it to go on longer, and the 'ah' for *Treasure of the Deep* was very satisfying to hear.

For once, I asked the BBC's presentation department to speak over the end credits (which they were very good at), but only to make an announcement that Compo's submarine should not be copied as it didn't really work. It worried me that some child might copy the crude submarine and drown. But, believe it or not, despite this caution, I received a letter from a twelve-year-old asking if there were any plans of the submarine available because he wanted to make one. He would obviously grow up to be one of those people who don't watch the end credits.

Before filming for the series had ended, I was asked by Gareth Gwenlan, the current Head of Comedy, if I could make another feature-length film for Christmas. I said that I didn't think that the films really worked for our audiences who expected to hear lots of laughter throughout them.

I said that it would be much better if we were to make an hour-long 'Special' over two recording days in a television studio. That way, we would get a long show with good laughter throughout from the two audiences. This was agreed, and Roy was commissioned to write a one hour Christmas Special which would bring Foggy back to the series.

It was with eager anticipation that I awaited the arrival of Roy Clarke's script to see how Foggy would return. The script of *CRUMS* (1988), which stands for the Christmas Resistance Underground Movement, was another Roy Clarke triumph.

It revolved around the appearance in town of a mystery Santa Claus who is eventually unbearded to reveal that it is Foggy. There was only one problem with the script which was that for most of the time, Seymour and Foggy were bickering between themselves as to who had been first to come up with an idea.

I sent the script to Brian Wilde and told him that I suspected that he would be disappointed with it. Brian's response was that it was a letdown, and proved conclusively that *Summer Wine* only works with a trio of males, not a quartet. He said he was very sorry, but he didn't think it was right for him – and this time, I had to agree.

It was a time when Roy was very busy writing other series, so I suggested to him that, with a little editing to delete Foggy, and with a few more lines, his excellent script would remain, more or less, intact. In the original script of *CRUMS*, Foggy, dressed as Santa Claus, is trying secretly to visit his Auntie Wainwright. My solution was simple: let Auntie Wainwright be Howard's aunt. This revised structure of the script was sent back to Roy for his approval and some additional lines.

The next thing was, who would I cast to play Auntie Wainwright?

It was a particularly good part and I wanted to cast someone who would give it that something extra. The answer again came from my wife, Constance.

After a long run playing Hilda Ogden, Jean Alexander had asked to be written out of *Coronation Street* so that she could do other things. Constance had seen her being interviewed on a television chat show and said that she was certain that Jean would want to play Auntie.

I made a call to Jean Alexander's agent and the answer was, in principle, 'Yes'. However, Jean was on a cruise and would naturally have to see the script first. It was such a good part that I knew the answer would definitely be 'Yes'.

Although the BBC's Artists Booker had trouble making contact with Jean's agent, I wasn't unduly worried because she was probably still on her cruise. With no knowledge at all of our enquiries, Jean Alexander returned home and was surprised to find in her letterbox the script for *CRUMS* along with my letter saying that I hoped she would like it enough to play Auntie Wainwright. Jean read it and was as expected, delighted by the character and especially the quality of the speeches that Roy Clarke had written for her. It was just as well that Jean liked the part so much as filming was only a fortnight away. I had been so certain that she would accept the part that, for once, I didn't have an alternative actress in mind.

An empty dilapidated shop that could be turned into Auntie Wainwright's second-hand emporium was found near our unit base in Marsden by Neil Banks who was briefly our location manager. It was a great find as it was in a quiet Marsden backstreet that was as typically Yorkshire as anyone could get. It had an unspoiled period look to it and was spot on for the story. It couldn't have been bettered.

A few days before the filming of the Auntie Wainwright scenes I went along to our temporary costume and make up room that had been set up in the Huddersfield Hotel. I was to meet Jean Alexander for the first time and check her costume and make up.

I'm afraid I had never seen an episode of *Coronation Street*, but I knew that Hilda Ogden was a very popular character in the series. When I arrived at the hotel, besides the make-up and costume staff, there was also an elderly woman standing nearby. Could this be Jean Alexander? I wondered. She didn't look at all like the Hilda Ogden character I had seen in photographs. I couldn't be at all sure if she was my guest star or just a family member of the hotel's management. To avoid the risk of embarrassing her, I carefully avoided saying her name just in case it wasn't Jean Alexander, and we talked generally about the series. She then said that she liked Michael Aldridge very much although she missed, of course, Brian Wilde. It was a good five minutes later, when she eventually asked me if I was happy with her wig, that I was certain that this was definitely Jean Alexander. Jean was a triumph as Auntie Wainwright and was so good that Roy subsequently wrote her into every series. Thanks, Constance.

Just for nostalgia sake, I cast James Casey and Eli Woods to play the two drunks in *CRUMS* who see a many-legged creature running down the street (actually a water bed being transported by the men). James Casey, a former BBC Radio Producer in Manchester, is the son of the legendary comedian Jimmy James, and Eli Woods (not the *Spiderman* actor) was one of Jimmy James' two stooges, the other being the versatile entertainer, the late Roy Castle. Some years later, it was a nostalgic meeting for Jimmy and Eli when Roy Castle's daughter, Antonia, was our stage manager. Needless to say, Jimmy and Eli have made regular guest appearances in the series.

CRUMS was finished and ready for transmission when I received a call from Gareth Gwenlan to ask why it ran for an hour when he had asked me to make a 50-minute special. I reminded him that actually he had asked me to make a 90-minute film and that it was I who had suggested we make a one hour special with an audience instead. But, inexplicably, he denied that any such thing had been discussed. Fortunately, after a great deal of angst, it was agreed that it would ruin the programme to arbitrarily delete ten minutes of the story, so it remained unspoiled at its proper length of 60 minutes.

It was customary for the Head of Comedy to travel up to Yorkshire and take the three *Summer Wine* principals and the producer to dinner. When Gareth Gwenlan visited, he told our principals what they wanted to hear: there would be another series the following year. A month or so later, back at the BBC rehearsal rooms in Acton, I received a panic phone call from Gareth. "I've got a problem," he said. "The Controller wants another series next year and I've told the cast that there won't be any more."

I replied: "No…, you told them that there would be a series next year." "Did I? Oh well, that's all right then," he said, and our forgetful Head of Comedy hung up.

To introduce Jean Alexander as Auntie Wainwright in *CRUMS*, I made a specially filmed 60-second cinema-style trailer. It would be at the end of *The Day of the Welsh Ferret* (1988) which would be the last episode in the current series. At the start, the trailer looked as if it was promoting a mystery film before it was revealed that it was actually about Jean Alexander being in our Christmas special. I had left the space for this trailer within the 29-and-a-half minutes of my allocated programme time, but the BBC Presentation Department objected to this on the grounds that it was their prerogative to make and show trailers. But this was a funny specially-filmed trailer that wasn't made up of excerpts and it was part of our programme time.

As expected, Gareth Gwenlan let us all down by agreeing with the Presentation Department, and my trailer was removed. Although it was shown on another evening on its own, we lost the opportunity to bang the drum to our *Summer Wine* audience that the wonderful Jean Alexander would be in our Christmas special.

CRUMS was a huge success at Christmas 1988 and, besides the enthusiastic appreciation of Jean Alexander, it was good to see that Michael Aldridge had now been completely accepted by the viewers as Seymour.

Who needs Californian sunshine, when we have such good weather in Yorkshire (filming Howard and Marina scenes).

CHAPTER 15
Mickey Rooney

I could tell from the many letters I received from America that *Last of the Summer Wine* was very popular there too. It had always been my wish to make an American version of our series with Mickey Rooney playing the American equivalent of Compo.

When Mickey was in London to appear in *Sugar Babes* at the Savoy Theatre, Roy Clarke came down from his home near Doncaster for a meeting with Mickey and his agent in the star dressing room at the theatre. Unfortunately the agent had broken his leg and couldn't attend, but Mickey, having seen *Last of the Summer Wine*, was very enthusiastic about the project and suggested that a town north of Los Angeles, near Bakersfield, would be a good location.

"I'll tell you who would be great to play the Clegg character," Mickey said. "Donald O'Connor. He's a great actor, you know. He isn't seen enough." I wasn't sure that Donald O'Connor was a very good suggestion to play a thoughtful Clegg-type character.

Mickey Rooney was so keen to talk about being in an American version of *Last of the Summer Wine* that he delayed the opening of *Sugar Babes* by five minutes, which is a long time in theatre land. The overture had to be played twice and the stage staff were panicking to get the understudy ready to take over Mickey's part. But Mickey Rooney was completely unconcerned and just wanted to continue talking about *Last of the Summer Wine*.

A couple of months later, I went out to Hollywood with Roy's concept of the American series which he called *Sweet September*. The great thing about the William Morris Agency is that it is very powerful. Numerous appointments were made for me to pitch the *Sweet September* idea. However, I had made a basic error. I had assumed that making an American version of the series would be done in the same way that we made *Last of the Summer Wine* in the UK. Here, we film for four weeks on location, and then return to London to complete the episodes in a multi-camera studio in front of an audience. In America, at that time, series were either all-film or all multi-camera in a live studio, and the two were never mixed. This was mainly because of there being different rates for multi-camera crews and for single camera film crews and using the two crafts in one show would have been prohibitive. That, and the fact that Mickey Rooney had a reputation for being Mickey Rooney and doing whatever he pleased, made the project as presented pretty well a non-starter.

Because I was unable to stay in Los Angeles, I had no time to adjust the concept of the series to be either all film or all multi-camera. But I had a good friend in Dick Blaney whose company had distributed around the world those *Crackerjack* 'Don and Pete' comedy films that I had made.

I asked him if he had a contact in the United States who might be interested in an American version of *Last of the Summer Wine*. Dick said that he was returning to Los Angeles the following week and would be playing golf with the head of Universal Television and another producer. He said that he would bring the subject up.

My telephone rang a week later and Dick reported the good news from Los Angeles that *both* of his American friends were very interested. A few weeks passed and then Dick called again to say that Universal wanted to take on the series. However, as the series was entirely new to them, the deal wasn't the best ever. Roy would let them make the series based on his scripts, with other writers to keep up the necessary flow. Roy would have a major say as an Executive Producer, as would I. Dick Blaney warned us again that it wasn't a great deal but, if the series worked, it would ultimately be great for all of us. Roy fully agreed, saying that the alternative was to let the scripts gather dust on a shelf.

Several weeks later, when contracts were about to be signed, Roy withdrew from the deal on the strenuous advice of Sheila Lemmon, his UK agent who had nothing to do with the project. And the scripts *have* gathered dust ever since. It was a great pity, but I had a series of *Last of the Summer Wine* to make in England and it was no time to draw swords.

CHAPTER 16
Making an Exhibition

Last of the Summer Wine was gearing up for its 83rd episode when Bill Owen mentioned to me that, at the age of 74, he was being asked to do things in the filming that were really too physical for him. Roy Clarke appreciated this, so wrote the action in the episodes to be carried out by Barry, played by Mike Grady. One such episode was *Getting Barry Higher in the World* (1989) where Barry hangs on to a kite for dear life.

With the help of a huge crane and very thin wires, Barry was transported across a field and over Edie's car while hanging on to the kite. Of course, Mike Grady didn't actually perform the stunt, as nor would have Bill Owen had it been Compo hanging on to the kite.

The audience reaction to Barry's flight over the heads of the ladies in Edie's car was, as expected, euphoric. Also, as expected, Bill Owen came to me and said that he had changed his mind and felt that Compo should do all the stunts.

Bill Owen could be seen as being a little selfish sometimes but, when it came to doing something for Holmfirth and its community, he was completely selfless and would go to considerable lengths to support them. When asked, a few years earlier, to help publicise the town, he would only agree to be interviewed on television if he was allowed to wear a 'Holmfirth' T-shirt. It worked, and tourist buses began to appear in the town.

To give the visitors something of interest to look at in addition to the well-known locations, it was announced that there was going be a *Last of the Summer Wine* exhibition at Compo's house which was immediately beneath Nora Batty's front door. It was really only a store room and had been used to keep dogs and other animals, so there was always a disgusting smell whenever the door was opened. It was so pungent that when Compo had to be seen coming from his house Bill would wait outside until the camera was running and the clapper board had identified the scene before he would enter. He would then take a deep breath, go inside and immediately turn round and come back outside again.

Bill Owen liked the idea of the exhibition very much and offered his services as its official curator. He would give his unfettered support to the project in return for having full control to make it a worthy exhibition.

A man of his word, Bill decided that what was needed was a gallery of photographs of various moments in the history of the series. To select them, he went with me to the BBC's picture library in West London and carefully selected stills from early episodes. He also felt that there should be a prominent display of good portraits of the actors. It was later observed that there seemed to be many more photographs of Bill Owen than anyone else, but that was how the curator wanted it to be.

When I offered the exhibition Seymour's homemade submarine from *Treasure of the Deep* (1988), Bill turned it down on the grounds that nobody would want to see 'that old rubbish'. In fact, it was exactly what the public *did* want to see and it proved to be the most popular part of the exhibition. So, to satisfy Bill, during all the weeks that he was in Holmfirth for our filming, the exhibition staff took the submarine and other recognisable props and hid them out of sight in a nearby lock-up garage.

Although the *Last of the Summer Wine* exhibition had quite realistically recreated Compo's basement home in the cleaned-up store room, Bill said that there was something missing. He decided that Compo would have a clothes horse in front of the iron stove with his underwear stretched out on it to dry. Bill was delighted to take his freshly-washed long johns and other items of underwear that he used when filming and formally present them to the exhibition. There, he ceremoniously draped them over the clothes horse in exactly the same way that Compo would have done.

One chilly morning a few weeks later, when he was about to film up on the moors, Bill was feeling quite cold, so he told Bob Eltrincham, his dresser, to get out his thermal underwear.

"You've given it all to the exhibition, Bill," Bob replied.

"Well, go and get it back, I'm cold," Bill instructed.

So Bob had to drive into Holmfirth in the early morning and get the exhibition opened up to retrieve Bill's underwear.

Another prop that Bill considered unsuitable for the exhibition was the mangle used in *Three Men and a Mangle* (1989). We all have our favourite episodes and for me, the most satisfactory episode of the 1989 series, and certainly one in my top ten, was *Three Men and a Mangle*. Compo, Clegg and Seymour do Nora Batty a favour by delivering her old mangle to a friend on the other side of the valley. At one point in the script they find an old iron bedstead and have to go to some lengths to lift the heavy mangle on to it to make it easier to push. It seemed to me that their difficulties in lifting the mangle on to the bedstead were a bit contrived.

The idea came to me that it would be funnier if they decided to take a short cut across the valley using a disused railway viaduct. When Seymour lassos the mangle and is in the process of hauling it up, two policemen appear on the viaduct to investigate. Seeing them, they let go of the rope and the mangle falls through the roof of the police car below. Unaware of this, before returning to their now demolished police car, the policemen warn the men to be careful. When the policemen return to their demolished car, one of them (Ken Kitson) doesn't notice the damage and boasts about the advantages of having local knowledge when dealing with difficult situations.

Having the idea was one thing but finding a disused railway viaduct over a quiet road was another, and it was the old problem of searching maps, but I couldn't find one anywhere. I was well and truly stumped and was about to abandon the idea when, one evening, I was having a drink with a friend who lived in Thornton, near Bradford. When I mentioned my frustration at not being able to find a disused railway viaduct over a quiet road, he immediately said, "There's a viaduct about half a mile from my house that has a quiet road beneath it."

I rushed over to Thornton and there it was: the absolutely perfect disused railway viaduct over a quiet road that I had been searching for. And they say drinking isn't good for you.

I am happy to say that, when the sequence of the mangle demolishing the police car was shown to an audience, the laughter completely obliterated all the dialogue of the two policemen that followed.

CHAPTER 17
Undercurrents

Despite the fact that I was making some of the best ever episodes of *Last of the Summer Wine*, including *Three Men and a Mangle*, there was a distinct feeling that the comedy department manager wasn't giving us the support that the series merited. It was pointed out that the equestrian interests of Gareth Gwenlan, our forgetful Head of Comedy, had resulted in his devolving many of his duties to David Lilley who appeared to be out of his depth.

By having little wine parties for the girls in the department, he made himself very popular with them. The inexplicable consequence of this was that the production assistants who were attached to *Summer Wine* were efficient but unhelpful, and seemed to be working to rule.

When I told one of my assistants that she wouldn't be required to go with us to film a mute background shot for titles where notes wouldn't need to be taken, she recited: "I am a production assistant. I am paid to do the work of a production assistant and I intend to do my work to the best of my ability." She then turned and climbed into the cab of the camera van. The only thing that was missing was a two-finger gesture at the end. The sound recordist observed, "That's put you in your place."

I was astonished that the girl had the audacity to disobey me openly, but I later learned that she acted with some considerable indemnity in that she was soon to become Mrs Gareth Gwenlan!

I have always frowned upon location romances where inevitably someone gets hurt. I had no wish however to interfere in the private lives of my staff, but when such relationships go wrong and affect their work it concerns me. In recent years, to avoid such situations, I tried to ensure that only assistants who either were married or had a strong relationship were used on the filming. Nevertheless, I would still find young assistants, distressed and weeping, behind the scenery in a corner of the studio. There can be no doubt that location romances are disruptive to the production.

But other matters were being far more disruptive to the usual smooth running of the production. Instead of being supportive, the comedy manager was being downright obstructive. Craft staff were allocated, whose mission it seemed, was to be unhelpful. I am fiercely critical of the 'New BBC' with its plethora of executives, but the 'Old BBC', with its protective departments, was by no means perfect and was sometimes inexcusably extravagant with my budget.

In a boatyard near where I live, I had seen some old decaying boats which prompted me to suggest a slightly different plot for an episode that was subsequently called *Das Welly Boot* (1989). I suggested to Roy Clarke that Foggy sees a sunken boat in the canal and decides that it should be refloated and refurbished so that they can operate a water taxi service.

Our set designer was given the address of the boatyard where there were quite a few shabby but watertight boats available for only the cost of taking them away. A few weeks later, I asked about the boat and I was told that it was 'nearly finished' at a different boatyard in Lower Sunbury. I couldn't see the logic in this because I wanted to use one of the old boats that I had first seen which would have cost us nothing. I was appalled when I learned that the designer had gone to a professional boat builder and had a shiny new boat built at a cost of over two thousand pounds! "Don't worry, I'll make it look old," was her response to my concern about the cost and the fact that it didn't look as if it was possible to sink it.

When it came to the seating in the boat, I said that I wanted an old and tattered three-piece suite that would look completely out of place. What was supplied was a black 'leather look' three-piece suite that made the boat look swanky enough for St Tropez harbour. The whole concept was a scandalous waste of money and I was justifiably angry, but the Design Department fully supported their designer's extravagance. Although I was able to ensure that the production of *Last of the Summer Wine* wasn't affected in any way by the mischievous actions of the comedy manager, I could only wonder what was going on. Why would anyone of sound mind want to cause trouble?

I then received some bad news that would be far more disruptive than the Comedy Department front office. Towards the end of that season's filming in 1989, I was at the Huddersfield Hotel one evening when Peter Sallis came over to me. Solemnly, he said that Michael Aldridge would like to see me in his room. It was very important and he wanted to tell me personally. I feared that something, or someone, had upset him, but when I went into his room, I could see that he had been crying.

Image is all, when you are running a personal messaging service.

Over recent years, Michael had told me about his dear wife Kirsty, who was suffering from Alzheimer's Disease. He said that even though he may have just told her about his day's filming in Yorkshire, she would immediately forget it and ask him what time he would be home for dinner that night. Michael said that he had now received some letters from his neighbours telling him how they had found Kirsty wandering around the town very late at night, looking for him. They felt that she needed his care and attention.

"I'm going to have to resign," Michael said. "This is the best job I've ever had, but Kirsty supported me when I was starting out as an actor, and now I owe it to her to look after her when she needs me." Michael was very tearful and said that he wanted to tell me personally of his decision which had been very difficult for him to make. It was a very sad moment for us both. So, for unavoidable circumstances, Michael Aldridge would not be with us for another series.

My immediate thought was to bring Brian Wilde back. He had been willing to come back to play Foggy for an episode, so I was certain that he would be willing to return as a regular,

Top: How to get Bill Owen (Compo) and Seymour (Michael Aldridge) to lift Peter Sallis (Clegg) into a tree for 'When you take a Good Bite, Yorkshire tastes Terrible' (1987). Bottom: Director of Photography, Robert Pascal prepares to film Compo (Bill Owen) in the famous runaway bath scene.

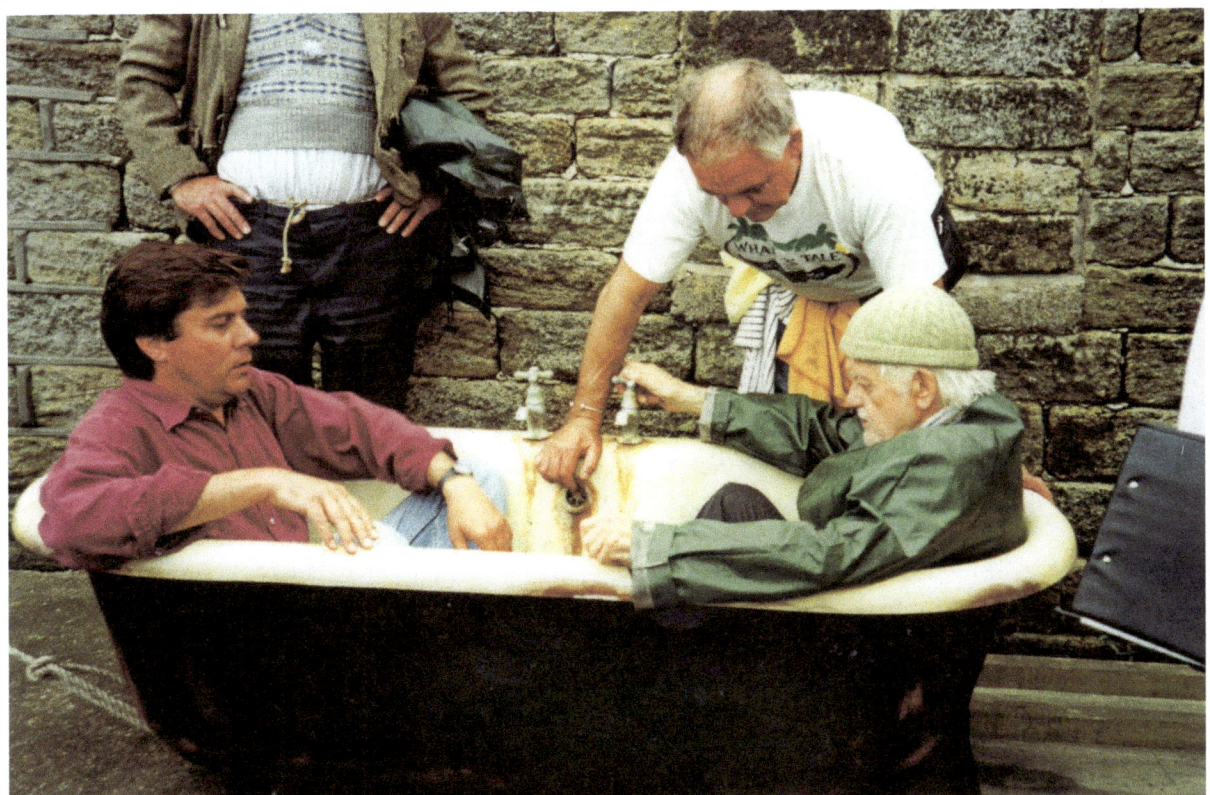

Top: The façade of Auntie's shop is bolted on to the domestic frontage. Bottom Left and Right: Filming a precarious part of "Give Us A Lift" (1991).

but I thought it wise to check with Peter and Bill. Surprisingly, they were both strongly against having to work with Brian again. It had all been so much fun with Michael Aldridge and the thought of going back to the awkwardness of Brian Wilde was not something they would want to suffer again. I told them both that it was going to be difficult to find yet another 'third man' who would fit the role and it was in the interests of ensuring the future of the series if Brian returned. For that reason only, both Peter and Bill reluctantly agreed to withdraw their objections.

I then telephoned Brian Wilde and told him that Michael Aldridge was leaving us and that I would be delighted if he would return to play Foggy again. Brian immediately thanked me for inviting him to return to the series, but said that he had been offered a stage tour of the classic play *Hindle Wakes*. Not for one minute did I believe that Brian would consider touring in a play. He disliked acting on the stage, and touring would be a major sufferance for him. With that in mind, I said that, as he obviously wanted to do the play, I wouldn't press him to return to the series. Brian quickly dispensed with the 'unavailable' ploy, and said that, perhaps, we should meet and talk about it – which we did.

I arranged to meet Brian at one of his favourite inns near his home in Ware. It was a beautiful sunny day, and the inn was on a typically English village green. It was easy to see why Brian couldn't wait to get back from filming in the North. As always, Brian was very good company when he wasn't filming. He was very sympathetic to Michael's predicament and agreed to return to the series with very few demands.

However, before Brian Wilde could return to the series, there was another Christmas Special to be made with Michael Aldridge. This time it had been firmly agreed that it would last only 50 minutes. It was entitled *What's Santa Brought for Nora, Then?* (1989) and it brought back Jean Alexander who had stolen the show a year ago as Auntie Wainwright in *CRUMS* (1988)

But there was now another major problem: the shop that was used as Auntie's emporium had gone. The building was still there, but during the year since we had used it the owners had turned it into another residential apartment in the block. The whole frontage of Auntie's had gone, including the shop window which had been bricked-up and replaced by two smaller domestic windows.

There was no point looking for an alternative location as the unique shop and the atmospheric surroundings had all been firmly established in *CRUMS*. So I told our designer, Stephan Paczai (long since forgiven for felling the Holmfirth tree), that the only solution was to make a false shop front identical to the original that could be bolted on to the new frontage. This was done and the false frontage was used, not only at the location but also in the studios in London for nearly twenty years. The only disadvantage now was that I could never shoot straight-on to the frontage with the door wide open as all we would see is the plain apartment corridor and not the cluttered interior of Auntie's shop.

By the time we were filming this Christmas episode with Michael Aldridge, Brian Wilde had been signed-up to return and play Foggy the following year. So at the very end of the episode, during a party scene in the café, I showed Ivy opening a present and finding that it is a decorated egg. Anyone who had faithfully followed the series would remember that in *Uncle of the Bride* (1986), Foggy left a note saying that he had gone off to take over a family egg-painting business in Bridlington. Quite a number of viewers did remember this and realised it was a subtle advance notice that Foggy was going to return to *Last of the Summer Wine*.

Return of the Warrior (1990) said goodbye to Seymour and welcome back to Foggy. We were all deeply saddened by Michael's enforced departure from the series. It had been great fun to work with him and we were all going to miss him very much.

Brian Wilde re-joined the series with ease and, although Michael Aldridge had been excellent, there was a good feeling that the series had returned to where it was with the perfect trio.

Captain Clutterbuck (Ron Moody) with 'Our Three' in Captain Clutterbuck's Treasure' (1995).

CHAPTER 18
The Sound of Music

Years before *Last of the Summer Wine*, Bill Owen had written *The Match Girls*, a much-performed musical about the industrial action taken by the female workers at the Bryant and May match factory. After 50 years, it is still a very popular production with amateurs, mainly because of the large number of parts for women, who tend to dominate amateur players. Besides *The Match Girls*, Bill had quite a reputation as a songwriter, with his songs being performed by the likes of Cliff Richard and Engelbert Humperdinck. Consequently, he was always very pleased whenever there was an opportunity for him to sing a song in an episode of *Last of the Summer Wine*.

Usually, Bill would sing the song unaccompanied and Ronnie Hazlehurst would write the orchestral backing after we returned to London. It was a routine that worked very well, but it wasn't without some considerable angst from Ronnie. "Have you ever heard of a metronome?" Ronnie once asked me, somewhat spikily. "He's all over the place with the tempo, and he changes key three times in the first few bars!"

I told Ronnie to forget the 'click track', which gives the musicians the exact tempo in their headphones, and just conduct the orchestra to follow Bill's singing as though he were in the studio singing live. This successfully overcame the problem of the ever-changing tempo, and somehow Ronnie managed to overcome the awkward key changes and make them sound intentional.

An appropriate opportunity for Bill to sing came in *The Last Surviving Maurice Chevalier Impression* (1990). The script had initially called for Compo to embarrass Nora Batty by singing to her at a crowded talent competition at a gala in the local park. The cost of a large crowd would have sunk our budget, so I suggested to Roy that we change the story so that the talent show is an item in a local television news magazine programme called, perhaps, *Outlook North* as there was a real programme called *Look North*. This would only require a few participants as Compo would be seen on television singing to Nora in Ivy's unusually crowded café.

Gorden Kaye, of *Allo, Allo* fame and who incidentally came from Huddersfield, played the presenter. This was Gorden's first appearance since his head was spiked by a piece of flying debris when he was driving his car in a storm.

I had the actors and a good script, but what about the news studio? We wouldn't be able to use a real television news studio as they were in constant use, so I asked the location manager to find me a largish hall somewhere that we could dress with lights and all the paraphernalia of a regional television news studio. The search revealed no suitable location. Huddersfield Town Hall wasn't accessible, and the church halls in the area were too small and looked like… church halls.

Then I thought of Huddersfield University. It would surely have a large lecture hall. I went to meet the University Administrator, and I was right. There was a large hall that could easily be turned into a TV studio. So I agreed a fee for the filming which would take place on a Sunday as it would take a considerable amount of time to set up our fake television studio with dummy cameras and other props.

I was well pleased with myself for deducing that I would find a large hall at the university but, just as we were about to part, the University Administrator said, "Oh, by the way, forgive me for asking but why aren't you using our television studio?" There was a long pause as I considered what he had just said.

"What television studio?" I asked.

"Oh, we have a fully equipped TV studio with cameras and lights," he replied. This was before the days of media studies being all the rage, so it never crossed my mind that we would actually find a practical television studio in the middle of Huddersfield. And it was, of course, perfect for Bill to sing 'You Must Have Been a Beautiful Baby' to Nora and wreck the programme when his pet ferret escapes.

There was a general feeling that the series was better than ever, and much of the credit for that was due to the enthusiasm of Simone Dawson, our assistant floor manager.

While we were making a quality comedy series, the comedy manager was still at it and arrows were being fired that could only have been motivated by a wish to frustrate the production. It is hard to believe that anyone would allow a non-creative office manager to cause so much trouble. One of my assistants offered up a clue. When he went for an interview before a BBC Appointments Board for promotion he was asked by Gareth Gwenlan if he thought that *Summer Wine* was too much for one man to produce and direct. The negative answer was, he said, not what Gareth wanted to hear, and my assistant didn't get the job. Although Gareth was head of department, he had 'badged' *Only Fools and Horses* (1981 – 2003) when its first producer left the BBC. It was suggested that he would like to have put his name to our series as well. I, of course, dismissed this theory as nonsense. Who would do such a thing?

When I was forced to dismiss a hopelessly incompetent and disruptive first assistant director, he retaliated by complaining about the super-efficient Simone. Inexplicably, the comedy manager tried to remove her from the production!

The women in the production – Thora Hird, Kathy Staff, Sarah Thomas and Jane Freeman were up in arms. Simone was the only person on the production that they could trust to give accurate information about the film schedule. Having been an actress herself, Simone had an excellent rapport with all the artistes and understood their needs.

After Michael Aldridge had left the series and returned to London, he wrote me a note to warn me about the now replaced first assistant director, saying that he didn't trust him as far as he could throw him. Peter Myslowski, our grip who had worked on many feature films, couldn't understand me for letting the troublemakers get away with it. "On features, they wouldn't last a minute. They would be told that they are now a memory, and booted out." My problem was that, with the departure over the years of Jimmy Gilbert and John Howard Davies, there was no longer anyone in charge who would support me.

Actually making the series was not a problem, but I was finding it difficult to have to put up with the constant sniping of the comedy manager. Even the usually supportive Robin Nash, now Head of Comedy was influenced by him to mistrust my judgement. Robin agreed with him that I was giving Simone too much responsibility. It was a foolish contention, for Simone was absolutely brilliant at re-scheduling and anticipating problems, and should have been promoted, not kicked.

Compo, Foggy and Clegg together again.

Test driving "The Thing In Wesley's Shed" (1995)

A one-time only picture of Foggy and Seymour with Clegg and Compo

Then it happened. For no apparent reason, the Design Department complained to David Lilley, the comedy manager, that I had used our effects crew to ride on some mobile steps and not stuntmen. In fact, it was the effects crew who insisted that *they* had to operate the steps as they would be too difficult for anyone else to control. The matter had nothing whatsoever to do with the Design Department and their interference was clearly mischievous. I felt that I had had enough. I went to see the BBC doctor and told her, with some embarrassment, that I, the producer/director of *Last of the Summer Wine*, was literally being bullied and frustrated by the front office, and I was beginning to find this undercurrent very stressful.

Within days, there was a change in attitudes, and a friendly, supportive atmosphere returned. I could concentrate on making the programmes again without having to put up with such nonsense. Nobody ever mentioned this affront to decency again, and I soon forgot all about it as there were more important things to deal with. One of them was the extravagance of the Costume Department.

Two of my actors asked me why, when the costume designer took them shopping to buy plain ordinary clothing for the series, they were taken to expensive shops in Bond Street in London's West End rather than to the type of shops where their characters would have shopped. It was an extravagance my actors couldn't understand when their fees were far from generous.

A few years later, there was the matter of replacing Compo's well-worn jacket and trousers. Bill Owen had complained that the jacket was falling apart so badly that it was a miracle that it held together in one piece. I agreed that the time had come for it to be replaced.

"Get them to go to C&A and buy them there," Bill sensibly suggested. But the costume designer didn't go to any of the High Street stores; she went to a Saville Row tailor to have them made. Each jacket, with a pair of ill-fitting grey trousers, cost £700 – and there were three of them. So for three Compo jackets with grey trousers, the sum of £2,100 was casually paid out of our budget.

The new jackets were then broken down – cut, torn and dirtied – to look like the original jackets. Bill Owen, who had been first to discover how much they cost, was understandably very cross at this arrant wastage of licence-payers' money.

CHAPTER 19
Principles

Although I knew the Holme Valley area better than any local there are always some particular locations that simply elude discovery. You know that there must be somewhere out there that is right for a scene, but finding it is very difficult. After many weeks of searching for a beautiful location that was quiet and accessible, I happened upon a track that wound its way around the side of a reservoir. At the end of this track was a pretty area with an abundance of heather that would be perfect for a reflective scene with Compo, Clegg and the newly returned Foggy Dewhirst. The owner of the site was contacted and he was pleased to give his permission for us to film there. All was well, and I had a new location that looked good and was exactly right for the scene.

Meanwhile, Bill was doing what he always did, and that was giving his full support to a local campaign. This time it was to stop a new quarry being opened up a few miles out of town. The local newspaper carried a picture on its front page of Bill Owen with 'Say No to the Quarry' banners. A telephone call from the landowner of the pretty location informed us that he was withdrawing his permission for us to film there, as he was the owner of the new quarry site that Bill was urging everyone to protest about.

Bill was unrepentant, and said that his principles were far more important than my locations. Thank you, Bill.

Having Brian Wilde back was a great pleasure, but some of his intransigent principles were still raging. Because of a shower of rain, filming at Intake Lane, high above New Mill had been temporarily suspended.

I saw a car arrive and the driver getting out. He looked around as though he was looking for someone. His case looked very much like a doctor's bag, and he looked like a well-dressed doctor. Fearing that there may have been an accident, or that someone on the unit was unwell, I went over to him and introduced myself. He, in turn, introduced himself to me as Andrew Duncan from the *Radio Times*. Suddenly it all came back to me:

I had agreed with the *Radio Times* that our actors would be interviewed on location by Andrew Duncan who was a much-respected in-depth journalist. It was for a feature about *Last of the Summer Wine* that would precede our first transmission and would obviously be good publicity for the series. The date for this interview was agreed but I, unfortunately, had completely forgotten about it and hadn't mentioned it to the men.

I welcomed Andrew Duncan to the location and introduced him to Brian Wilde who just happened to be walking past at that moment, holding a plastic cup of tea.

"Oh, Brian, this is Andrew Duncan who is writing a feature for the *Radio Times*," I said.

"I don't speak to the *Radio Times*," Brian replied tersely, ignoring Andrew's proffered hand. "When they start giving me equal billing with Ronnie Barker, I'll talk to the *Radio Times*."

This was a new one on me, but it emerged that, for the repeats of *Porridge* on BBC1, it was only Ronnie Barker's name that appeared above the title in the *Radio Times* billings. It was no slight on Brian. It was just that there was no room for all the leading actors to be credited as these were repeats. Anyway, Brian went on his way to join Peter and Bill in the Winnebago without saying any more. I apologised to Andrew for Brian's behaviour but he wasn't in the least bit offended.

Andrew Duncan's published interview in the *Radio Times* was a triumph of observation and wit, reporting the fact that, although Brian wasn't talking, he couldn't resist correcting Peter and Bill when they got their facts wrong.

Brian Wilde was a very good actor, and his return to the series was welcomed by everyone. He underplayed his character and squeezed every bit of comedy out of Foggy's speeches.

Many people have asked me why Clegg and Howard moved homes in the series. The reason was that, for eight years, we had used two cottages that were located behind the church clock tower in Holmfirth. They were at opposite ends of a row of three cottages. The cottages, with their Gothic windows, stand out in their imposing position overlooking the centre of the town. They looked good, but they didn't lend themselves easily to the business of filming. The landing that ran along the front of the houses was far too narrow for our equipment. To overcome the problem and accommodate the lights and the camera, every year we would build an expensive scaffold platform alongside the landing and over the steep garden below. It was quite an expensive operation, but it was a very atmospheric location and well worth the trouble. But this year, there was to be unexpected trouble.

The owner of the middle house (which we never used) demanded a fee that was three times what the other two households were getting. This woman was adamant that we couldn't film there without paying the amount she demanded. Here was the analogy that I had given Bill – about the three properties on a Mayfair site, actually being played out.

I didn't want to give in to ransom, so the solution was to find another location. I remembered seeing a row of weavers' cottages at Jackson Bridge that would make an excellent location. There was a wide forecourt that would easily accommodate all our equipment, and there were pretty views of the valley all around. However, Ron Backhouse, the landlord of The White Horse inn below them, said that there was no chance whatsoever of filming there because the owner of the house at the end of the row of cottages was a Mr Noble who didn't like *Last of the Summer Wine*. In fact, he was on record as saying that he wouldn't have a film unit within a mile of his house.

The other owners of the cottages were all agreeable to letting us film there, but they all repeated that Mr Noble at the end house, who happened to own the right of way, would never relent.

With nothing to lose except a good location, I went to see Mr Noble and his wife. As I had been warned, he was adamant that he didn't want anything to do with *Last of the Summer Wine* and he wasn't interested in the money. Defeated, I politely thanked Mr Noble and his wife for their courtesy and left. Mrs Noble followed me outside and, quietly closed the door behind her. She signalled me to wait a moment.

"He always watches *Summer Wine*, you know," she confided. "And you know what? He really loves that Marina. Thinks she's marvellous."

An hour later, I knocked on Mr Noble's door and introduced Jean Fergusson to him. Mr Noble was completely overwhelmed by this surprise visitor and immediately withdrew his objections to our filming there. The only condition was

Top: Peter Sallis copes with the narrow landing outside Clegg's original house. Left: Marina (Jean Fergusson) learns that she has a fan who 'open doors' for us.

that we wouldn't divulge the whereabouts of the location as he didn't want tourists on his private roadway. This condition we were very happy to observe. God bless Marina.

When we informed the house owner in Holmfirth that we wouldn't be coming back again, she formally complained to the BBC about the way she had been treated. She revealed that she had worked for the BBC Drama Department in the past and knew what they paid for locations. Drama Department budgets, for no sensible reason are always much larger than those in Light Entertainment. But I should add that what we paid for our locations was always fair. So my sincerest gratitude goes to the ex-BBC lady for causing us to move to Jackson Bridge which was a more accessible and attractive location with lots of room for filming.

Plenty of room for filming, but we aren't welcome.

To address the unlikelihood of Clegg and Howard still living next to each other at a different location, Roy Clarke wrote:

Howard: How does it feel, Cleggy – being re-housed?
Clegg: Well… I'm still next door to you. It's a lot like it never happened.

All of the houses at this new location had one thing in common: the ground floor of each house was the kitchen/dining room. Behind every window was a sink and draining board. So every time we filmed there, net curtains were put up to mask them. This also meant that we couldn't film an exterior scene where we would see completely inside, for what we would see wouldn't be the living room, it would be the kitchen. The only way to overcome the problem was by having a duplicate exterior built in the studio.

CHAPTER 20
Posterity

Much of the success of *Last of the Summer Wine* was due to the beautiful Yorkshire scenery. Unfortunately, in the early days of the programme, it was always noticeable that the picture quality of the exterior scenes when using 16mm film didn't match the quality of the multi-camera studio scenes. Film had a much wider tonal range than the studio cameras and the two merged together uneasily. As an experiment, I shot all of the location scenes for the 1991 series using a video camera instead of a film camera. For the first time, the exterior scenes matched the studio scenes, but unfortunately the video pictures of the Yorkshire countryside were lacklustre and less impressive. And worse, on more than one occasion, the damp atmosphere clogged the recording heads of the video recorder. Much time was wasted, waiting until the condensation had dried off before we could start shooting.

Kodak were demonstrating their new high quality T-Grain 16mm film stock at the BBC Television Centre in Wood Lane. Their representative suggested that I should make one episode of *Last of the Summer Wine* entirely on film, for posterity. He wasn't just selling the film stock. He genuinely felt that there should be at least one episode that would be future-proof.

It always seemed to me that it was very fortuitous that celluloid film was developed before video. If Charlie Chaplin or Buster Keaton had used video rather than film, the masters wouldn't have lasted for more than a few years. With film, every time a new digital recording process comes along (and there have been quite a few over the last 40 years), the film can simply be copied again – and always with a huge improvement in quality. At the moment there is much talk of the demise of film, but we should remember that film lasts, and the longevity of digital storage is unknown.

Kodak was right to think of posterity, but it wouldn't be practical or economic to put in place all the requirements for shooting only one of the episodes entirely on film. However, the thought of making not just one episode but <u>all</u> of the episodes entirely on film began to take root. What if we could afford to shoot the whole 1992 series on film? There were quite a few very good reasons why it would make sense. Mainly, there were fewer and fewer live studio interiors for the audiences to see being recorded (although there were never any complaints). And the actors – Bill Owen in particular, were always really tired having to hang around the Television Centre from eleven in the morning until nine at night, just to perform six or seven minutes of an episode in front of the audience.

I worked out that it wouldn't cost significantly more to make the series entirely on film. It was certainly on a par with the cost of the established method of using 16mm film for location shooting and using the very expensive multi-camera studio for the few minutes of interiors.

There were also the outside rehearsals that they had to attend which would take as many days for six minutes as for thirty minutes.

Abandoning the established way of making the series after twenty years was so radical that I discussed it with my past mentor Robin Nash, who was now Head of Comedy. Gareth Gwenlan had gone and, according to Robin Nash, he left no scripts in development. Robin approved of the change, providing that nothing was lost in the transition.

Filming on location for the all-film 1992 series using Kodak's new film stock was very successful and produced some classic episodes. And, as a bonus, they were all filmed in Super16 widescreen. However, as widescreen hadn't yet arrived in the UK, the series was initially transmitted in standard 4x3 format.

One of the most memorable episodes that year was *Happy Birthday Howard* (1982). It was memorable because of the repercussions from our being responsible and respectful to the countryside. The latter was important to us, and we would always go to enormous lengths not to spoil one of the programme's most important assets. Wherever we filmed, we always left the locations as we found them and possibly better. However, sometimes good intentions can go wrong which could have left an unfavourable impression of the whole unit.

In *Happy Birthday Howard* (1992), Marina gives Howard a giant panda as a birthday present. To add to Howard's dilemma of having to hide the present from Pearl, an extra-large panda was made. The script was good and needed no adjustment, but when I saw the marshy location I had found for a scene featuring the two policemen (Ken Kitson and Tony Capstick), I asked Roy Clarke if he would mind my adding an extra bit of visual comedy it. Roy was happy about it and the effects department went to work.

The scene involved the two policemen stopping their car to investigate the unusual sight of a very large panda sitting on a dry stone wall. I thought that it would be funny if one of the policemen, while making a note in his book, slowly sinks up to his knees in the bog.

In order not to scar the countryside, the effects department was reminded to make sure that we should leave the site looking exactly as it was when we arrived. Very carefully, they dug out a hole that was just big enough to take the small hydraulic lift that would lower one of the policemen in the scene. The earth that they had removed in digging the hole was carefully hidden a few feet away out of sight of the camera. The hole with the hydraulic lift inside was then filled with a mixture of peat and water. The clump of moorland long grass removed to dig the hole was replaced on top to blend in.

The effect worked extremely well and was very funny. When we were finished, the hydraulic lift was removed from the hole and taken away. This left behind a nasty slurry of peat and water. However, the effects crew had thought about that, and had made special arrangements with the Holme Valley Council, at a cost of £60, to have a drain-cleaning tanker come along later to suck out the slurry and replace the earth and the marshland grass. They would ensure that the site would be left exactly as we had found it: no unsightly scars or a hole to trip up hapless walkers.

That should have been the end of a successful day's work for everyone. It should have been – were it not for a sequence of events that was completely out of our control.

An hour after the unit had packed up and gone, a man was walking his dog in this remote area known as Hade Edge, when he saw an unmarked tanker slow down and stop. The dog owner, a good citizen, suspected that the unmarked tanker is up to no good and he hid behind a wall. He saw the tanker driver get out of the cab, look around and consult a piece of paper which was, in fact, a map made by the effects department to identify the location of the hole. The dog owner wondered what a tanker is doing in the middle of nowhere and what the driver is looking for. The tanker driver searched around and eventually found the hole filled with the peat slurry. He went back to the tanker and unrolled a large flexible tube which he carefully dropped into the hole. The dog owner now knew what was going on: the man was clearly dumping waste from the tanker into the countryside!

The tanker driver then switched on the pump and sucked out the slurry, looking around as he did so for the pile of earth that he has to put back in the hole. When the driver finished, he carefully shovelled the earth back into the hole. The final touch was when the driver replaced the clump of moorland grass and patted it down with a shovel to ensure that the incision is well and truly masked. Obviously late for his dinner, the tanker driver quickly packed up and made off at breakneck speed. To the dog owner, this was conclusive proof that some poisonous liquid had been dumped.

On receiving the dog owner's report of his sighting, Holme Valley Council called in investigators from ICI who, wearing full protective clothing – masks and Geiger counters – carefully roamed the area searching for the hole which had now, of course, been filled in and was blending in nicely with the rest of the area. They then took samples from the site for analysis. The National Rivers Authority was alerted in case the unknown substance contaminated the water courses that ran into the nearby reservoirs.

The police set about trying to identify the tanker (the dog walker had been too far away for him to see its registration number), and the public were cautioned to be on the alert for similar occurrences.

The *Huddersfield Examiner*'s headline, 'Toxic Waste Fears over Chemicals Dumped on Moors', added to the drama. It also alerted our effects team who quickly pointed out the error to the council, quoting their reference number of the fully paid bill for the work that it had carried out so efficiently.

Then the *Huddersfield Examiner* headline changed to 'Moorlands Mystery as Water Turns into *Summer Wine*' with an article that gave voice to a well-known anti-*Summer Wine* local who condemned the BBC's recklessness. The man with the dog had very sensibly reported what he saw, but it was just unfortunate that there was no marking on the tanker. On reflection, it would have been better to have left a scar on the countryside.

Back in the studio in London to film the interior scenes, it became clear that there were other advantages in making the episodes entirely on film. It helped the storytelling immensely. It meant that whenever required, I could put in position the 'fourth wall' of the interior sets where the live cameras and the audience had previously looked into the set. The fourth wall of Ivy's café for instance, had never been seen before, and it was good to be able to film the characters wherever they would naturally be in a scene. From her position behind the café counter, Ivy could now look across at the three men silently plotting in the corner, and we would be able to see exactly what she sees from her point of view.

The only problem I had was a practical one. Previously, a café scene would be recorded with a variety of shots from four or five live cameras. Now, the same scene would have to be filmed with just one film camera, shot by shot.

I told the cast that, in order to conserve time, I would have to shoot all the similar set-ups completely out of order and that I, personally, would sometimes have to give them the cue lines and tell them where to look. Fortunately, the actors in *Last of the Summer Wine* are the best, and they easily adapted to this pragmatic means of getting the episodes made. It was the penalty for shooting 'all-film' and it proved to be a real burden on me personally.

We were at Fountain Studios in Wembley and at the end of the first day's filming I was so tired that I sat behind the steering wheel of my car in the car park and just stared ahead for about an hour until I was able to concentrate on driving. Surprisingly, the end results were perfectly acceptable, but I soon realised that it was better to slow down and stop rushing.

I had previously had some experience of showing finished films to audiences to record the laughter and they hadn't been at all successful.

For *Ripping Yarns* (1979), Michael Palin introduced the films and, although there was a good audience response, it still ruined the finished soundtrack. Thankfully, the non-audience versions were used on the DVD releases.

For *By the Sea* (1982), in the large Preview Theatre 7 at Pinewood Studios, Ronnie Barker had entertained an audience for about ten minutes before the screening. Their reaction to the film was of course, excellent, but only for about fifteen minutes, and then it began to lose its strength. The reason was clearly that, after a while, the audiences began to ask themselves: 'What are we doing here watching a screen when we could watch it just as well at home?'

The answer to the problem was obvious: make the audience feel that the cast are around them all the time, especially when the films are being shown.

For the first previews at the Picturedrome in Bradford, Peter Sallis offered up a script of a short scene to be performed before the audiences by Bill Owen and himself. It was very much in the style of Roy Clarke but, dare I say it, without the wit. There is only one Roy Clarke. I politely vetoed Peter's contribution on the grounds that it would be too similar to the episodes that the audience had come to see.

Instead, remembering the failure of the Royal Command Performance sketch, I devised some short scenes with Howard and Marina (who was dressed as an ice cream girl), Peter reading out fake fan letters, Bill Owen performing a song and Eli getting lost amidst the audience, all of which were performed with the necessary close contact with the audience. It was all very much pantomime but it was on the right level to entertain the audience and not conflict with the episodes that would be shown on the big screen. I received a letter from a gentleman in Bradford who thanked me for taking the trouble to entertain his family at what they had expected to be just film previews with themselves as 'audience fodder'.

On the second day of the previews, after the first performance at which two episodes had been shown, Bill Owen announced that he was getting the four o'clock train back to London. Despite my protests that he would leave a gaping hole in our live show, and that he would be letting everyone down, Bill went back to London on the four o'clock train.

The following year, Bill Owen was not invited to be a part of the previews in Bradford and other items were added to the live performances instead, like a blooper reel and a pre-recorded telephone call to Wesley (Gordon Wharmby) from Edie (Thora Hird). The form of the preview screenings was beginning to take shape, and we were beginning to get good *real* laughter tracks. But in truth, although the laughs were fine, the quality wasn't nearly as good as the live studio recordings had been. This was mainly because the microphones are better placed in television studios and what we had for our previews was what a film sound recordist was able to set up in the time available.

By the summer of 1993, the business of making the series all-film had become routine. One of the episodes that year was *Stop That Bath* which became the stock put-down by junior critics of the series who saw Compo travelling down the hill in a bath as representative the whole series. In fact, the original script called for the bath and Compo to roll down a hill into a ditch. I adjusted the stunt to show it travelling along a pavement and down some steps where a gutter pours water over him. The reason I did this was because there weren't any ditches around, but there was, at a disused garage, a pavement with some steps down and a loose gutter. It made the audience laugh, which is what it was there for. But ever since then, that one scene, out of the 285 episodes that have been made, has been identified as typifying *Last of the Summer Wine* by the alternative brigade – 'Alternative to being funny,' as Ronnie Barker correctly observed.

Whether it is a bath, one of Wesley's contraptions or Seymour's submarine, props have always been a feature of episodes. They provided the backbones of the plots. One, which was as far from a bath as you could get, was in *Aladdin Gets*

Top: Just the place for a spaceship to land. Bottom: Standing Stones awaiting the arrival of a space ship.

on Your Wick (1993). The original script had them buying an old wardrobe from Auntie Wainwright to turn it into a large sailboard. I suggested to Roy Clarke that we should make it a large steel office cabinet instead: the back has been cut open because the cabinet doors have been locked shut and the key lost. When they are testing it on a lake as a sailing boat, Compo finds a key that he tries in the lock. The doors of the cabinet open and they fall though the bottom into the water.

I then thought that we should explain where they got the sail. I suggested to Roy that Edie (Thora Hird) summons Wesley (Gordon Wharmby) into her front room (quickly inserting an old newspaper to shield the door frame from his oily hands), and confronts him.

> |Edie: Do I go poking around YOUR things?
> Wesley: Well, no.
> Edie: NO!
> Wesley: What makes you ask?
> *Edie holds up a white linen napkin with greasy fingerprints all over it.*
> Edie: What have you done with my double-damask tablecloth?

Behind her, we see her tablecloth being carried past the window attached to the mast of the steel cabinet boat.

I scribbled this on a page of the script and sent it to Roy for his words. It was returned with 'This is O.K.' written on it. This was a first. Roy would always completely change and improve the guide script. I felt highly honoured, even if it was only five short lines. My guide scripts were only ever to indicate to Roy the sort of lines needed to link scenes when something had been cut, or a piece of action didn't fit. It was always a firm rule that new lines came from Roy Clarke and nobody else.

Another interesting prop was a special off-the-road bicycle made by Wesley for *Welcome to Earth* (1993). It was a Christmas Special and featured Paul Bown as its guest star. Paul had starred in *Watching* (1987-93), a comedy series about birdwatchers made by Granada Television in Manchester.

Paul played a member of the Barnsley Extraterrestrial Society who is convinced that an alien spacecraft is going to land locally in a field near some ancient Stonehenge-like standing stones.

As with ditches, canals and deep rivers, there are no standing stones in the Holme Valley, so we would have to make them. I wanted these standing stones to look as real as possible, not cut from giant blocks of a lightweight polystyrene material which would wobble in the slightest breeze.

To make our replica stones as realistic as possible, the designer Richard Brackenbury had them made by the plaster shop at Pinewood Studios. The end result was so realistic that a local man walking his dog past the field said to me, "You know, I've been walking past here for over forty years and never noticed them stones."

To film *Welcome to Earth* the unit had to travel up to Yorkshire for a third time that year. It was scheduled to take place in mid-October which was a bit of a gamble weather-wise. It could be very cold and wet at that time of the year, and most of the story in this episode was set in the hills in an exposed field beside the Holme Styes reservoir.

Bill Owen, remembering the snow storm that had interrupted the filming of *Barry's Christmas* (1990) three years earlier, was quick to point out that it was going to be a tough location for the actors, and warned that he would not under any circumstances stand around in the cold. But helpfully, he had worked out a solution to the problem: "Get me a small tent where I can sit down between takes," he said. "Just big enough for me to shelter from the wind." It was a very

Top: Instead of a spaceship, Our Three arrive on Wesley's Special Bicycle. Bottom:"Just give me a little tent to keep me out of the wind".

good idea, so a small easily-assembled tent was bought for Bill Owen's exclusive use. The one thing that was paramount in Bill's mind wasn't really his comfort; it was his resolve never to put the continuation of the series at risk. The tent would save Bill from the icy-cold winds that swept up from the reservoir.

As sometimes happens, the weather didn't follow form, and it turned out to be one of the mildest and sunniest Octobers ever and there was no need for Bill's tent. But it was erected all the same, and the crew lost no time in teasing Bill by making a small camp fire and a 'Compo's Catering' sign.

At the end of *Welcome to Earth*, expecting aliens, the whole town turns up at the standing stones only to discover that the extraterrestrial lights seen there are only Howard and Marina on another secret assignment. Compo, Clegg and Foggy then cycle off together on Wesley's special bicycle. End of episode.

I thought that it would be a stronger ending if the brakes fail and the bicycle flies over a low wall and lands in the field below. There, another sci-fi enthusiast, having seen them landing, shines his torch on them. He waves an olive branch and says, "Welcome to Earth". Roy accepted this suggestion for a revised ending.

To play the one-line part of the sci-fi enthusiast, I asked John Cleese who had made a cameo appearance in *Golden Gordon*, the second of the two *Ripping Yarns* films that I directed in 1979. John was pleased to accept my invitation to be in my film this time too.

To film the John Cleese part of the sequence – which had been devised in a matter of days, I used the bushes in the grounds of the Old House (production offices) at Shepperton Studios. When it was dark, John, who was at the studios filming for Kenneth Brannagh's *Frankenstein*, came out on to our set. As all of my conversations had been with his agent, John revealed that he had no idea whatsoever what he had to do or what the episode was about. I know I have a reputation for being laconic, but this was probably going too far. However, John Cleese coped and made his very small appearance the highlight of the episode. He tentatively dangled his olive branch at our three extra-terrestrials and delivered the "Welcome to Earth" line. He was then pelted with turnips and, taking cover, he added: "Makes you wonder which planet they come from."

So that we could see the three men on a bicycle flying through the air into the field, I had used three stunt doubles on the bicycle which was suspended by thin wires from a huge crane. It was while we were actually filming this at a quarry on a hillside above Holmfirth that I decided to make it like the 'E.T. flying across the moon' shot, which was very much in keeping with the theme of our episode. Had I thought of it earlier, I would have filmed the moon shot differently and certainly better, but it was still funny, all the same.

I was very pleased with the programme. Ronnie Hazlehurst's pastiche of the ET music was excellent, the director of photography, Robert Pascall, did an excellent job, as did the film editor, John Wilkinson. In fact, so did everybody, especially the production manager, Charles Garland, who got into the spirit of marshalling a lot of cars and a horde of villagers by wearing his Territorial Army combat suit. When he called for silence, he got silence!

When John Wilkinson decided that our long editing schedule was interfering with his home life, he laudably stood down in order to spend more time with his family. To replace John, I decided that Brian Wilde's son Andrew, who was an assistant film editor, should be given the opportunity to edit our films. Over a period of 16 years, Andrew Wilde took us from physically cutting the film with a splicer and sticky tape to the wonders of digital editing.

At this period in BBC Television there were rumblings of change. Odd things were happening at Television Centre. The best studio camera crews were being disbanded and made redundant, the best vision mixers were similarly being paid-off. Production staff were being offered generous cash redundancies at age 55 on full pensions. Senior posts were beginning to be filled by executives from ITV. And worst of all, the BBC's prized

Ealing studios and Lime Grove studios were sold off at giveaway prices. Nobody would discuss these goings on – it was like a fifties' science fiction film where aliens infiltrate a community and remove everyone's brains. The only difference here was that it was the BBC, a cherished institution that was being disassembled, and it was for real.

The name of John Birt, the hatchet-minded deputy Director General from London Weekend Television, curdled on the lips of loyal Corporation staff. ITV executives were being liberally placed in senior positions throughout the BBC. One of them was David Liddiment who had produced *Albion Market* and *Coronation Street* at Granada Television. I had briefly worked for him on an Anita Dobson series called *Split Ends* and had regretted taking the job, mainly because of the weak chain of command that Liddiment had put in place. Astonishingly, this ITV executive was now Head of Light Entertainment at the BBC and he made his mark by bringing to the BBC *Men Behaving Badly* (1992-8), a series that began life at Thames Television where it had been cancelled.

Curiously – or should I say scandalously? – at a tribute event held at the Television Centre, *Men Behaving Badly* was held to be the best situation comedy in the history of the BBC! Really? It wasn't in any way a BBC comedy. It was an independent production and the first six episodes were made for Thames Television at ITV! This was an outrage that deeply offended Bill Owen, Peter Sallis and Thora Hird who wondered why on earth they had been invited along to witness such an affront to the integrity of the once trusted BBC.

David Liddiment was settling in when he announced that he was dropping the 'Light' from 'Light Entertainment'. This major contribution to television was celebrated with a party: 'To say Goodbye to Light.'

As John Wilkinson, our film editor, said, "It's goodbye to light, and hello to an age of darkness."

David Liddiment also decreed that there would be no more residuals (repeat fees) for directors, and it wasn't negotiable. I felt that this clearly demonstrated contempt for the contribution that directors make to productions. To underline the thoughtlessness of this, another director was standing by to take over from me. It would have been interesting to see how another director would have approached the job.

Surprisingly, it was Brian Wilde who offered to support me if I were to resist David Liddiment's new 'take it or leave it' style of negotiations. Brian said that he would refuse to work with anyone else. Could this be the same Brian Wilde who wouldn't work with me ten years earlier? Bill and Peter wholeheartedly agreed with Brian, although they were more than a little surprised by their fellow actor's unexpected show of solidarity.

Those of us who had (and continue to have) deep concerns for how the BBC is managed are those that still possess a deep regard and understanding for what the BBC is and should be. We love the BBC and hate to see what is happening to it.

CHAPTER 21
Norman Wisdom

One of the greatest joys of working on *Last of the Summer Wine* was the arrival of Roy Clarke's scripts which were always funny. But there were two or three which I had put aside. It wasn't that they weren't good; it was because they were either too expensive or too difficult to film.

One such script was a story about Compo, Clegg and Foggy helping Wesley deliver an upright piano for Auntie Wainwright. A man, seeing the piano on the back of Wesley's truck, flags it down and asks if he can borrow it. He wants to play on it, 'When granddad dried his socks on the radiator overnight' (or some such title) at a village hall concert. That is a very rough summary of the story but the basic elements are there.

Although I have to admit that I wasn't keen on the episode, the reason for setting the script aside was that it was an episode within the series, and a village hall concert would mean having to have a crowd. I felt that the story wasn't strong enough to justify this cost, so Roy wrote a new episode to replace it which was less demanding.

Then the BBC decided that it wanted a Christmas Special, or rather a 'Special for Christmas'.

Seven years earlier, away from the BBC, I had been invited to make a silent film comedy with Norman Wisdom. Unfortunately, the character that Norman had written for himself was totally unlikeable and the script, called *He Who Laughs Last*, was far too ambitious and expensive to make. Despite my lack of interest in this silent film (which was never made), Norman and I had remained good friends.

I asked Norman if he would be interested in making a guest appearance sometime in *Last of the Summer Wine*. The answer was a firm and enthusiastic "Yes – not half!" which he qualified by adding: "And do you know why? It doesn't have big 'up your nostrils' close-ups all the time." Here was my sort of actor.

When I discussed with Roy Clarke the idea of having Norman Wisdom as our guest star in the Special, Roy said he would be delighted to write for him. I then suggested that we take the abandoned piano episode and tailor it to Norman. I suggested that, instead of an upright piano, we have a grand piano on which Norman expertly plays a dazzlingly impressive introductory opening. But that is <u>all</u> he can play – just the opening and nothing more. I suggested this because, as a child, I used to be able to play a wondrous opening on the piano with lots of rich chords that really impressed visitors. But that was <u>all</u> I could play, not another note.

My suggestion to Roy was that Foggy, impressed by hearing Norman playing this marvellous opening, decides to become an impresario intending on organising a big concert at the village hall. Roy liked the premise and started to write a complete one-hour script for Norman Wisdom. As this was a special programme, the expense of the village hall sequences was no longer a problem.

The new script was called *The Man Who Nearly Knew Pavarotti* (1995) and arrived in a remarkably short time, and it really was in every way excellent. I couldn't wait to see how Roy had overcome the pianist's inability to play anything beyond the impressive introduction. Well, what happens is now no secret: Billy Ingleton (Norman Wisdom) plays the grandiose intro at the concert, then faints! Billy has barely hit the floor before Foggy and Clegg rush on to the stage and carry him off on a convenient stretcher. Compo is then called upon to perform an accomplished musical ending to the concert – and the episode.

Bill Owen was delighted and asked if he could sing 'Lulu's back in town' which was the song he sang with his stage partner, Charlie Burton, when he first started out as a song-and-dance man many years ago. So for Bill, it was enjoyably sentimental.

Roy's script of *The Man Who Nearly Knew Pavarotti* was very funny but deep down, I was a little worried. John Howard Davies' warning years ago, about the risk of casting Norman Wisdom was playing on my mind. So I sent Norman a copy of the script and went over to his home on the Isle of Man to discuss it with him.

Norman picked me up with my wife Constance from the airport and gave us a hair-raising ride to his house near Kirk Andreas. I say hair-raising because it was over some of the TT motorcycle racecourse, and Norman was having a great time going round the bends at alarming speeds. Later that evening, I was horrified to discover that Norman Wisdom was eighty years old! Eighty years old and driving like a lunatic!

I made it absolutely clear to Norman that we are in television where there is neither time nor money to waste on egos. He looked very hurt that I could even suggest such a thing, and assured me that I would not be disappointed in him. He would obediently do whatever I asked of him. But now, knowing that he was eighty years old, I was more concerned that he might not have the stamina for our filming.

"Course I'm fit," he said indignantly when I broached the subject. "Look, you know the bit where I faint? Can I do it this way?"

Norman sat at the grand piano in his lounge and played a few simple chords. He then froze, stood up, then fell backwards like a plank on to the hard floor. Thinking that he must have hurt himself, I immediately rushed over to help him.

"Don't be daft, I'm alright," he said as he leapt up off the floor. "Mind you, if you'd rather, I could do it *this* way," and he immediately fell backwards again on to the floor, this time raising his legs in the air like an upturned turtle. I asked him to stop doing that because he could hurt himself, but he assured me that falling over was part of his act. He said that if it hurt him on the filming, he would just think of the money.

Norman was very proud of his house in Kirk Andreas which he had designed himself. He pointed to a huge wooden beam that crossed part of the ceiling.

"What about that?" he asked.

"Looks good," I replied.

He then reached up and tapped it with his knuckles. It sounded hollow. "It's made of plaster. The boys in the plaster shop at Pinewood made it for me," he revealed.

It really did look real. Those plasterers at Pinewood are very talented: oak beams, standing stones, anything.

Then came another surprise. He opened a cabinet to reveal a large screen television – not a modern flat screen, just a large screen. Although it was quite late, Norman demonstrated the television by showing one of his films that just happened to be at hand. I had seen *A Stitch in Time* (1963) many times before. However, he pointed out that a shot where he drives a motorised trolley through a hospital ward has a couple of frames of

Chapter 21 – Norman Wisdom – 141

Top Left: Norman Wisdom joins the established cast to play Billy Ingleton. Top Right: Billy Ingleton (Norman Wisdom) is stuck inside the piano. Bottom: Norman Wisdom and the Grand Piano with Foggy.

film too many and you can see the set beginning to collapse when he accidentally bumped into it.

After what seemed like hours, the film finally came to an end. "Would you like to see another one?" he asked. There was a 'Yes/No' situation as Constance said 'Yes' and I said 'No', but, with carefully-tuned selective hearing, Norman only heard the 'Yes'.

I came away from the Isle of Man tired, but pleased that Norman was going to be very good for *Last of the Summer Wine*.

Just before we started filming *The Man Who Nearly Knew Pavarotti*, a session pianist was engaged to pre-record the impressive opening in one of Yorkshire Television's studios in Leeds. At this session, Bill Owen also pre-recorded 'Lulu's

Top: Norman Wisdom and a worried Auntie Wainwright. Centre Left: I give Norman Wisdom some notes. Centre Right: There seems to be a conspiracy to keep Norman Wisdom out of this picture. Bottom: In 'A Musical Passing for a Miserable Muscroft', Ivy (Jane Freeman) and Nora (Kathy Staff) help Billy Ingleton (Norman Wisdom) regain his confidence.

back in town' as 'Nora's back in town' for playback at Foggy's big concert scene.

An early scene in *The Man Who Nearly Knew Pavarotti* is where the three men see Billy Ingleton (Norman Wisdom) approaching along the canal side. Norman apologetically said that he didn't think much of the location that had been chosen. Norman wasn't saying that he wouldn't film there; he just felt that we could have done better. He was right. It was a particularly dull section of the canal in Marsden, and was close to a quite busy road bridge. Norman asked if he could have twenty minutes to see if there was anything better nearby. I told him that I had been assured by the location manager that there was nowhere better that had access for the unit. "Oh, please let me look…. Please….please," he pleaded. I said that it was all right by me, but it had to be somewhere where the generator and the lights can have access. Norman went off and returned less than three minutes later. "Come and see this," he said triumphantly as he steered me across the road and through an opening in a hedge that led to the continuation of the canal. Norman had found somewhere much better that looked really beautiful, was quiet and had easy access for the generator and the rest of our equipment.

Norman Wisdom, besides being good at finding locations, was the perfect film actor and was never far from the camera. He lived for

Right: The ending of 'The Man who nearly knew Pavarotti 'with Compo singing. Bottom: "I think we've cracked it, this time" Howard and Marina in disguise.

Top: Rehearsing with Norman Wisdom and Josephine Tewson (2006). Centre: Billy Ingleton is confused by the poetic language of the librarian (Josephine Tewson). Right: Some locations are not easy to organise.

filming and making people laugh, and there was nothing that he wouldn't do if it was going to make a scene funnier.

For a shot where his character Billy Ingleton gets stuck inside the grand piano on Wesley's trailer, Norman could easily have stood behind the camera and spoken his lines while a double within moved about inside the piano but, no, Norman wanted to do it himself, no matter how uncomfortable it may be. But, for a scene where the grand piano passes by at speed with Billy still inside, I had to be firm to prevent him from doing the stunt himself. It was very dangerous for anyone, let alone an octogenarian.

Brian Wilde, always surprising, told Norman that it was a great honour to work with him as he admired his work so much. Bill Owen, rather predictably, was very polite, but he was noticeably aware that the spotlight had moved off him, and that he had some serious competition in the popularity stakes. And Peter Sallis, bemused by Norman's enthusiasm and discipline on the set, would, first thing in the morning, mimic Norman by running from his caravan to my side. There, Peter would stand rigidly to attention and say, "I'm ready, Sir. Ready for my next scene." He would salute and click his heels.

My only disappointment was that I wanted Ernie Wise to make a brief cameo appearance in the film with Jean Alexander but, because he had recently suffered a stroke, he couldn't do it. I was very sorry that I wouldn't have the pleasure of working with Ernie ever again.

It was while we were filming for 'Pavarotti' that Thora Hird told me of a strange occurrence. For the first time in over 50 years, her husband Scotty (James Scott) had said that he would like to come filming with her. Thora was astonished for, until then, he had never ever visited a film set or paused to chat with the other actors. He had simply delivered Thora to the rehearsal rooms or the locations, wherever, and gone straight home. Now, for no obvious reason, he had decided to come up from London with Thora and be part of the filming. He joined in socially and was even very happy to be in the audience at the filming of Foggy's concert. How strange.

Sadly, a few weeks later, Thora returned home to their mews house in Bayswater one day to find that her beloved husband had died from a stroke. Everyone thought that without Scotty's support behind her, Thora would go to pieces but far from it. Thora drew on her faith and found the strength to carry on.

Norman Wisdom's guest star appearance in *The Man Who Nearly Knew Pavarotti* was a highlight of the whole series, and for a few years afterwards he made other cameo appearances as Billy Ingleton: *Extra! Extra!* (1996), *Gnome and Away* (2001), *The Coming of the Beast* (2001) and the main guest part in *A Musical Passing for a Miserable Muscroft* (2002) in which, as Billy Ingleton, he is restoring a fairground organ.

For a scene in this episode where Billy Ingleton falls out of the back of the mobile organ and down a bank, Norman desperately wanted to do the stunt himself and promised that he wouldn't get hurt, but I refused. Very reluctantly, Norman accepted that our stuntman Riky Ash would do the stunt. I had no doubt that, if I had let Norman fall down the banking, he would have done it very well but, at the age of 86, it would be, to say the least, reckless.

To get the sound of a fairground organ, it gave me great pleasure to have Phil Kelsall play the music on the versatile Wurlitzer organ in the Blackpool Tower Ballroom. I was very pleased, too, that he let me rise out of the floor actually playing the Wurlitzer but, after the first few impressive chords, I had to stop because that was all I could play.

Norman Wisdom's last appearance on *Last of the Summer Wine* was in *Variations on a Theme of the Widow Winstanley* (2004). In this episode, Norman, as Billy Ingleton again, recites a poem at the poetry group in the local library. For this he used a poem that he had written himself called Falling in Love, about an ageing pensioner, that was witty and poignant. Norman surprised us all by the way he movingly performed the poem so well to the accompaniment of an off-stage piano (Ronnie Hazlehurst's orchestra would be added later). When Norman came along to our preview shows at Teddington Studios, he brought the house down with his signature song 'Don't Laugh at Me' and a rendition of his poem, Falling in Love again. He really was a great talent. I was very sad to learn that, shortly after his ninetieth birthday, when he returned from a cruise on which he entertained the passengers at two concerts, he was put into a non-show business retirement home where he was cut off from all his friends. It was a very sad situation.

Norman Wisdom died on October 4th 2010. He was without doubt Britain's most famous and best-loved comedian. Norman lived for making people laugh and the whole business of filming was his life. His face would noticeably light up at the sight of a film camera. I am pleased and honoured that I had the pleasure of using Norman Wisdom in *Last of the Summer Wine* in his later years.

CHAPTER 22
Beware of the Good Idea

'Beware of the Good Idea' isn't an episode, but it should be at the top of every director's list of "Don't do's".

In *Bicycle Bonanza* (1995), there was a scene where Smiler (Stephen Lewis) jumps out in front of a cyclist to hand him a flyer advertising Auntie Wainwright's shop. The man is so startled that he wobbles and falls off his bicycle. To fall off a bicycle isn't at all easy as the road is hard and the bicycle has many jagged parts, all designed to cause maximum damage to a falling cyclist. A good stuntman knows how to fall safely, but just falling off a bicycle is visually unexciting. So I looked around for an alternative. I noticed that, in the road that leads down the hill from Auntie Wainwright's shop, the gardens were divided by six-foot-high wooden fences. One of these fences wasn't in great condition, so I asked one of my assistants to knock on the door and ask if we could demolish the fence and replace it with a better one.

There was no one at home, but a helpful neighbour said that the lady owner worked down the road in a video hire shop. The woman was contacted and her permission obtained. I thought that it would be a good idea if our cyclist, when he is surprised by Smiler, wobbles into and through a section of the fence.

The fence was pre-sawn to allow a section to collapse easily and everybody stood by to film the stunt. A few onlookers paused to watch the proceedings including some lady shoppers who were asked to stand a bit further back for safety's sake. The clapperboard was put on and the stuntman was cued to cycle down the hill. Smiler jumped out with his flyers and startled the cyclist who, as planned, wobbled towards and through the weakened section of the old fence. Thanks to the stuntman, the shot looked very good and was a lot funnier than seeing the man just fall off his bike. One of the lady shoppers stepped forward, looked at the partly demolished fence and said, "What do you think you're doing with my fence?" When she was told that the woman in the video hire shop had given her permission, she revealed that the woman in the video hire shop lived next door to her. We had obtained permission to knock down a different fence! Well, it was a good idea, and in the end the lady was quite happy with her new fence and I was happy with the scene, but it was nonetheless very embarrassing.

A *Last of the Summer Wine* episode that was a little more ambitious was another Special for Christmas. *Extra! Extra!* (1996) was a film within a film, so to speak. Foggy, Clegg and Compo are engaged as extras in a period movie being made in the area. To play the part of the film director, I engaged George Chakiris, famous for *West Side Story* for which he had won an Oscar.

To provide an economic period background, I hired a full-size circus tent from Chipperfield's Circus Company, along with a huge caravan that had formerly been the travelling home of the circus boss. Strangely enough, this giant caravan added only a few pounds more to the cost of hiring the circus tent. This would be George Chakiris's caravan and I was absolutely certain that it would become an issue with my three stars who shared a relatively small Winnebago mobile home, but surprisingly it was never mentioned.

Peter Sallis recalled that when George Chakiris was starring in the original stage version of *West Side Story* at the Theatre Royal, Drury Lane, he had felt very privileged to be introduced to him in his dressing room after the show. Peter said that he never thought that one day he would have billing above George Chakiris.

Believing that *Extra! Extra!* might well be the final episode of *Last of the Summer Wine*, I made a brief non-speaking appearance as the man to whom Nora Batty proudly boasts that Compo is her neighbour. I'm afraid I wasn't very good.

It was as we were about to film *Extra! Extra!* that I asked Mike Cager to come out of retirement and direct the documentary *25 Years of Last of the Summer Wine* (1996). Mike had originally suggested that a documentary should be made to celebrate 20 years of the series, but the BBC Documentary and Entertainment Departments weren't interested. By the time I had persuaded the BBC to make *25 Years of Last of the Summer Wine* (1996), Mike had retired. However, as it was his idea, I thought it only fair to bring him back to direct it.

To show what this documentary would cover, I wrote a script which was based entirely upon what the actors had told me in the past, but it was only meant to be a guide and the actors were asked to put the speeches into their own words. Surprisingly, most of them preferred to learn my script, which was, of course, all right because it was what they had previously said to me.

One day, Bill Owen came to me with the documentary script in his hand. He said that he didn't want to say the bit about him wanting to be buried in Holmfirth when he died. "It's just something that I said."

This was surprising, as he had often been quoted as saying that he wanted to be buried at St. Johns Church in Holmfirth – and he had often said it to me personally, too. Looking back, I think it was because he was 82 at the time, and the prospect of his actual death was something he didn't want to think about.

Besides the documentary, the longevity of the series was also marked by a dinner for the cast and crew at the Television Centre to celebrate 25 successful years.

Thora Hird, aged 83, asked the young man sitting next to her what he did. "I'm Head of Comedy," he replied. Thora, much impressed, said, "But you look as though you've just finished school." The young man was Geoffrey Perkins who had produced the radio version of *The Hitchhiker's Guide to the Galaxy*. By this time in his short life (in 2008 he fell and was tragically run over by a lorry), he had produced a fair number of very successful comedies, mainly for ITV. The divide between BBC and ITV had by now been totally erased.

Probably the best episode in that series, and certainly the most memorable, was *Destiny and Six Bananas* (1996) where Brian Wilde stole the show with his 'Jungle-Hunter' leadership. When Foggy tells Clegg and Compo that he is going to capture a wild gorilla using a blow dart, he assures them that it will work:

Foggy: Don't worry, I've seen the natives do this in the jungle.
Clegg: Yes, they've got poisons growing in the jungle. What have you got?
Foggy: The trained soldier learns to make do with whatever's available – you have to use whatever comes to hand.
Compo: All right, what is it you've got that tha' soaks the dart in that's going to put it to sleep?
Foggy: If you must know, it's Horlicks.

Chapter 22 – Beware of the Good Idea – 149

Top Left: The Film Director (George Chakiris) pleads with Wesley (Gordon Wharmby to fix the generator quickly. Top Right: As Wesley fixes the generator, The Director checks with his Extras: Clegg and Foggy. Right: Geoge Chakiris and 'Our Three' share a joke.

Compo: That's supposed to make it sleep?
Foggy: It makes me sleep.

Brian Wilde was at his best, delivering some of the best of Roy Clarke's lines. Little did we know then that it would be Brian's swan song on the series.

A few years previously, Brian Wilde had suggested the popular actor Trevor Bannister to co-star with him in an amusing series called *Wyatt's Watchdogs* (1988) that I had produced and directed. It was written by Miles Tredinnick, a new writer, and was about a local Neighbourhood Watch group. Brian had worked with Trevor Bannister on *The Dustbin Men* (1969/70); a comedy series made by Granada Television, and had enjoyed working with him. Trevor, subsequently, became a semi-regular guest star in *Summer Wine*, playing the Golfing Captain, and we also became very good friends.

While we were dining together one evening, Trevor Bannister observed that *Are You Being Served* (1972-85), a very successful, comedy series about a department store, was surprisingly never repeated on BBC1. Trevor had played Mr. Lucas in that series. During our conversation, Trevor mentioned Frank Thornton and what a good reliable actor he was. It occurred to me that I should bear Frank Thornton in mind as a future guest actor in *Last of the Summer Wine*.

The following morning, I looked at Frank Thornton's photograph in *Spotlight*, the actors' photo gallery, and mentally noted that he would be very good for us to have as a guest actor sometime. I was walking home that same day when I received a call from Christine Mellor, my assistant, to say that Brian Wilde wouldn't be able to film with us because he was suffering from an attack of shingles. I immediately asked Christine to check Frank Thornton's availability.

Brian Wilde then confirmed that he wouldn't be well enough to film for at least, the first half of the series of ten episodes and suggested that it might be safer to recast his part entirely. I didn't want to do this, for Brian was a valuable asset to the series and would be a great loss.

I arranged for Frank Thornton to come into the BBC to have lunch with me. I knew of course, that Frank was a good actor, but I needed to be certain that he was fit enough to undertake the exhausting location filming in the uneven hills and valleys of Yorkshire. As I struggled to keep up with him on the long walk from the Television Centre reception area to the restaurant block, I could see that Frank Thornton was in very good physical condition indeed.

Right: The new trio – Clegg (Peter Sallis), Truly (Frank Thornton) and Compo (Bill Owen). Bottom: Truly (Frank Thornton) joins Compo (Bill Owen) and Clegg (Peter Sallis).

Frank had assumed that I was only interested in him for a guest part in the series, so he was astonished and delighted to be offered a lead part as one of the trio in *Last of the Summer Wine* for five episodes.

It was a stroke of fate that Trevor Bannister had praised Frank just at the moment that some unexpected emergency re-casting was looming.

A 50-minute Special to introduce Frank Thornton's character was then commissioned from Roy Clarke, but this raised a logistical problem. If Brian Wilde were to be well enough to return for the second block of five episodes, then both he and Frank would be on location at the same time when the scenes for Frank's Special were being filmed. Besides being expensive, it would be impractical.

Brian Wilde had made it clear only recently that he was tiring of going up to Yorkshire for the filming. He said that he had worked out that if we filmed all his shots together, he would only need to be away from home for a few days rather than seven or eight weeks. Although this was a preposterous observation that couldn't be taken seriously, it was an indication that Brian was not enjoying being away from home.

Warning signs of difficult times ahead began to flash when, a few weeks earlier, Brian gave me a list of contractual provisos:

On location: To be picked-up from his hotel no earlier than 9.a.m. (Agreed)
The drivers should not talk to him on the journey to the locations and the hotel. (Agreed)
The location filming day should not go beyond 5.30 p.m. (Agreed)
His dressing room at the film studios should have a couch, a bathroom and an open view from the window (not the side of a building). This was asked for because last time, Bill Owen, the eldest of the trio, had been given the dressing room used by Madonna for the filming of Evita – (Not agreed)
He wouldn't be called to be at Shepperton Studios before 10. a.m. (Agreed – but only because we would probably be filming at Elstree Studios next time).

There were other conditions, but best not to examine them in this politically correct world. Sadly, I decided that, in order to avoid an uncertain situation arising later when we were in mid-production, it would be sensible to let Brian go. I was very sorry to lose him for a second time, but I really had no other choice.

Roy Clarke wrote *There Goes the Groom* (1997) with Lloyd Peters as the groom and Michele Whitehead as the bride. This longer episode would introduce Frank Thornton as retired policeman Herbert Truelove, known affectionately to himself alone, as 'Truly of the Yard'. This Special would be followed by a series of ten episodes.

Frank was clearly enjoying filming for *Last of the Summer Wine* and his infectious enthusiasm lifted the atmosphere of the production in the same way that Michael Aldridge had nine years ago. Once again, I had the full co-operation of all the actors.

Frank Thornton's acting career had been long and illustrious and he was firmly established as one of this country's most versatile actors, going back long before *Are You Being Served?* and the famous Tony Hancock *Blood Donor* episode (1961), but he was content to be the first-rate character actor for which he was renowned. Frank soon proved to be an excellent addition to the cast in 135 episodes over the following twelve years.

Besides introducing Frank Thornton, *There Goes the Groom* (1997) saw the introduction of wide screen (16x9) transmissions. At last, the whole picture would be seen.

Like Michael Aldridge, Frank was also a very popular member of the company who embraced all the disciplines of filming with fresh enthusiasm. For a scene at a lakeside, Frank wanted to run into the lake himself, but he reluctantly accepted that for safety's sake his double should do it. However, undeterred, he insisted on dunking himself under the water to match what the double had done. This was going way beyond the call of duty and was a degree of commitment to the series that must have sent shivers down the spines of Bill Owen and Peter Sallis. The new boy might be going a bit too far with his willingness to endure such extremes of discomfort.

Meanwhile, the 'New BBC' set-up, with executives from ITV taking the reigns, was beginning to take its toll. 'Producer Choice' encouraged producers to use cheaper external resources. An instruction to reduce our budget by £200,000 seemed impossible to achieve without marring the production values of the series, but I found that by moving out of the BBC Television Centre completely and using the same facilities at Teddington Studios, which had been abandoned when Thames Television lost its licence to broadcast, I could at a stroke save the whole £200,000.

It was an absurd situation, for here was I, spending a vast amount of licence-payers' money on outside resources that were available and better at the BBC and which would, as a result, be left lying unused. In reality, I hadn't saved £200,000 of the BBC's money – I had thrown it away.

It amazed me that there was no public outcry at this wastage of money.

CHAPTER 23
Healthy and Safe

We all shudder at the mention of health and safety which so often just means that some simple action has to be unnecessarily examined and assessed, but, in truth, it does make people conscious of the consequences of a stunt going wrong, or the risk of a badly erected platform collapsing, etc. and sometimes it happens that things go wrong, even when health and safety matters have been fully considered and assessed.

Oh, Howard, We Should Get One of Those (1998) was about a motorised bed that Wesley has made for a competition. Compo can't believe his luck when Nora Batty is forced to accept a lift from him on the bed. In reality, there was no actual engine on the bed as a mild incline would be enough for it to roll on its own. The steering and the braking were in the hands of an experienced effects man hidden beneath the mattress.

The wide shot of the motorised bed as it moved along the road looked very good. To get a closer shot of the beaming Compo and the coy Nora Batty, our director of photography Pat O'Shea and I then sat on the bed too. Because the background of this closer shot had to match the position on the road of the wide shot, I told Bill and Kathy to do nothing until they heard me say 'Action'. The bed was released and, as the camera turned over, the bed slowly rolled down the hill. However, I was suddenly aware that the sound of the wheels on the road surface was different. They were beginning to screech as they revolved at an alarming speed. The brakes had failed and the bed was now rolling down the hill out of control.

Equipment was quickly moved off the road as everyone scattered out of the way of our runaway bed. To try and stop it, I reached out to the grass bank with my leg and, for the first time, did the splits, which wasn't a pleasant sensation.

The bed was eventually brought to a halt by a couple of strong members of the crew. Bill Owen was wide-eyed and speechless, but Kathy Staff just looked at me blankly and said, "Did you say 'Action'?"

The whole duration of the 'runaway bed' shot was only about four seconds, but it was a very long four seconds.

I should confess here that the brakes failed because of the extra weight on the bed when Pat and I jumped on board. The effects man, who was steering the bed, did protest about the extra weight on the bed, especially as a proper towing hitch was in place, but nobody heard his voice from his concealed position beneath the mattress. This hazard hadn't been taken into account on the risk assessment form, but how often do you hear of the brakes failing on a bed?

There were other mishaps to contend with, and not always to do with the programme.

Thora Hird, now Dame Thora, asked me if I would accompany her to the tenth anniversary celebration of *The Richard and Judy Show*. I was worried when I rang the bell of her mews home in Bayswater and there was no reply. I tried again, and this time I heard Thora's voice, very weakly, saying: "Is that you, Alan?" She then threw down to me the front door keys and told me to let myself in. When I went upstairs to her apartment, Thora was lying on the floor near her armchair. I said that I would get an ambulance, but she said, "No, don't do that. Just help me up into my chair." Thora said that she had fallen over in her kitchen and couldn't get up off the floor. She had dragged herself into the lounge, but she was unable to raise herself up into her chair to use the telephone.

I telephoned a neighbour who, despite Thora's protests, insisted that a doctor be called. To attend to her, two very young girls arrived. Could they really be fully qualified medics at their age?

They checked Thora over and without further ado, called for an ambulance. When it arrived, Thora was then carefully carried down the perilously steep and very narrow steps of her mews flat. As the ambulance turned out of the mews on to the main road, Thora was getting noticeably weaker. The ambulance then stopped while the medics checked her over again. When a tube and a mask were pulled down from above her, she firmly refused them. "No oxygen. I don't want any oxygen." The medic said, "All right, no oxygen" as he put the tube and mask away. He then pulled up a different tube and mask from below which was attached to another cylinder marked 'Oxygen'. Satisfied that Thora was all right, the ambulance continued on its ways to St. Mary's Hospital at Paddington. I must say that the two ambulance medics were marvellous and handled Thora in a comforting and reassuring way. They had no idea that the Mrs Scott that they were looking after was Dame Thora Hird.

It was found that Thora had a circulation problem and a week or so later, the hospital seriously considered amputating her foot. Any such action would have unthinkable consequences for Thora who treasured her mobility, as limited as it was. And also, dare I say it; she still had quite a few scenes to film for me at Pinewood studios.

Prompted by Thora, who just wanted to get back to work, her daughter Jan (the film actress Janette Scott) worked out a plan with the hospital that would be acceptable to the doctors and still allow her to film her scenes for me. At Pinewood Studios, I would shoot the main body of Thora's scenes in her absence, and then film all of her shots when she arrived. That way, she would be able to return to the hospital without any delay.

When the day came, the specialists, who still had the amputation of her foot in mind, were not at all happy about allowing Thora to leave the hospital, but Jan assured them that she would be carefully looked after in a private ambulance which would take her from the hospital in Paddington to Pinewood Studios, some twelve miles away.

On the nominated day, the ambulance, with Thora and her daughter, arrived at Pinewood Studios a little late, due to the medics having a legal obligation to attend an accident that they happened upon on the way. Jan reported that Thora had not been in the best of spirits during the journey until the ambulance drove through the famous main entrance of Pinewood Studios. It was as though some magic dust had been sprinkled over her; Thora immediately brightened up and was her usual self again.

After she had been to costume and make-up, Thora arrived on the set and I filmed her set-ups with Glenda (Sarah Thomas) for all six episodes. No one would ever know that here was a lady making us laugh, who was in acute pain and who was at serious risk of having her foot amputated.

Thora Hird had stayed with the series since her first appearance in *Uncle of the Bride* (1985). There is no doubt that she brought with her a huge following of viewers who enjoyed her playing of Edie, Wesley Pegden's unforgiving wife. Her vast experience in film and television, and her gift of being able to make all of her characters subtly different yet recognisable, made her a very

Chapter 23 – Healthy and Safe – 155

Top Left: Frank Thornton (Truly). Bottom Left: Bill is noticeably less active. Above Top: Clegg, Compo and Truly search for the missing groom. Above Centre: Milkman (Sportsman Kris Akabusi) is consoled by Truly (Frank Thornton) and the Post Lady (Brenda Kempner) when he loses his milk float. Above Bottom: Frank Thornton gets into the swing of filming by dunking himself in a lake.

popular member of the *Last of the Summer Wine* cast. Thora was everybody's memory of their mother, and was loved as much for that as for all the humour she brought to the part.

Dame Thora died on the 15th March 2003 aged 91 at Brinsworth actors' home. She always held that playing Edie in *Last of the Summer Wine* had been her favourite part. A few days before she passed away, she said to me that she wakes up every morning and is uplifted by the prospect of going off to Yorkshire again to film for the next series. And she meant it.

It was surprising then, that at her memorial service in Westminster Abbey, none of the speakers mentioned *Last of the Summer Wine* in which she had appeared for eighteen years.

CHAPTER 24
Compo

The new millennium was fast approaching and it was decided that we should make a Special to mark the arrival of the 21st century. Roy Clarke wrote *Last Post and Pigeon* (2000), a really touching and funny film that was respectful to all those who had lost their lives in the Second World War. Roy had done it again. No one else in the world could write almost to order, such a wonderfully human script. However, the Head of Comedy, Geoffrey Perkins, wasn't happy with it and said that Roy should re-write it. No one in management had ever questioned the quality of Roy's scripts before, and Geoffrey's appraisal of this one was most definitely wrong. I assured Geoffrey that it was one of the best *Last of the Summer Wine* scripts that Roy had ever written, and it was exactly right for the Millennium. A little reluctantly, Geoffrey agreed to let it go ahead without re-writes, and the old problem of 'too many cooks' was averted.

Last Post and Pigeon was completed without a single alteration to the script – well, not intentionally, for a catastrophic situation arose, the consequences of which would affect everyone on the production.

The last scenes of the film were set in France on the Dunkirk beaches where allied troops were rescued in World War Two. We discovered on the recce that Dunkirk is a generic name for the whole stretch of beach north of Dunkirk harbour. It would be impossible to film in the town of Dunkirk itself as it had been built up in the decades since the war and there was no easy access to the beaches. I settled for an attractive seaside village called Bray-Dunes about five miles away where a memorial stands in honour of the troops who lost their lives on the beaches there.

Bray-Dunes had no hotel which was essential for the story, so our designer Stephan Paczai turned the exterior of a family home on the main street into an *auberge*. Further along the road was a typically French café, ideal for our filming. However, I observed to the Bray-Dunes representative that there was quite a lot of passing traffic which could be a problem for us.

The first scene to be filmed of *Last Post and Pigeon* would be Compo, Clegg and Truly aboard a P&O cross-Channel ferry on their way to France. It was crucial that it was filmed with the white cliffs of Dover in the background as they were what the scene was all about. P&O Ferries were giving us an enormous amount of assistance for our filming, but they wouldn't go so far as turning the ferry back for another take.

If we didn't get it right, it would be too bad: they had a strict timetable to maintain and couldn't be delayed.

It was a short scene, but to save time in the morning, I rehearsed it the day before at Teddington Studios in a conference room in the restaurant block overlooking the Thames. The rehearsal was a little worrying because Bill Owen, always on top of his lines, was uncertain of them and was looking unusually tired and frail. The thought crossed my mind that this could be advance warning of serious health problems ahead for Bill. Was this the beginning of the end of *Last of the Summer Wine* I wondered?

In order to get to the early morning ferry on time, the actors and the entire crew stayed at a hotel not far from Dover Ferry Port. In the forecourt car park, besides the cars and our equipment, there was the motor cycle and sidecar that would play an important part in the story. I wasn't at all happy with the sidecar as it didn't look right, and it wouldn't be easy to achieve some of the shots that I wanted to get of Truly sitting in the sidecar holding the pigeon. But if that was all that could be found, I would have to accept it, although it was a great pity.

In the morning, we went down for breakfast at the hotel and looked outside to see what looked like a battlefield. Despite the fact that the hotel reception had an enormous 20-foot-high window frontage, during the night thieves had ransacked all of the cars, all twenty-odd of them, stolen the wheels from two of them, and left a trail of discarded personal items belonging to other hotel guests. Our vehicles had been spared being ransacked except for the motor cycle and sidecar on its trailer which had been stolen. This was clearly the work of a gang as no one person could cause so much devastation.

I telephoned the police and was surprised to be told that we should just claim on our insurance! I asked if the police were going to attend the scene but the answer was 'No'.

We couldn't understand how such a mammoth robbery could possibly have taken place only a few feet from the hotel reception's huge window. The night porter said that he must have been attending to a room service order at the time and didn't see anything. It was another example of truth being stranger than fiction.

On board the P&O ferry our filming on a side deck was all set up with the camera, the generator and the lights in place. As the ferry pulled away from the Dover ferry terminal, I quickly rehearsed the scene with Bill, Peter and Frank. It was to be filmed as one continuous shot. Again, I was alarmed that Bill Owen was struggling with his lines. The optimum point for playing the scene had arrived and the clapperboard was put in front of the lens for the first take, but Bill couldn't complete the scene. I tried three more times but without success. Because the white cliffs of Dover were now rapidly disappearing into the distance, I split the scene into three parts. This was something that I had never had to do in the 18 years that I had worked with Bill. Alarm bells were beginning to ring loudly.

Next day at Bray-Dunes in France, Bill, now rested after a good night's sleep, was looking much better and his delivery of the lines was as good as ever. And there was some good news: another motorcycle and sidecar – much more suitable than the stolen one – was on its way to us from England. Fate again.

I went with the representative of Bray-Dunes to look at the *auberge* location. I noticed that the road had been closed with a large DIVERSION sign across it.

"Is there something on?" I enquired.

"It's for your filming," he replied.

"But that's in two days time."

"I want them to get used to it."

And so the filming proceeded unhindered, thanks to the kindest of co-operation from the elders of Bray-Dunes. But Bill Owen wasn't himself. Something was wrong. Unlike in the past, he declined an invitation to join Peter and Frank for dinner – and we were near some of the best restaurants in France.

A scene where Bill is on the wide Bray-Dunes beach looking out to sea was very emotional for him, and a genuine tear came to his eyes as he delivered Roy's lines about the soldiers that had died there in the Second World War.

Roy and I had disagreed about one of the speeches, where Compo recalls that he won at a game of cards. He had kept the money because he didn't want a soldier to drown because of the weight of the coins in his pockets. It seemed to me that it was a tasteless reference to a dying soldier, but Roy was adamant that it should stay. I didn't argue my case, and the line remained in the scene. Although it worried me a lot, and still does, it didn't upset anyone else, so Roy was obviously right.

After four days of filming in France, we regrouped in Yorkshire. Again, Bill wasn't well and asked me to take him out of any scenes where he wasn't absolutely necessary. This wasn't the Bill Owen I knew: Bill would always want more lines, not fewer.

Filming at Nora Batty's was tiring for Bill Owen at any time because of the amount of stair-climbing involved, but even so, this time Bill seemed to be much more exhausted than usual. To get into position to play a scene where he entertains Nora with a homemade glove puppet, Bill had to climb up a ladder and stand on a scaffold platform. It wouldn't usually be a tiring task, but he was clearly having trouble. On the take, however, he brightened up and gave his usual impish performance taunting Nora Batty. In mid-afternoon, Bill, completely exhausted, sat at the bottom of Nora Batty's steps and asked me if we could call it a day. I agreed and said that we could easily film the abandoned scenes in the next block of filming.

Although he was unwell, Bill Owen, who was totally loyal to the series, wasn't going to let us down – for any reason. He worked for over two weeks in Yorkshire filming for the first few episodes of the series and for *Last Post and Pigeon*, our Millennium film. When his pain worsened, he was taken to a hospital in Wakefield for an emergency check-up. While he was away, I filmed as much as I could of the *Magic and the Morris Minor* (2000) episode without him.

The news from the hospital wasn't good, but there was no definitive prognosis. When Bill

Top: A café in Bray Dunes, France. Bottom: The last picture of Compo for 'Lipstick and other Problems' (2000).

returned to the set, he was just well enough to film his close shots that would be dropped in to the otherwise completed scenes.

Everyone on the unit was deeply concerned about Bill's worsening health, and none more so than Peter Sallis who insisted that Bill should go down to London straight away and see a specialist that he knew.

The next day Bill was taken back to London to see the recommended specialist and have some tests done. I deleted Bill entirely from scenes that we hadn't yet started to film, and to explain his absence I filmed some unscripted shots with a double of Compo going into a betting shop.

Francis Gilson, a very capable production manager, arranged that I would be telephoned with the results of Bill's tests as soon as they were known. On the following day, a Saturday, I was shocked to be told that Bill had pancreatic cancer and had only a few weeks to live.

With such devastating news – that I couldn't share with anyone – it wasn't at all easy to decide the ethical course of action to take. Bill Owen was a friend and deserved every bit of my respect and care, but as the producer, I had a responsibility to consider the unfinished programmes and the expensive Millennium film. Bill had to be in most of the scenes in *Last Post and Pigeon* as they were all mainly about Compo. Without him, the film and the first three episodes couldn't be finished, and well over a million and a half pounds would be lost.

I decided that I would have to preserve as much as possible of what had been filmed so far and keep Bill's participation to the minimum. In order to do this, Bill's condition would have to remain secret. If news of his illness got into the press, we would be sunk.

A crucial café scene would have to be filmed inside the real café in Holmfirth and not, as planned, on the stages at Shepperton Studios when we returned from Yorkshire. This café scene, for *Last Post and Pigeon*, is where Compo receives a letter from the local council telling him that he is unsuitable to formally represent the town in France. Without this scene, there was no story.

I had filmed inside the real café in Holmfirth 16 years ago for *Getting Sam Home* (1983). Although there wasn't as much space as in the café set in the studio, it was certainly possible, but Bill would surely want to know why I was filming this unscheduled scene on location and not in the studio. So I sent a memo to everyone, including Bill, telling them that the film was required to be completed sooner, so I was bringing the café scene forward and filming it in Holmfirth. Bill accepted this excuse, but his wife, Kathy, who had come up to Holmfirth to look after him, was very cross that Bill should be bothered by production memos. Deeply concerned for Bill and his deteriorating health, she said that all Bill wanted to do was get the filming finished and get back to his home in London.

The café scene in the real Holmfirth Café was completed, but Bill looked very tired. It eased my conscience considerably to know that it was Bill's declared wish to continue filming although it is always possible that had he known the extent of his illness, he may have thought otherwise.

As insurance, I filmed Bill against a green screen in our makeshift Holmfirth studio which was a large garage in an old mill building at Thongsbridge, not far out of town. These shots could be digitally inserted into scenes later. One of them was a vital shot of the trio as Compo plays his bugle at the *auberge*. This was also originally scheduled to be filmed on the stages at Shepperton Studios. And there was a series of shots of Compo sleeping on a bed, dead drunk, in the *auberge* bedroom. These would explain why he doesn't take part in the bedroom scene when they frantically attempt to capture the escaped pigeon.

The final scene in *Last Post and Pigeon* is set on the outskirts of Dunkirk where Compo had spent the night, before being rescued from the beaches.

I had intended to film this scene in the grounds of either Pinewood or Shepperton studios and it was going to be a huge risk leaving this important scene, the conclusion of the film, for three weeks with no certainty that Bill would still be with us. I decided that we would find somewhere in the Holme Valley to film it.

Francis Gilson found a copse just outside Holmfirth that could be adapted for the scene. A pond was dug out, a waterfall installed and some additional trees planted to augment those that were already there.

The actual countryside around Dunkirk and Bray-Dunes was almost entirely flat, but there were a few copses in the area. I felt that a pretty scene in a wooded area would be more appropriate than the reality of endless fields reaching out to the horizon and, besides, there was no way that we could possibly re-create that in the Holme Valley.

As this copse was on gated private land, we were able to keep away any onlookers who would have been sorry to see a very ill Bill Owen.

For the final shot in the film, Bill mimed playing 'The Last Post' on a bugle. He was still feisty enough to get angry with me when I said that he didn't look as though he was blowing hard enough to play the bugle. "Don't you start telling me how to play a bugle – I've been playing one for 70 years," he said.

Bill mimed to a commercial recording of 'The Last Post' which was used as a guide by a session musician in the music studio. Towards the end of the piece, sensitively recorded by Tony Philpot, the solo bugle was augmented by Ronnie Hazlehurst's orchestra. Then, as the camera slowly moved in for a big close-up of Compo's tearful eyes, Ronnie ends the music (and the film) with a final chord that is truly heart-rending. This final scene is, for me, one of the most touching that Roy Clarke ever wrote, and was also a fitting farewell to Bill Owen. On the evening of the filming in the copse, a dinner for Bill was hurriedly arranged at an inn 20 minutes away from Holmfirth at Emley Moor. There, he wouldn't be on display to people who knew him so well. Besides Bill and his wife, there was also Peter Sallis, Frank Thornton and Roy Clarke. Only Roy knew that it would be the last time that he would see Bill Owen who was beginning to look uncomfortably emaciated. The pain he was experiencing was alleviated a little by propping him up in his chair with cushions.

The following day, Bill Owen filmed a short scene with Peter and Frank at the rear of the Co-operative supermarket in Holmfirth. With so much beauty abounding in the Holme Valley, it was sad that Bill's final scene was played at such an ignominious location. My last sight of Bill was as he looked out from the rear passenger window of the production car. I waved goodbye, but it was only a faint gesture of recognition that was returned. Bill Owen was taken back to the unit base where he would take off his Compo outfit for the last time.

When the unit returned to London to film the interior scenes, Bill went into the Wellington Hospital for treatment. I managed to see him in the hospital, but he was lying on the bed motionless with his eyes closed. I reached out and touched his hand, but there was no reaction from him. So many memories of Bill came flooding in, and I felt no shame in shedding a tear that he was leaving us forever. His wife Kathy then told me that there would be a small family funeral. I was concerned that Bill would hear what she was saying, but she assured me that he wouldn't hear anything at this point of his illness.

The interior sets of the *auberge* had been built at Pinewood Studios three weeks earlier than planned in the hope that Bill would still be with us, but it wasn't to be: Bill Owen died on July 12, 1999, aged 85.

The world lost a great actor and I lost a good friend. I shall always remember his looks to me when I laughed at his delivery of a funny line, or applauded his singing of a song. He was, without doubt, a great performer.

Truly and Clegg 'and then there were two.'

CHAPTER 25
The Trilogy

There was great sadness on the production at the loss of such a huge talent and friend, but we were in the middle of a series and had to complete the first three episodes and *Last Post and Pigeon*.

It was relatively easy to film the scenes of Compo in the *auberge* using a double, but there were also lines that he had to speak in other scenes and getting them wasn't so easy. When all the filming at Pinewood and Shepperton studios had been completed and edited by Andrew Wilde, I called upon the considerable talents of Enn Reitel who, besides being a first class actor in his own right, has made a name for himself with his vocal impressions on *Spitting Image* and numerous commercials. He gave as good an impression as anyone could get of an irascible old codger with a very distinctive and recognisable voice. I doubt if anyone noticed that it wasn't always Bill's voice and that Compo doubles were used quite liberally in scenes.

Thankfully, the first three episodes and the millennium film, *Last Post and Pigeon* (2000), were successfully completed with relatively little financial loss, but we had seven more episodes to make. Everything was in place to make them, but all the remaining scripts featured Compo There was only one option: we would have to abandon the seven scripts and have new episodes written.

Roy decided that he would write three new linked episodes to acknowledge the passing of Compo. Over a period of about a fortnight, Roy wrote a trilogy of three truly outstanding episodes that would explain Compo's death, the preparations for his funeral, and the funeral itself.

The first episode in this trilogy, *Elegy for Fallen Wellies* (2000), began with the female harridans of the series rehearsing a dance routine for a local concert. Edie (Thora Hird) played the piano while the ladies of the troupe – Pearl (Juliette Kaplan), Ivy (Jane Freeman) and Nora Batty (Kathy Staff) – danced to a number from *Cabaret* choreographed by Juliette Kaplan.

In the story Nora reluctantly accepts Ivy's challenge to show herself to Compo in her flapper costume, complete with fishnet stockings. Later we learn that it was too much for Compo and sadly, he passed away.

It was a superb script and nothing was changed except for having the giant message 'See ya Compo' on the hillside spelled out with people wearing the painters' white overalls rather than having these laid out on the grass as described in the script. Getting the local scouts, ramblers and other volunteers to climb up the side of a steep hill, and putting them in place to spell 'See ya Compo' was a fair challenge but Phil Hartley, a masterful first assistant director, achieved the near impossible using walkie-talkies.

The emotions expressed by Peter Sallis and Frank Thornton at Compo's passing were, of course, exactly what they were really experiencing at the loss of Bill Owen. Their farewell to Compo was as sincere and touching as anything achieved in a prestige drama production.

After *Elegy for Fallen Wellies* (2000) was transmitted, a record number of viewers wrote in or contacted the BBC to say how moved they had been by the episode, and quite a few tears were shed across the nation.

The second film in the trilogy, *Surprise at Throstlenest* (2000), is where it is discovered that Compo had a secret girlfriend he met every Thursday. It gave me great pleasure to cast Liz Frazer who is so much a part of the British comedy establishment.

The unit base for the filming was in the car park of the Burnlee Club which had been the subject of Barry Took's film way back in 1966 that had suggested Holmfirth as the home of the series. Now the Burnlee clubhouse was derelict and the only sound was that of Liz Fraser shouting at her errant dog. "Bracken!" she would scream in a way that was guaranteed to get the attention of every living thing except Bracken who delighted in totally ignoring her. Liz Fraser's failure as a dog trainer was overshadowed by her skill at driving a vintage tractor. It wasn't easy, for her view was obstructed by the cameraman, lights and me on a specially constructed platform at the front.

The third film, *Just a Small Funeral* (2000), took us up to Compo's funeral and was again a very emotional script which brought the era of Compo to a respectful end. The fact that these three episodes, besides being touching, were also very funny is a lasting tribute to the unmatched brilliance of Roy Clarke.

The impact that *Last of the Summer Wine* had on the residents of Holmfirth was demonstrated when the town formally requested that there be a preview of the trilogy at the local cinema. This was arranged and the turn-out was a clear indication of the respect that the town had for Bill Owen. We all lamented that he had never won a BAFTA award for his comedy performances as Compo, but this was by far a tribute that was much more honest and meaningful. He would have been very proud indeed.

We were all very much aware that had Bill Owen died between series, it would have been a good excuse for the series to be killed off. There was still a small festering faction within the BBC that resented the lasting popularity of *Last of the Summer Wine*. Here was a series that had been commissioned nearly 30 years ago by Duncan Wood and Bill Cotton. It was still attracting huge audiences and international sales while more modern comedies lasted for only a few series before they ran out of steam.

The negative reaction was compounded later by the *Radio Times*, the BBC's listings magazine. It issued a grossly disingenuous press release to say that a poll had revealed that *Last of the Summer Wine* was the programme most people wanted to see the end of. What it didn't say was that the poll was carried out by the *Radio Times'* brand new internet site. The kind of people who would be inclined to wade through the internet to vote on such a feeble question are not the kind of people who would be likely to understand the humour of *Last of the Summer Wine*. Douglas Adams, the writer, once summed up the *Radio Times* thus: "The combined intelligence of the *Radio Times* staff is equal to that of one – not particularly bright – plank."

CHAPTER 26
Like Father

Here we were, with three classic episodes dealing with Compo's passing that could not have been bettered and four new episodes still to be written that would set the series off in a new direction. But how?

When Bill Owen died, I asked Roy Clarke to bear in mind that Bill had a son, Tom, who was also an actor and had made a small appearance in *Cashflow Problems* (1991). Tom Owen looked so remarkably like his father that a few years ago, I had suggested to Bill that Tom might like to double for him, but Bill didn't think that it was a good idea and the suggestion was dropped.

At Bill's funeral in Holmfirth I daresay that Roy saw for himself the likeness, for he rang me and asked if I thought that Tom would be good for us playing Compo's long lost son. I said that I thought he would and that I would speak to him to see if he was interested. Tom was very pleased to be asked to play Compo's son and he accepted eagerly.

Tom had spoken to me immediately after his father's death to say that there was to be a small family funeral. Only Roy Clarke and Peter Sallis from the production were being invited because they had worked with his dad for so long. I was surprised and disappointed, but I had to accept the family's wishes. Unfortunately, quite a few people assumed that my absence indicated ill feelings between Bill Owen and me but nothing could be further from the truth as Bill and I would often meet up between series, or he would stay over at my house. I was of course, very disappointed not to have been invited, but that is how the family wished it to be.

On our first day back in Holmfirth for the continuation of the filming, in order that we could pay our respects to Bill, I arranged for the production to attend a special service at the Church of St. John's in Holmfirth where Bill is buried. It was a very emotional experience, especially when the sound of the *Last of the Summer Wine* signature tune, played by the Holme Brass Band, echoed across the misty valley at the end of the day.

The millennium film was transmitted on 2nd January 2000 and in order to retain the mood of that final scene with Bill Owen playing 'The Last Post', I put all of the credits at the front of the film. This allowed me to fade to black slowly at the end – an emotional and tasteful farewell to a much-loved friend. Sadly, the BBC continuity department, with its usual level of sensitivity, banged in with a crass trailer for a forthcoming programme complete with loud raucous music. The respectful atmosphere of our film was instantly and tastelessly shattered.

I am sorry to say that on the DVD, a 'Made by BBC' credit is tastelessly superimposed before the fade out is finished. That and also a trailer for an unfunny alternative comedian, spoil the DVD release.

Tom Owen, playing Compo's son Tom Simmonite, made his entrance into the series in *From Here to Paternity* (2000). He arrived in a dilapidated white van with his lady-friend Mrs Avery (played by Julie T. Wallace) and her hippy daughter Babs (played by Helen Turaya).

The script had also included another daughter who was having a deep relationship with a married man. I felt, very strongly, that this would be a leap in the wrong direction. Roy said that it was the current way of the world, and of modern comedy, but I said that we would lose a huge section of our audience if we featured such a salacious storyline in *Last of the Summer Wine*. The second daughter was duly cut from the script and it made no difference at all to the episode.

Roy could have been right, of course, as modern comedy has ventured into territories that would have been grounds for dismissal from the BBC not so long ago. Being smutty and obscene was becoming all the rage.

It was at Shepperton Studios a few years earlier that Thora Hird, dismayed by the modern trends in comedy, asked if she and the other ladies could show me an 'alternative' version of the coffee morning scene that was about to be filmed. She warned that it would of course, have liberal measures of course language and crude gestures. I said 'No' – under no circumstances, as it would undoubtedly find its way into the wrong hands. The women all felt that I was being over-protective. I don't know how far they had got in working out their 'alternative' version of the scene, but it would have been a bad idea to let them perform it, as funny as it may have been.

It took Tom Owen some time to settle down into the part of Compo's son but he fulfilled the objective of proving that the series could continue without his father. Had I cast another actor to replace Bill Owen, no matter how good he was, he would have been savaged by ruthless comparisons. But by having Bill's own son the audience would view his replacement with some compassion.

Unfortunately, the combination of Tom, Mrs Avery and Babs, who lived like travellers in a converted bus, wasn't at all popular with the viewers. It just wasn't in the tradition of *Last of the Summer Wine* which featured a gentler way of life that we all believe once existed. We were in Summer Wine Land (as Peter Sallis once described it) and it didn't countenance the abrasive side of the real life that Tom Simmonite and his acquired family depicted. It wasn't long before the old bus was ditched in order to have Tom and Mrs Avery living in Compo's old house beneath Nora Batty. But it was still an awkward combination, for Tom could never logically have the exchanges with Nora that Compo once had. Likewise, the younger Mrs Avery character eliminated any possibility of having the references to the past that had sparked the biting exchanges between the older characters. Eventually, Mrs Avery would disappear from the series.

An actress who fitted in with the series perfectly was Dora Bryan who played Ros, the wayward sister of Edie. Dora was another star of stage, film and television who had all the right credentials to make her fit like a glove into the series. When Dora joined us for *Last Post and Pigeon* (2000) her long-time friendship with Thora Hird was firmly enhanced. Together they played the scenes like real sisters and enjoyed the occasional 'mistakes' on the set where Thora would deliberately get something wrong for the sake of making everyone laugh.

Dora Bryan was very much a one-off, a real star who was as individual as they come. It was very sad for us all when, in her fourth year of playing Ros, just a few days before she was due to film for us again, Dora had to drop out because of ill health.

Once again, I was left with the problem of losing one of our key actors at the last minute. A quick solution was required if we were going to keep to the film schedule. But where would I find instantly, a replacement that would bring

Chapter 26 – Like Father – 167

Top Left: Tom Owen arrives to play Compo's long lost son Tom Simmonite. Top Right: Trevor Bannister plays Toby, the Golfing Captain. Bottom: Billy Hardcastle and Alvin (Keith Clifford and Brian Murphy) are not sure about the new recruit to the Band Of Merry Men (Valerie Leon).

Top: Pearl (Juliette Kaplan) with Nellie (June Whitfield). Inset: Thora's cream cake. Dora Bryan laughs as Thora Hird gets some cream on her nose. Bottom: Tom (Tom Owen) and Smiler (Stephen Lewis) delivering furniture for Aunty Wainwright (Jean Alexander).

something special to the series in the way that Dora Bryan had? Again, it was my wife Constance who suggested her replacement, June Whitfield.

With only three days to go, I realised that I was going to have to break my strict rule of never having an actor play two different characters in the series. The versatile and hugely experienced June Whitfield had played in *Potts in Pole Position* (2001), a Christmas Special, playing Warren Mitchell's overbearing wife. High winds had stopped us from filming an important scene on the moors, so it wasn't my favourite episode, but June had been such a pleasure to work with on the episode, it made up for my disappointments elsewhere. If the versatile June were to be available, all my problems would be solved at a stroke. I telephoned her and asked if she would be interested in returning to play a different character in *Last of the Summer Wine*. She said that she was very interested indeed, but when was it likely to be? I told her that it was in three days' time.

Happily, June Whitfield was available and was soon on a train journeying up to Yorkshire. As she was travelling to the location, Roy Clarke was writing a new character into the episodes. June would play 'Nellie', who had an unseen husband and who saw herself as being much more upper class than the other ladies in the series. Nobody has mentioned that she looks very much like Warren Mitchell's wife in the *Potts in Pole Position* (2001) episode.

Someone else who had to look different in the series was Valerie Leon. Valerie had been a James Bond girl and had appeared in *Up Pompeii* as a strikingly glamorous and sexy handmaiden. She was tall, alluring and every man's idea of the perfect woman. In *Who's That Merry Man With Billy, Then?* (2007) I wanted Valerie to play a tall frumpish recruit in Billy Hardcastle's troupe of Merry Men. But could she – would she – abandon the glamour make-up to play an unattractive character?

I asked Valerie if she would like to come along to meet me at Teddington Studios without wearing any make-up. She was horrified at the thought (of not wearing make-up that is, not of meeting me), but she soon realised that she was being considered for a character part that for once, wouldn't trade on her glamour. It was entirely different from the sexy parts that she was accustomed to playing. If she wanted this part, she would have to throw away her false eyelashes.

Although Valerie was excellent as Billy's frumpish recruit and made the episode very funny, I am sure that having to wear commodious layers of padding didn't please her fans.

My very brief appearance in *Extra! Extra!* (1996) hadn't fired within me any desire to become an actor. However, when it was necessary to record someone as the singing voice of a gnome in *Gnome and Away* (2001), I volunteered. This was only because I didn't mind looking foolish singing 'I Want to be Happy' above the rooftops of Jackson Bridge one lunchtime. Thankfully, because the recording had to be treated to make it sound mechanical, there was no risk of me being discovered as a new singing talent.... although I don't know though.

Entwistle (Burt Kwouk) worries about his truck when Auntie (Jean Alexander) is driving.

CHAPTER 27
Just Like in Real Life

Something that I noticed early on was that Roy Clarke's scripts often seemed to include something that was happening in his surroundings. When I went to see him one day at his home near Doncaster there was a telephone engineer up a telegraph pole. Sure enough, in the next script to arrive, there was a scene with a telephone engineer up a telegraph pole. It is obviously very sensible to reflect real life in the scripts of *Last of the Summer Wine* as so many interesting and recognisable situations are suggested.

One day, I received from Roy the script of *The Coming of the Beast* (2001), that had the men using a hydraulic digger. It was to appear from behind a bush and looking like a dinosaur, it would startle a cyclist so much that he wobbles into a ditch. I couldn't see this working as the actions of the hydraulic arm wouldn't be fast enough to look like anything other what it was, a large hydraulic digger. I told Roy that it wouldn't work, but Roy took me to the side of his house where some building works were being done. He showed me the actual digger that had been his inspiration and assured me that it had moved very fast when the operator was using it. I was proved wrong.

But there was another problem that I had with the script. For the first time, the trio would be doing something deliberately to cause a calamity, even if it was only a cyclist wobbling into a ditch.

I suggested that the storyline be changed slightly to have Wesley innocently wrapping a tarpaulin around the hydraulic arm to keep it out of his wife's sight. Then, when the policemen are driving along, what they see when the digger is accidentally operated, does look a bit like a dinosaur. Our two petrified policemen swerve off the road and into a pond with a big splash. Cut to Norman Wisdom, who was already in the episode. He is sitting on the roof of his little mini-car in the pond, having obviously met with the same fate. Holding a mobile phone in his hand, he looks at the policemen in their sinking car and says, "Blimey, that was quick! I've only just finished dialling."

The pond was an old mill reservoir that we had used extensively in the past, particularly for *From Wellies to Wetsuit* (1982) and *The Thing in Wesley's Shed* (1995) when Compo drives Wesley's homemade car into it.

Filming these pond scenes took quite a bit of time as the stuntmen had to get out of the police car to be replaced by the actors, but it was well worth the trouble for it was a very funny episode. However, a mischievous local resident reported us for spilling oil in the pond. The effects men had steam cleaned the oil off the two cars, but even the smallest drop of oil spreads out to be a wide film on the surface of water and of course, it couldn't be ruled out that it was merely an empty sardine tin that had spilled its oil.

Always aware of the importance of health and safety, it has to be admitted that sometimes a controlled chance is taken. When we were filming *Beware of the Hot Dog* (2002) Wesley is supposed to have built a mobile barbeque that has flames that go ten feet into the air. When he pumps up the pressure it's like a jet plane taking off. Needless to say, although the flames looked pretty fearsome, they were safely controlled by Ian Rowley, an effects expert who was famous for having built something called 'Dusty Bin' for a Yorkshire Television game show.

In a scene with the flaming mobile grill in the background, Wesley, who is wearing a chef's paper hat, exits from the shot to go and make a hot dog. A few moments later, he reappears proudly holding the hot dog – all very simple, all very safe. However, Gordon's creative brain cells were raging and he suggested that when he leaves the shot, some lighter fuel is poured over his hat so that when he returns, his hat is on fire, presumably by the barbeque flames.

"It's too dangerous," I said.

"No, it's not, I've tried it out. It's quite safe," Gordon assured me.

He then demonstrated what he had in mind, and I had to admit that it did look very funny. So I agreed to this improvement to the scene as long as they were very careful and a fire extinguisher was standing by ready for any mishap.

The clapperboard was put on and the scene began. As Wesley left the shot to have his hat set on fire, I glanced over and saw the BBC's health and safety person approaching. It was too late to do anything about it now. Wesley's paper hat was being liberally splashed with lighter fuel. I quickly asked our location manager Sylvia Kendall, who was guaranteed to take anyone's eyes off the ball, to go over and keep our visitor talking. Wesley's hat was now ablaze as he returned to the shot to say his line. I said "Cut" and the flaming hat was quickly removed from his head and the flames doused. But Gordon's hair was still smouldering and likely to re-ignite, so a tea towel was quickly thrown over his head.

Sylvia brought the man over and I asked him if all was well. "Oh, yes", he said. "Everything's fine." Well done, Sylvia.

CHAPTER 28
Gains and Losses

Years ago, I had wanted to cast Brian Murphy to play Billy Hardcastle, a distant relative of Robin Hood, in *How Errol Flynn Discovered the Secret Scar of Nora Batty*. (1999). Because of a misunderstanding with Brian's agent about his availability, I had cast instead my second choice, Keith Clifford. Keith had demonstrated a good sense of comedy for me in *Lost for Words* (1999) and I was pleased to take advantage of it in *Last of the Summer Wine*. Roy Clarke liked Keith and eventually made Billy Hardcastle a regular in the series but, although he was often the 'third man' in scenes with Clegg and Truly, he never really became a comfortable member of the trio. He didn't look like a contemporary of Peter and Frank. He was simply, believe or not, too young, but he played Billy Hardcastle very well and gave us many funny moments. Sadly, a minor accident at the unit base when he fell down the steps of a trailer forced him to leave the production.

When the opportunity arose for a second time to bring Brian Murphy into *Last of the Summer Wine*, I was delighted to find that he was every bit as good as I had hoped – and better. He had originally flown in on his hang-glider as Alvin Smethurst in *The Lair of the Cat Creature* (2003) and demonstrated what a fine comedy actor he was. Brian was widely known for *George and Mildred*, a hugely popular Thames Television series that topped the ratings for many years.

When Roy moved Alvin into Compo's old house – hey presto! Nora Batty had a new sparring partner. Whereas Compo pursued Nora relentlessly, Alvin would insinuate that every innocent move that she made was an advance that had to be resisted at all costs. I'm pleased to say that Brian Murphy was seen by everyone to be very good casting.

Roy Clarke doesn't usually get involved with the casting. He writes the characters and leaves it to me, but in the script of *Ancient Eastern Wisdom – An Introduction* (2003), the name 'Burt Kwouk' appeared. Roy wanted him to play Entwistle, a Chinese electrician from Hull, and he was going to be a semi-regular character in the series.

The idea of having Burt Kwouk in *Summer Wine* was interesting and exciting. However, I had to point out to Roy that our cast budget was already over-burdened and we couldn't afford another regular character. As much as I admired Burt's work, and he has done much more than the relatively few *Pink Panther* films for which he is rightly famous, I had to be practical. If there was no money left in the budget, that was it. Then, out of the blue, the whole situation was up-ended.

A month before filming for the 2002 series would begin, Gordon Wharmby telephoned Sylvia Kendall, our location manager who lives in Holmfirth, to say that, rather than stay at the unit hotel in Huddersfield as he usually did, he wanted her to help him find a cottage to rent in the Holme Valley. Nothing at all strange in that as other actors in the series had done the same over the years. As well as having some freedom, it gave them the benefit of enjoying the peace and quiet of the countryside on their days off.

But Sylvia reported to me that she was concerned by the sound of Gordon's voice on the telephone, which was strained and weak. She urged me to see him to make sure he was all right. Sylvia arranged that Gordon would meet us at a service area on the M62, which wasn't too far from his home in Rhyl in North Wales.

When we met, I was shocked to see that Gordon had lost a lot of weight and was clearly in great pain. He was sucking a succession of ice-lollies to ease the discomfort of what was obviously throat cancer.

Gordon tried to brush aside his problem and talked only about the cottage he wanted to rent in Holmfirth for the duration of the filming, but it was very clear that his illness was far worse than he wished to admit. No longer was he the cheerful Northerner with sparkling eyes. He was intense and fidgety.

Gordon told us that he had taken care of his wife's future financially, and that all was well with him other than this minor throat problem. Gordon then pronounced his theory on how to be rich: "Only buy what you need, not what you want." He also stressed that he hadn't had any alcohol for ages. "Not since that business in Holmfirth, which we all remember," he said rather pointedly. Sylvia discussed the accommodation she had found for him in Holmfirth, but we were very much aware that the chances were slim of his being able to make use of it.

Sylvia and I waved farewell to Gordon as he disappeared out of the motorway service area in his car. We wouldn't see him again. Gordon died a few weeks later of throat cancer. Why does anyone smoke?

Gordon's sudden passing cast a different light on Burt Kwouk's appearance in the series. Wesley, with his trusty Land Rover, had provided transportation for our characters as well as being the means of delivering a variety of contraptions that had to be either carried or towed.

It was only a matter of replacing the little Chinese van that Roy had described for Burt with a pick-up truck that would fulfil all the functions of Wesley's Land Rover. And it meant that we could now have Burt Kwouk as a regular in the series, if he would agree.

Roy was very saddened at the loss of Wesley but delighted when we found that Burt was going to be available as a regular. Although it is some years since his last appearance as Cato in the Pink Panther films, he is still remembered by everyone for that role.

Entwistle, the Chinese electrician from Hull, opened up a new avenue of comedy from Roy's limitless imagination. It should be noted that, if Roy hadn't wanted Burt in the series, I would have had another example of emergency casting to replace Wesley.

Burt Kwouk, besides being a popular member of the cast with a warm and generous personality, is in every way a gentleman. As an actor he displays all the modesty and patience of someone who has long since come to terms with the demands of filming.

In a scene on the moors with Auntie Wainwright, he had to jump out of the cab of his truck quickly. After the first take, I complained to him: "You're getting out of the cab like a 70-year-old." Burt thought for a brief moment, and then said, "Alright. How old do you want me to be?"

"About 30 years old," I replied.

On my cue, he leapt out of the cab like Cato did in the Pink Panther films.

"Make it 50 years old, Burt."

I hadn't realised that at the time Burt was in reality 72.

Peter Sallis initially refused to go near a chicken, but when he overcame the problem, they became good friends.

Top: Alvin (Brian Murphy) enters the series by Hang-glider and is welcomed by Truly Clegg and Billy Hardcastle. Bottom Left: Burt Kwouk plays Entwistle the Chinese Electrician from Hull. Bottom Right: Suddenly a new romance threatens.

CHAPTER 29
Stars

Responding to the request of Peter Fincham, the then Controller of BBC1, to have more guest stars in the episodes, the brilliant comedian Brian Conley joined us for *Enter the Finger* (2007) to play a fitness fanatic.

Brian Conley was always a favourite with the viewers and, whenever I work with these popular and really funny comedians, I have to ask: where are the variety shows that were once so popular on television?

Our audiences enjoyed the appearance of popular guest stars, so when I was approached by an agent who suggested his client Bobby Ball of the comedy duo Cannon and Ball, to be in the series, I was very interested. I had been at a London Palladium show 30 years ago when Cannon and Ball were on the bill, and I remember thinking that they were a very good double-act. London Weekend Television signed them up, and they made several successful series there. Now, nearly 30 years later, I was looking for someone to play 'Lenny from the pickle factory' in *The Swan Man of Ilkley* (2006) and Bobby looked as though he might be a good choice.

The tapes that his agent had sent to me showed him in some small dramatic roles. He was good, but the over-riding question was, would a star comedian be a strong enough actor to play a leading part in *Summer Wine*? There were a lot of good lines in the script, and they needed a good actor to play them.

One Sunday evening, in order to see Bobby Ball performing on stage, I went to the Grand Theatre in Blackpool where Cannon and Ball were top of the bill. So popular are they with the public that their show was a sell-out. When they came on stage, the audience erupted. Anyone who says that variety is dead should go and see Cannon and Ball. From my box, I could see the faces of the audience, young and old, each one of them thoroughly enjoying a good clean comedy act. I immediately thought that, with a good scriptwriter, they would be every bit as good as Morecambe and Wise were at the height of their success, and I still think so. But in the meantime, I cast Bobby Ball in Summer Wine. At the end of filming a scene with Bobby, Peter Sallis patted me on the back and whispered, "Well done. Good casting."

To his great credit, Bobby had asked if there was anything that his partner Tommy Cannon could do in the episode and, of course, there was. I gave Tommy the part of a narrow-boat owner who finds himself towing Bobby up the canal on his inflatable swan. Bobby was pleased to perform the stunt himself, or rather, he didn't complain.

Bobby Ball was so good that I brought him back a year later to play Lenny again in *Who's That*

Talking to Lenny? (2006) and then again in *Get Out of That* (2007).

The following year, long-time favourite Eric Sykes joined us to play the title role in *The Second Stag Night of Doggie Wilkinson* (2007). Having recently played an important part in the latest Harry Potter film, Eric was enjoying his continued success as an actor. Of course, for our filming he would have to be comedic which was really what he did best. Like all seasoned players, Eric was happy to put up with all the discomforts of the part which in this case meant playing a drunk and being tossed around on a bumpy handcart.

When he had finished filming his scenes, I asked Eric how he had found the experience of working with us. He replied that it was exactly as he had expected it to be. If only I knew what he'd expected!

As Warren Mitchell remarked when he played in *Potts in Pole Position* (2001): "For an actor, *Summer Wine* is like National Service. You know you're going to have to do it sometime."

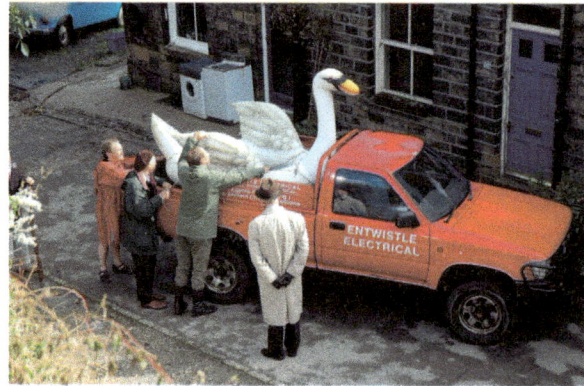

Top Right: Bobby Ball plays 'The Swan Man of Ilkley. (2005). Bottom Left and Right: The men are intrigued by this idiot who wants to travel the canals by inflatable swan.

Top: Guest star Eric Sykes (Doggie Wilkinson) is welcomed to the series. Bottom: Eric Sykes' friends provide suitable transportation for a second honeymooner.

Top: Howard and Marina enjoying the joys of the countryside. Bottom Left: PC's Cooper and Walsh (Ken Kitson and Louis Emerick) are always on the look out. Bottom Right: Howard and Clegg up a tree for 'Watching the Clock '2005'.

CHAPTER 30
Goodbye Nora

After two series of making *Last of the Summer Wine* in High Definition, for which we were the first all-film comedy series to use this super-sharp system, a salesman in a television showroom in Holmfirth said that his customers loved watching *Last of the Summer Wine* in HD because of the way it captured the scenery. However he asked why the BBC didn't have extracts from it in its HD demonstration programme instead of scenes from fast moving dramas where HD didn't matter.

It was a good question, like: Why was the series so badly scheduled for transmission at teatime in the height of summer?

Shooting in High Definition would at last let us show the detail in the beauty of the Yorkshire scenery. But there was a disadvantage: whereas, for long shots of the men in the hills, it used to be acceptable to use doubles, now we had to use the real actors. We could see their faces! There was no possibility that we could get away with using doubles any more.

Meanwhile, Roy had written a pilot for a spin-off series featuring the two policemen played by Ken Kitson and Louis Emerick. It was made as an episode within the main series and was called *A Short Introduction to Cooper's Rules* (2008). The policemen were, without doubt, two of the most popular characters in the series and there was always a murmur of anticipation from the audience the moment their police car appeared on the screen.

In *A Short Introduction to Cooper's Rules* (2007) they were given names for the first time: P.C. Cooper (Kitson) gives his mobile partner PC Walsh (Emerick) expert tuition on how not to get involved with problems. The episode, which also featured Nicholas Smith from *Are You Being Served?* was a great success and proved that they could easily carry their own series, but so far the opportunity to see more of them just hasn't happened. We remain ever hopeful.

In April 2007, the BBC celebrated the continued success of *Last of the Summer Wine* by having a formal dinner in the Council Chamber at Broadcasting House. The whole cast and key production personnel were there including Roy Clarke and Ronnie Hazlehurst who was at the time, recovering from a stroke.

The Controller of BBC1, Peter Fincham, was also there, and he confirmed that he was going to re-launch *Last of the Summer Wine* with a more sensible evening transmission time. At last, we had a Controller who cared about content, not just filling slots. When, a few years ago, the series was shown in the autumn or winter months, it was always in the top ten 'most watched' programmes.

Peter Fincham gave a short uplifting speech which left no doubt in anyone's mind that here was a Controller who valued the series and was going to protect its future. This was very good news indeed. It was comforting to know that all the hard work of the cast, the crew and the production team was being appreciated from above.

But fate was lurking negatively around the corner and the production of *Last of the Summer Wine* was about to encounter severe turbulence.

The American photographer Annie Leibowitch had been commissioned to take some official portraits of Her Majesty the Queen and the BBC covered the photo session as part of a programme about a day in the life of Buckingham Palace. Unfortunately, a trailer advertising the programme showed Miss Leibovitch asking the Queen if she would mind taking off her crown for one of her photographs. Sharp cut to Her Majesty walking stridently down a palace corridor expressing her extreme displeasure about what had just happened. But, in fact, her annoyance had absolutely nothing whatsoever to do with Miss Leibowich and was the result of misleading editing which had certainly made it appear to be so.

The BBC was called to answer for such an unthinkable situation, and as a result both Peter Fincham as Head of BBC1 and Stephen Lambert, chief creative officer of the production company RDF Media, honourably resigned. Sadly, when Peter Fincham left the BBC, so too did our champion.

An accident while filming *Would the Genuine Racer Please Come In?* (2007) brought home the high risk of working with older actors and was a contributory factor in my deciding to rejuvenate the series. In a set-up where Clegg was standing next to a track bike, Truly's overcoat caught on the handlebars and pulled the bike off its stand. It pushed Peter backwards and on to the ground, hitting his head on the tarmac.

Our unit nurse was immediately on the scene and telephoned for an ambulance. "There has been a motorcycle accident," she said. This was accurate but misleading. She changed it to: "A motorcycle has knocked over one of our actors." By the time she got it right, the ambulance was well on its way, but it must be said that Peter Sallis was very complimentary about the nurse's care and her reassuring manner. Fortunately, Peter was completely unharmed, but it was more through luck than anything else. However, this accident was a reminder that we were working with elderly, vulnerable actors.

Age is not a great problem in a series like *Last of the Summer Wine*. It was after all created to reflect the enduring spirit of older men in their firm resolve never to grow up, but I felt that the time had now come to rejuvenate the series and give it a lift.

After all the negotiations and persuading to get Russ Abbot to join the series, the result was that we had another trio with Russ playing Luther 'Hobbo' Hobdyke, Burt Kwouk playing Entwistle and Brian Murphy playing Alvin. We were, as they say, on a roll!

We were about to enter this new phase in the history of the series when, a couple of days before we went filming in Yorkshire, Kathy Staff was unwell and couldn't do any more work for us.

This was another calamity! There were quite a few Nora Batty scenes that had to be changed, but who could replace her? I suggested to Roy that we could use Barbara Young who had played Bobby Ball's wife in two episodes and was very good. All we would have to do is have a short scene with her saying goodbye to Lenny and saying that she is looking after Nora's house while she was away. Roy said, "She's an actress, she can play other parts. Give her a wig and I'll make her Nora's sister." And that is what was done. Simple.

It all happened so quickly that when Barbara arrived in Yorkshire, she thought that she had been booked to play Bobby's wife again. Like June Whitfield, she played a completely different character and merged seamlessly into the series.

Filming was finished for another year when it was announced that our marvellous Kathy Staff had suffered a brain haemorrhage. I went to see her at her home, but she was a shadow of the powerful actress we all knew and loved.

Chapter 30 – Goodbye Nora – 183

Kathy Staff passed away on 13th December 2008. She was a good friend and an irreplaceable member of the company. It was a great loss to the series and to everyone who knew her.

Top Left: Barbara Young (Stella) takes over from Kathy Staff. Top Right: Clegg – an unwilling decoy – on Howard's track bike. Bottom Left: Truly, Entwistle and Alvin give Clegg advice on how to use Howard's Track Bike. Bottom Right: Truly shares a nostalgic moment with Auntie.

Nora Batty (Kathy Staff) an icon of Last of the Summer Wine.

CHAPTER 31
Celebrating the Series

Welcomed back by Director General Mark Thompson from her stopover at Channel Five, Jay Hunt took up the reigns of running BBC1 and began to demonstrate her strength by throwing out cherished, popular programmes with all the care of a bulldozer at an archaeological site.

At this point, there was every indication that my strategy in casting Russ Abbot would take the series forward for at least another couple of years.

The preview audiences had given Russ a resounding welcome and Mark Freeland was enthusiastic about the development of the series. Everything was upfront and good. At least I thought so. Here I was, reading in disbelief, an email from Mark Freeland telling me that the new BBC1 Controller had in effect, axed the series.

What I couldn't understand was, why couldn't there have been a meeting with Mark Freeland and Jay Hunt to discuss their plans to end the series? After all, I had been producing and directing the series for 28 years. But, an email?

Later, I received a call from *The Huddersfield Examiner* saying that the BBC press office had strenuously denied the axing, saying "It just wasn't true". My reply was that if there is no filming next year, it will effectively have been axed, and I had been formally told that there will be no filming next year.

A few days later on the Thursday, I was invited to a meeting at Television Centre. At the meeting was Mark Freeland (Head of Comedy), Jay Hunt (Controller BBC1), Lucy Lumsden (Commissioning Editor, Comedy) and George Dixon (Planning). Jay Hunt said it was unfortunate that the matter had been taken to the press as she had "got in the neck" as a result. I can't say I felt bad about that. What about the artists and crew who were to be suddenly abandoned? She then assured me that the series most definitely had *not* been 'axed'. No decision would be made until the latest series was transmitted. I pointed out that if the production is dormant for a year, it would be difficult to get its well-oiled machinery to start up again. It was the efficiency of our unit that kept the series coming in on budget, to which Jay Hunt replied: "This is not about money. There's plenty of money." Really?

"And what about the scenery and the props?" I asked. Without a moment's hesitation, Lucy Lumsden replied, "The scenery is in storage and the props are all safely locked up in Holmfirth." This accurate knowledge revealed that it was no sudden decision to end the show, as there must have been discussions with lesser members of staff to get that information. Why didn't they have a meeting with me?

I said that if Jay Hunt was serious about not making a decision until the latest series had been shown, why didn't she commission a one-off Special, which at least would keep the company together for another year? After a great deal of debate, during which Jay Hunt observed that we were arguing on different planes and getting nowhere, she suddenly said, "All right, I'll do a deal with you. You stop saying the series has been axed and I'll give you your Special." There was a sharp intake of breath from Lucy Lumsden, accompanied by her wide-eyed look of disbelief. Jay Hunt had obviously strayed from the agreed agenda but nonetheless she shook hands with me to confirm the arrangement. A deal had been struck.

Jay Hunt then said that she would 'work it out' with Lucy, and ring me next morning with the details. I said that I would talk to the press office and issue a statement withdrawing my allegation that the series had been axed as it now clearly hadn't been.

Both Roy Clarke and Mike Hughes, Russ Abbot's agent, were delighted when they heard of the agreed Special. It was better than nothing. Throughout the following morning, I waited for Jay Hunt's call. And I waited, and waited. At about three o'clock, I started making calls to the BBC but no one was available. Then, at five-thirty, I received a call from Mark Freeland to apologise for the fact that there would in fact, be no Special after all as there was no money to pay for it. What about Jay Hunt's statement yesterday that "there's plenty of money"? Obviously, not for programmes.

It seemed to me that, if Jay Hunt found that she was unable to go through with her side of the bargain, she should have telephoned me personally. Mark told me that there would be a meeting in the New Year with Roy Clarke, his agent and myself to discuss the situation. I told them that I wouldn't go to any meeting where Roy's agent, Stephen Durbridge, was in attendance. He had ruined the chances of developing a series that Roy Clarke had written for me that was to star David Jason.

In 2009, the first series starring Russ Abbot was transmitted slightly earlier in the year from April to June and, despite the usual teatime slots, it attracted very acceptable viewing figures.

Then in early June, I received a call that was entirely unexpected. It was from Mark Freeland enquiring if I could make a series of six episodes this year. My answer was a definite 'Yes'. I asked if this was likely to happen, and he said, "Let's say that conversations are taking place." So Jay Hunt had kept her word – the series really hadn't been axed.

In order that Roy Clarke could be prepared for this unexpected decision I drove up to Yorkshire to see him. He would have to write the scripts very quickly if we got the go-ahead. I started to tell him about the strong possibility of our making another six episodes, but he already knew and had already started writing them! It seemed odd to me that 'conversations are taking place' was as certain as Mark could be with me, but with Roy he had actually given enough assurance for him to start writing. But this wasn't the time for any contention. It looked like the show was back in production.

Roy said that he had asked Mark Freeland if he was to put a 'full stop' at the end of episode six, and the answer was "No – there's no such thing in television as 'never'." On June 17th 2009, I received a call from Television Centre saying: "You know about the six episodes?"

I said, "Yes." In truth, all I knew was that "conversations were taking place".

"Well, can you give us the filming dates as soon as possible?" This was the confirmation I needed. We were on for another series, albeit a short series of six episodes.

Simone Dawson, my first assistant director, alerted the cast and crew, and I set the first filming day to be August 17th, just eight weeks away. Roy's scripts for this short series were very good and, for the first time, they were in the form of a serial.

We hadn't long started filming in August 2009 when, at the unit base near Scholes, about a mile out of Holmfirth, Russ Abbot came to see me.

"Forgive me for asking," he said, with the usual twinkle in his eye, "but I have been elected spokesman for the actors. Because episode six is

Chapter 31 – Celebrating the Series – 187

Top Left: Filming in High Definition at the top of Cheesegate Nab. Top Right: Roy Clarke and Russ Abbot.
Bottom: The final trio: Entwistle (Burt Kwouk), Alvin (Brian Murphy) and Hobbo (Russ Abbot) give advice to Howard (Robert Fyfe).

*Top: The final trio: Alvin (Brian Murphy); Hobbo (Russ Abbot); and Entwistle (Burt Kwouk) above Jackson Bridge.
Bottom: Hobbo reminisces about his glory days in MI5 to Alvin, Enwistle and Ivy (Jane Freeman).*

very much like the walk-down at the end of a show, everyone thinks it's the final episode to end the whole series." I assured Russ that no decision was going to be made until the series had been shown and, as Roy had been told not to end this series with a full stop, episode six wouldn't be the end. I honestly believed that this was the truth and that the future of the series would depend upon the success of the episodes we were filming. On the daily call sheet, in good faith, I reassured the cast thus:-

There has been some speculation that the end scene in Episode 6 denotes a final curtain for the series. This is not so and the programme will continue if the BBC feels that it still merits re-commissioning. This has been the case since series one, and I have every hope that the BBC will be impressed by its huge world-wide following, which has been earned by the cast and the crew over the years. If it was intended to end the series with episode six, the bus with all the cast would most certainly have crashed into the reservoir!

Alan J W Bell

The last scene in episode six had all of our characters waiting for a coach that would take them to a wedding. The scene was originally written to take place in Ivy's Café which would have been filmed at Shepperton Studios. However, getting 22 characters into the small café set would be impossible, especially as there was so much movement in the scene. So the setting was changed to being an inn where there was more room, but even so, it was still cramped when all the crew and the equipment were moved in.

The following day, I filmed the scenes of the policemen, Ken Kitson and Louis Emerick, and their encounter with the coach that was carrying all our characters. It never occurred to me that I was shooting the last scene in the final episode, but that is what it turned out to be.

It was while I was in America the following year, fund-raising at a Public Broadcasting Service station in Illinois (the series is still hugely popular in the US), that rumours began to appear on the internet that the series had ended. Eventually, I was able to contact Mark Freeland who sent me an email saying that he had previously discussed with Roy *and me* that the six episodes were almost certainly the last. Maybe he did with Roy but most definitely, not with me. All I had been told was that "conversations are taking place". He added that we should all stick together on this to avoid the upset of last time when the situation went nuclear. What about the upset to the crew and the cast? What of Russ Abbot in particular who had been persuaded to join the show and who was now being unceremoniously dumped?

I returned from America and was in France when it was formally announced that the series of six episodes were the last ever, and that the end would be celebrated by the programmes *Countryfile* and *Songs of Praise from Holmfirth*. There would also be a special tribute on radio. The lid was being firmly screwed down on the coffin. The assurances that the series had not been axed were exposed as being completely untrue, and I was very angry that I had been duped into misleading the cast. In an interview, I openly criticised the BBC for having no regard for that huge audience of the over-40s, the largest section of the viewing public, who had avidly followed the series both in the UK and overseas. I also mentioned that there were too many overpaid executives at the BBC, so many in fact, that they were practically falling over themselves at Television Centre.

The interview must have ruffled a few feathers for, when I returned to London, I was invited to another meeting at the Television Centre. Besides Jay Hunt, there was Mark Freeland, George Dixon (of Planning) and Cheryl Taylor, a new and impossibly young Commissioning Editor of Comedy. Lucy Lumsden, her predecessor, had in the meantime landed in a lucrative chair at Sky Television.

I said at the meeting that I wholly accepted that neither I nor anyone else had a right to dictate what programmes the BBC made, but why hadn't there been a meeting to discuss it, rather than sending emails? Why hadn't this handled competently and professionally?

I wasn't at all angry that the series had ended because the end had been decided, and that was that. And I was comforted to have the BBC's agreement that our sets would be offered to Holmfirth to set up a bigger museum. However, due to a delay caused by the death of the man who was providing the transport, the sets were destroyed, which left a bad taste in the town.

A kind gesture of a farewell lunch was given in the Council Chamber at Broadcasting House. It was certainly appropriate, for it was in this very room that, barely two years previously, the then Controller of BBC1, Peter Fincham, had praised the series and assured its future. The idea of presenting all the actors with a cup-and-saucer set as an icon of Ivy's Café was abandoned when I pointed out that in the circumstances, the actors would see this as being rather derisory.

Alan Yentob, Creative Director of Television (and some suggest the instigator of the series' demise) spoke in glowing terms of the brilliance of the programme and how proud the BBC was to have made it for 37 years. I was tempted to stand up and ask: "Why then, if it's so wonderful, are you ending it?" The answer was given later by the new comedy commissioner, Cheryl Taylor: "It is to make room for younger talent."

Invited to be interviewed on radio on the last day of the Edinburgh Festival, I gave my honest opinion of the 'New BBC': that it has too many highly paid executives, it is a monument to wastage, and it doesn't deserve to retain the licence fee. I said that it was gross incompetence to end a series that satisfies that huge section of the viewing public that doesn't like embarrassment comedy and gratuitous foul language. I commented that, instead of having conferences about the appropriate use of 'four letter words' in programmes (as they had), the Director General [Mark Thompson] should step in and say, 'No more four letter words at all on the BBC'. He would gain overwhelming respect as a result.

My criticism of the musical chairs executives – that they have no loyalty – was demonstrated again a few weeks later. Jay Hunt, barely two years after joining the BBC, had jumped into a lucrative vacant chair at Channel Four. She was off, leaving behind her a channel that seems to have lost its unique reputation as a broadcaster of quality programmes and a harbinger of good taste.

It should be noted that the ubiquitous David Liddiment from ITV had also swapped chairs, and was now back at the BBC, despite being a shareholder in a production company, as a member of the BBC Trust. Wow! What a game.

The final *Last of the Summer Wine*, transmitted at 8 p.m. on 29th August 2010, had an audience of 5.3 million and was the top comedy programme that week. To dump a programme with such a strong following is in every way, grossly incompetent and the BBC executives involved should be ashamed of how they had failed to ensure the BBC fulfilled its remit.

At the end of 2010, there was much excitement and enthusiasm from an unexpected quarter to make a continuation of *Last of the Summer Wine*. The satellite broadcaster UKTV, which is half-owned by the BBC and was at that time half-owned by Virgin Media, expressed a keen interest in making more episodes. This was appropriate as the channel had flourished with repeats of *Last of the Summer Wine* while paying very small repeat fees.

The Controller of UKTV was Matthew Littleford who had successfully opened up other channels such as UK Gold that made use of the BBC's huge archive of programmes. Matthew said that *Last of the Summer Wine* was the most popular series that they show. I was delighted by his enthusiasm when he said, firmly, that he wanted it. Not "I'm interested in making it", but "I want to make it". This enthusiasm was most welcome.

Sadly, although it would mean making the series for much less money, the plan was vetoed by the finance committee and one can only speculate what happened at that meeting. In correspondence, I alluded to it as being the work of the dark hand of the BBC which strangely enough, was not contradicted. At the same time, Matthew Littleford resigned from UKTV to

The last picture of the company at Shepperton Studios, October 2009

'pursue other interests'. I would like to think that he resigned because of the finance committee's interference. I can only speculate who was behind the decision. Was it the Director General of the BBC who didn't like my remarks on radio about the validity of the licence fee? For whatever reason, the plug was pulled on the venture and we all suffered a double whammy.

My apologies go to the cast of *Last of the Summer Wine* for misleading them into believing that the series would continue, and especially to Russ Abbot who took the episodes to new heights and who found that a jobbing executive had set her mind on axing his series before it had even been transmitted.

The wisdom of the decisions made by the BBC is best judged by the events of the past few years. The Television Centre, custom built and in pristine condition, has been sold off to a developer. Staff and programmes have been moved into the brand new and wondrous billion-pound media centre in Salford Quays in Greater Manchester. Millions of pounds of licence-payers' money is now thrown away on the expense of taxis, trains and hotel bills to bring artists and production personnel the two hundred miles from London. Amid such bizarre extravagance, who cares about a popular comedy series that was only there to entertain?

I shall forever respect Roy Clarke as a great writer. Every script starts with blank pages, and over the years he has started with at least six thousand blank pages for *Last of the Summer Wine* alone. Every script is an outstanding masterpiece of prose.

And what about me? Well, I believe that I was the very last in the long line of traditional comedy producer/directors who made programmes – with little or no interference – from a production office run by only four people and not an executive producer in sight.

After making 250 episodes of *Last of the Summer Wine* over a period of 28 years, I was naturally disappointed to be thrown on the scrapheap, aged 73 – just when I was getting the hang of it all.

Appendix

FIRST TRANSMISSIONS

COMEDY PLAYHOUSE PILOT EPISODE
Filmed in 1972 Producer/Director James Gilbert
Starring Bill Owen, Peter Sallis and Michael Bates

Of Funerals and Fish	04/01/1973	8:00p.m.	1.	JG1

FIRST SERIES – A – 1973
Filmed in 1973 Producer/Director James Gilbert
Starring Bill Owen, Peter Sallis and Michael Bates

1.	Short Back and Palais Glide	12/11/1973	9:00p.m.	2.	JG2
2.	Inventor of the Forty Foot Ferret	19/11/1973	9:00p.m.	3.	JG3
3.	Pate and Chips	26/11/1973	9:00p.m.	4.	JG4
4.	Spring Fever	3/12/1973	9:00p.m.	5.	JG5
5.	The New Mobile Trio	10/12/1973	9:00p.m.	6.	JG6
6.	Hail Smiling Morn or Thereabouts	17/12/1973	9:00p.m.	7.	JG7

SECOND SERIES – B – 1975
Filmed in 1974 Producer/Director Sydney Lotterby
Starring Bill Owen, Peter Sallis and Michael Bates

1.	Forked Lightning	5/03/1975	9:00p.m.	8.	BT1
2.	Who's That Dancing with Nora Batty, Then?	12/03/1975	9:00p.m.	9.	BT2
3.	The Changing Face of Rural Blamire	19/03/1975	9:00p.m.	10.	BT3
4.	Some Enchanted Evening	26/03/1975	9:00p.m.	11.	BT4
5.	A Quiet Drink	2/04/1975	9:00p.m.	12.	BT5
6.	Ballad for Wind Instruments and Canoe	9/04/1975	9:00p.m.	13.	BT6
7.	Northern Flying Circus	16/04/1975	9:00p.m.	14.	BT7

THIRD SERIES – C – 1976
Filmed in 1976 Producer/Director Sydney Lotterby
Starring Bill Owen, Peter Sallis and Brian Wilde

1.	The Man from Oswestry	27/10/1976	9:00p.m.	15.	SL1
2.	Mending Stuart's Leg	3/11/1976	9:00p.m.	16.	SL2
3.	The Great Boarding House BathroomCaper	10/11/1976	9:00p.m.	17.	SL3
4.	Cheering-up Gordon	17/11/1976	9:00p.m.	18.	SL4
5.	The Kink in Foggy's Niblick	24/11/1976	9:00p.m.	19.	SL5
6.	Going to Gordon's Wedding	1/12/1976	9:00p.m.	20.	SL6
7.	Isometrics and After	8/12/1976	9:00p.m.	21.	SL7

FOURTH SERIES – D – 1977 – 1978
Filmed in 1977 Producer/Director Sydney Lotterby
Starring Bill Owen, Peter Sallis and Brian Wilde

1.	Ferret Come Home	9/11/1977	9:00p.m.	22.	SL8
2.	Getting on Sidney's Wire	6/11/1977	9:00p.m.	23.	SL9
3.	Jubilee	23/11/1977	9:00p.m.	24.	SL10
4.	Flower Power Cut	30/11/1977	9:00p.m.	25	SL11
5.	Who Made a Bit of a Splash in Wales, Then?	7/12/1977	9:00p.m.	26.	SL12
6.	Greenfingers	21/12/1977	9:00p.m.	27.	SL13
7.	A Merry Heatwave	1/01/1978	10:00p.m.	28.	SL14
8.	The Bandit from Stoke-On-Trent	4/01/1978	9:00p.m.	29.	SL15

CHRISTMAS SPECIAL 1978
Filmed in 1978 Producer/Director Sydney Lotterby
Starring Bill Owen, Peter Sallis and Brian Wilde

Small Tune on a Penny Wassail (30mins)	26/12/1978	10:00p.m.	30.	SL16

FIFTH SERIES – E – 1979
Filmed in 1979 Producer/Director Sydney Lotterby
Starring Bill Owen, Peter Sallis and Brian Wilde

1.	Full Steam Behind	18/09/1979	8:00p.m.	31.	SL17
2.	The Flag and its Snags	25/09/1979	8:00p.m.	32.	SL18
3.	The Flag and Further Snags	2/10/1979	8:00p.m.	33.	SL19
4.	Deep in the Heart of Yorkshire	9/10/1979	8:00p.m.	34.	SL20
5.	Earnshaw Strikes Again	6/10/1979	8:00p.m.	35.	SL21
6.	Here We Go Into The Wild Blue Yonder	23/10/1979	8:00p.m.	36.	SL22
7.	Here We Go Again Into The Wild Blue Yonder	30/10/1979	8:00p.m.	37.	SL23
8.	And a Dewhurst up a Fir Tree	27/12/1979	8:00p.m.	38.	SL24

CHRISTMAS SPECIAL 1981
Filmed in 1981 Producer/Director Alan J.W. Bell
Starring Bill Owen, Peter Sallis and Brian Wilde

Whoops (30mins)	25/12/1981	7:00p.m.	39.	AJW1

SIXTH SERIES – F – 1982
Filmed in 1981 Producer/Director Alan J.W. Bell
Starring Bill Owen, Peter Sallis and Brian Wilde

1.	In The Service of Humanity	4/01/1982	9:00p.m.	40.	AJW2
2.	Car and Garter	11/01/1982	9:00p.m.	41.	AJW3
3.	The Odd Dog Men	18/01/1982	9:00p.m.	42.	AJW4
4.	A Bicycle Made for Three	25/01/1982	9:00p.m.	43.	AJW5
5.	One of the Last Few Places Unexplored by Man	1/02/1982	9:00p.m.	44.	AJW6
6.	Serenade for Tight Jeans and Metal Detector	8/02/1982	9:00p.m.	45.	AJW7
7.	From Wellies to Wet Suit	15/02/1982	9:00p.m.	46.	AJW8

SEVENTH SERIES – G – 1982 – 1983
Filmed in 1982 Producer/Director Sydney Lotterby
Starring Bill Owen, Peter Sallis and Brian Wilde

1.	All Mod Conned	25/12/1982	6:00p.m.	47.	SL25
2.	The Frozen Turkey Man	30/01/1983	7:00p.m.	48.	SL26
3.	The White Man's Grave	6/02/1983	7:00p.m.	49.	SL27
4.	The Waist Land	13/02/1983	7:00p.m.	50.	SL28
5.	Cheering-up Ludovic	20/02/1983	7:00p.m.	51.	SL29
6.	The Three Astaires	27/02/1983	7:00p.m.	52.	SL30
7.	The Arts of Concealment	6/03/1983	7:00p.m.	53.	SL31

FIRST TV MOVIE SPECIAL 1983
Filmed in 1983 Producer/Director Alan J.W. Bell
Starring Bill Owen, Peter Sallis and Brian Wilde

Getting Sam Home (85mins -No on-screen sub-title)	27/12/1983	8:00p.m.	54.	AJW9

EIGHTH SERIES – H – 1985
Filmed in 1984 Producer/Director Alan J.W. Bell
Starring Bill Owen, Peter Sallis and Brian Wilde

1.	The Loxley Lozenge	30/12/1984	7:00p.m.	55.	AJW10
2.	The Mysterious Feet of Nora Batty	10/02/1985	8:00p.m.	56.	AJW11
3.	Keeping Britain Tidy	17/02/1985	8:00p.m.	57.	AJW12
4.	Enter The Phantom	24/02/1985	8:00p.m.	58.	AJW13
5.	Catching Digby's Donkey	3/03/1985	8:00p.m.	59.	AJW14
6.	The Woollenmills of your Mind	10/03/1985	8:00p.m.	60.	AJW15
7.	Who's Looking After the Café, Then?	17/03/1985	7:00p.m.	61.	AJW16

SECOND TV MOVIE SPECIAL 1986
Filmed in 1985 Producer/Director Alan J.W. Bell
Starring Michael Aldridge, Bill Owen, Peter Sallis and Thora Hird

Uncle of the Bride(85mins)	1/01/1986	8:00p.m.	62.	AJW17

CHRISTMAS SPECIAL 1986
Starring Michael Aldridge, Bill Owen, Peter Sallis and Thora Hird
Filmed in 1986 Producer/Director Alan J.W. Bell

Merry Christmas, Father Christmas (30mins)	28/12/1986	7:00p.m.	63.	AJW18

NINTH SERIES – J – 1987
Filmed in 1986 Producer/Director Alan J.W. Bell
Starring Michael Aldridge, Bill Owen, Peter Sallis and Thora Hird

1.	Why Does Norman Clegg Buy Ladies ElasticStockings?	4/01/1987	7:00p.m.	64.	AJW19
1.	The Heavily Reinforced Bottom	11/01/1987	7:00p.m.	65.	AJW20
2.	Dried Dates and Codfanglers	18/01/1987	7:00p.m.	66.	AJW21
3.	The Really Masculine Purse	25/01/1987	7:00p.m.	67.	AJW22
4.	Who's Feeling Ejected, Then?	1/02/1987	7:00p.m.	68.	AJW23
5.	The Ice-Cream Man Cometh	8/02/1987	7:00p.m.	69.	AJW24
6.	Set the People Free	15/02/1987	7:00p.m.	70.	AJW25
7.	Go With the Flow	22/02/1987	7:00p.m.	71.	AJW26
8.	Jaws(Danny O'Dea's first appearance as Eli)	1/03/1987	7:00p.m.	72.	AJW27
9.	Edie and the Automobile	8/03/1987	7:00p.m.	73.	AJW28
10.	Windpower	15/03/1987	7:00p.m.	73.	AJW29
11.	When you take a Good Bite, Yorkshire Tastes Terrible	22/03/1987	7:00p.m.	74.	AJW30

THIRD TV MOVIE SPECIAL 1987
Filmed in 1987 Producer/Director Alan J.W. Bell
Starring Michael Aldridge, Bill Owen, Peter Sallis,Ray McAnally and Thora Hird

Big Day At Dream Acres (80 mins) 27/12/1987		7:00p.m.	75.	AJW31

BRITISH RAIL CORPORATE VIDEO
Filmed in 1987 Producer/Director Alan J.W. Bell
Starring Michael Aldridge, Bill Owen, Peter Sallis and Keith Marsh

Ernie's Pension Fund

TENTH SERIES – K – 1988
Filmed in 1988 Producer/Director Alan J.W. Bell
Starring Michael Aldridge, Bill Owen, Peter Sallis and Thora Hird

1.	The Experiment	16/10/1988	7:00p.m.	76.	AJW32
2.	The Treasure of the Deep	23/10/1988	7:00p.m.	77.	AJW33
3.	Dancing Feet	30/10/1988	7:00p.m.	78.	AJW34
4.	That Certain Smile	6/11/1988	7:00p.m.	79.	AJW35
5.	Downhill Racer	13/11/1988	7:00p.m.	80.	AJW36
6.	The Day of the Welsh Ferret	20/11/1988	7:00p.m.	81.	AJW37

CHRISTMAS SPECIAL 1988
Filmed in 1988 Producer/Director Alan J.W. Bell
Starring Michael Aldridge, Bill Owen, Peter Sallis, Jean Alexander and Thora Hird

CRUMS (50mins)	24/12/1988	8:00p.m.	82.	AJW38

ELEVENTH SERIES – L – 1989
Filmed in 1989 Producer/Director Alan J.W. Bell
Starring Michael Aldridge, Bill Owen, Peter Sallis and Thora Hird

1.	Come Back Jack Harry Teesdale	15/10/1989	7:00p.m.	83.	AJW39
2.	The Kiss and Mavis Poskitt	22/10/1989	7:00p.m.	84.	AJW40
3.	Oh Shut Up and Eat Your Choc-Ice	29/10/1989	7:00p.m.	85.	AJW41
4.	Who's That Bloke with Nora Batty, Then?	5/11/1989	7:00p.m.	86.	AJW42
5.	Happy Anniversary, Gough And Jessie	12/11/1989	7:00p.m.	87.	AJW43
6.	Getting Barry Higher in the World	19/11/1989	7:00p.m.	88.	AJW44
7.	Three Men and a Mangle	26/11/1989	7:00p.m.	89.	AJW45

CHRISTMAS SPECIAL 1989
Filmed in 1989 Producer/Director Alan J.W. Bell
Starring Michael Aldridge, Bill Owen, Peter Sallis and Thora Hird

What's Santa Brought for Nora, Then? (50mins)	23/12/1989	8:00p.m.	90.	AJW46

TWELFTH SERIES – M – 1990
Filmed in 1990 Producer/Director Alan J.W. Bell
Starring, Bill Owen, Peter Sallis, Brian Wilde and Thora Hird

1.	Return of the Warrior	2/09/1990	7:00p.m.	91.	AJW47
2.	Come in Sunray Major	9/09/1990	7:00p.m.	92.	AJW48
3.	The Charity Balls	16/09/1990	7:00p.m.	93.	AJW49
4.	Walking Stiff Can Make You Famous	23/09/1990	7:00p.m.	94.	AJW50
5.	That's Not Captain Zero (with Trevor Peacock)	30/09/1990	7:00p.m.	95.	AJW51
6.	Das (Welly) Boot	7/10/1990	7:00p.m.	96.	AJW52
7.	The Empire that Foggy Nearly Built	14/10/1990	7:00p.m.	97.	AJW53
8.	The Last Surviving Maurice ChevalierImpression (with Gorden Kaye)	21/10/1990	7:00p.m.	98.	AJW54
9.	Roll On	28/10/1990	7:00p.m.	99.	AJW55
10.	A Landlady for Smiler	4/11/1990	7:00p.m.	100.	AJW56

CHRISTMAS SPECIAL 1990
Filmed in 1990 Producer/Director Alan J.W. Bell
Starring, Bill Owen, Peter Sallis, Brian Wilde and Thora Hird

Barry's Christmas(30 mins.) No on-screen episode title)	27/12/1990	8:00p.m.	101.	AJW57

THIRTEENTH SERIES – N- 1991

Filmed in 1991 Producer/Director Alan J.W. Bell
Starring, Bill Owen, Peter Sallis, Brian Wilde and Thora Hird
(All-video captured)

1.	Quick Quick Slow	18/10/1991	8:00p.m.	102	AJW58
2.	Give Us A Lift	25/10/1991	8:00p.m.	103	AJW59
3.	Was That Nora Batty Singing?	1/11/1991	8:00p.m.	104	AJW60
4.	Cashflow Problems	8/11/1991	8:00p.m.	105	AJW61
5.	Passing The Earring	15/11/1991	8:00p.m.	106	AJW62
6.	Pole Star	29/11/1991	8:00p.m.	107	AJW63

SPECIAL 1991

Filmed in 1991 Producer/Director Alan J.W. Bell
Starring, Bill Owen, Peter Sallis, Brian Wilde and Thora Hird
Situations Vacant (30mins.)   22/12/1991   7:00p.m.   108   AJW64
(Last TVC studio recording)

FOURTEENTH SERIES – O – 1992

Filmed in 1992 Producer/Director Alan J.W. Bell
Starring, Bill Owen, Peter Sallis, Brian Wilde and Thora Hird
All-film Super16 widescreen programmes, but transmitted in 4x3

1.	By The Magnificent Thighs of Ernie Burniston	25/10/1992	7:00p.m.	109	AJW65
2.	Errol Flynn used to have a Pair Like That	1/11/1992	7:00p.m.	110	AJW66
3.	The Phantom of the Graveyard****	8/11/1992	7:00p.m.	111	AJW67
4.	The Self-propelled Salad Strainer	15/11/1992	7:00p.m.	112	AJW68
5.	Ordeal By Trousers	22/11/1992	7:00p.m.	113	AJW69
6.	Happy Birthday, Howard	29/11/1992	7:00p.m.	114	AJW70
7.	Who`s Got Rhythm?	6/12/1992	7:00p.m.	115	AJW71
8.	Camera Shy	13/12/1992	7:00p.m.	116	AJW72
9.	Wheelies	20/12/1992	7:00p.m.	117	AJW73
10.	Stop That Castle	26/12/1992	7:00p.m.	118	AJW74

FIFTEENTH SERIES – P – 1993

Filmed in 1993 Producer/Director Alan J.W. Bell
Starring, Bill Owen, Peter Sallis, Brian Wilde and Thora Hird
All-film Super16 widescreen programmes, but transmitted in 4x3

1.	How To Clear Your Pipes	24/10/1993	7:00p.m.	119	AJW75
2.	Where There's Smoke, There`s Barbeque	31/10/1993	7:00p.m.	120	AJW76
3.	The Black Widow	7/11/1993	7:00p.m.	121	AJW77
4.	Have You Got A Light, Mate?	14/11/1993	7:00p.m.	122	AJW78
5.	Stop That Bath	21/11/1993	7:00p.m.	123	AJW79
6.	Springing Smiler	28/11/1993	7:00p.m.	124	AJW80
7.	Concerto For Solo Bicycle	5/12/1993	7:00p.m.	125	AJW81
8.	There are Gypsies at the Bottom ofour Garden	12/12/1993	7:00p.m.	126	AJW82
9.	Aladdin Gets On Your Wick	19/12/1993	7:00p.m.	127	AJW83

CHRISTMAS SPECIAL 1993
Filmed in 1993 Producer/Director Alan J.W. Bell
Starring, Bill Owen, Peter Sallis, Brian Wilde, Thora Hird and John Cleese
All-film Super16 widescreen programme, but transmitted in 4x3

Welcome To Earth (30mins)	27/12/1993	8:00p.m.	128	AJW84

SPECIAL 1995
Filmed in 1994 Producer/Director Alan J.W. Bell
Starring, Bill Owen, Peter Sallis, Brian Wilde, Thora Hird and Norman Wisdom
All-film Super16 widescreen programme, but transmitted in 4x3

The Man Who Nearly Knew Pavarotti (60mins)	1/01/1995	7:00p.m.	129	AJW85

SIXTEENTH SERIES – Q – 1995
Filmed in 1994 Producer/Director Alan J.W. Bell
Starring, Bill Owen, Peter Sallis, Brian Wilde and Thora Hird
All-film Super16 widescreen programmes, but transmitted in 4x3

1.	The Glory Hole	8/01/1995	7:00p.m.	130	AJW86
2.	Adopted By A Stray	15/01/1995	7:00p.m.	131	AJW87
3.	Defeat of the Stoneworm	22/01/1995	7:00p.m.	132	AJW88
4.	Once in a Moonlit Junkyard	29/01/1995	7:00p.m.	133	AJW89
5.	The Space Ace	5/02/1995	7:00p.m.	134	AJW90
6.	The Most Powerful Eyeballs In West Yorkshire	12/02/1995	7:00p.m.	135	AJW91
7.	The Dewhirsts of Ogleby Hall	19/02/1995	7:00p.m.	136	AJW92
8.	The Sweet Smell of Excess	26/02/1995	7:00p.m.	137	AJW93

SEVENTEENTH SERIES – R – 1995
Filmed in 1995 Producer/Director Alan J.W. Bell
Starring, Bill Owen, Peter Sallis, Brian Wilde and Thora Hird
All-film Super16 widescreen programmes, but first transmitted in 4x3

1.	Leaving Home Forever – Or 'till Teatime	3/09/1995	7:00p.m.	138	AJW94
2.	Bicycle Bonanza	10/09/1995	7:00p.m.	139	AJW95
3.	The Glamour of the Uniform	17/09/1995	7:00p.m.	140	AJW96
4.	The First Human Being To Ride A Hill	24/09/1995	7:00p.m.	141	AJW97
5.	Captain Clutterbuck's Treasure (with Ron Moody)	1/10/1995	7:00p.m.	142	AJW98
6.	Desperate for a Duffield	8/10/1995	7:00p.m.	143	AJW99
7.	The Suit that Turned Left	15/10/1995	7:00p.m.	144	AJW100
8.	Beware of the Elbow	22/10/1995	7:00p.m.	146	AJW101
9.	The Thing In Wesley's Shed	29/10/1995	7:00p.m.	147	AJW102
10.	Brushes At Dawn	5/11/1995	7:00p.m.	148	AJW103

SPECIAL 1995
Filmed in 1995 Producer/Director Alan J.W. Bell
Starring, Bill Owen, Peter Sallis, Brian Wilde and Thora Hird
All-film Super16 widescreen programme, but first transmitted in 4x3

A Leg-Up For Christmas (50mins) (Fuji)	24/12/1995	7:00p.m.	149	AJW104

SPECIAL 1996
Filmed in 1996 Producer/Director Alan J.W. Bell
Starring, Bill Owen, Peter Sallis, Brian Wilde, Thora Hird and George Chakiris (and Norman Wisdom)
All-film Super16 widescreen programme, but first transmitted in 4x3

Extra, Extra (45mins.)	29/12/1996	6:00p.m.	150	AJW105

EIGHTEENTH SERIES – S – 1997
Filmed in 1996 Producer/Director Alan J.W. Bell
Starring, Bill Owen, Peter Sallis, Brian Wilde and Thora Hird
All-film Super16 widescreen programmes, but first transmitted in 4x3

1.	The Love Mobile	20/04/1997	6:00p.m.	151	AJW106
2.	A Clean Sweep (with Keith Marsh)	27/04/1997	6:00p.m.	152	AJW107
3.	The Mysterious C.W. Northrop	4/05/1997	6:00p.m.	153	AJW108
4.	A Double for Howard	11/05/1997	6:00p.m.	154	AJW109
5.	How To Create A Monster	18/05/1997	6:00p.m.	155	AJW110
6.	Deviations with Davenport (with Jack Smethurst)	25/05/1997	6:00p.m.	156	AJW111
7.	According to the Prophet Bickerdyke	1/06/1997	6:00p.m.	157	AJW112
8.	Next Kiss Please	8/06/1997	6:00p.m.	158	AJW113
9.	Destiny and Six Bananas	15/06/1997	6:00p.m.	159	AJW114
10.	A Sidecar Named Desire	22/06/1997	6:00p.m.	160	AJW115

SPECIAL 1997
Filmed in 1997 Producer/Director Alan J.W. Bell
Starring, Bill Owen, Peter Sallis, Frank Thornton and Thora Hird
First all-film Super16 widescreen programme to be transmitted in 16x9

There Goes The Groom (50mins.)	29/12/1997	7:00p.m.	161	AJW116

NINETEENTH SERIES – T – 1998
Filmed in 1997 Producer/Director Alan J.W. Bell
Starring, Bill Owen, Peter Sallis, Frank Thornton and Thora Hird
All-film Super16 widescreen programmes transmitted in 16x9

1.	Beware of the Oglethorpe	4/01/1998	6:00p.m.	162	AJW117
2.	Tarzan of the Towpath	11/01/1998	6:00p.m.	163	AJW118
3.	Truly and The Hole Truth	18/01/1998	6:00p.m.	164	AJW119
4.	Oh, Howard, We Should Get One Of Those	25/01/1998	6:00p.m.	165	AJW120
5.	The Suit That Attracts Blondes	1/02/1998	6:00p.m.	166	AJW121
6.	The Only Diesel Saxophone In Captivity	8/02/1998	6:00p.m.	167	AJW122
7.	Perfection – Thy Name Is Ridley	15/02/1998	6:00p.m.	168	AJW123
8.	Nowhere Particular	22/02/1998	6:00p.m.	169	AJW124
9.	From Audrey Nash to the Widow Dilhooley	1/03/1998	6:00p.m.	170	AJW125
10.	Support Your Local Skydiver	8/03/1998	7:00p.m.	171	AJW126

TWENTIETH SERIES – U – 1999
Filmed in 1998 Producer/Director Alan J.W. Bell
Starring, Bill Owen, Peter Sallis, Frank Thornton and Thora Hird
All – film Super16 widescreen programmes transmitted in 16x9

1.	The Pony Set	18/04/1999	8:00p.m.	172	AJW127
2.	How Errol Flynn Discovered the Secret Scar of Nora Batty (introducing Keith Clifford)				
		25/04/1999	8:00p.m.	173	AJW128
3.	Who's Thrown her Tom Cruise PhotographsAway?	2/05/1999	8:00p.m.	174	AJW129
4.	What's Happened to Barry's Nose?	16/05/1999	8:00p.m.	175	AJW130
5.	Optimism In The Housing Market	23/05/1999	8:00p.m.	176	AJW131
6.	Will Barry Go Septic Despite Listening to Classical Music?	30/05/1999	8:00p.m.	177	AJW132
7.	Beware The Vanilla Slice	6/06/1999	8:00p.m.	178	AJW133
8.	Howard Throws a Wobbler	13/06/1999	8:00p.m.	179	AJW134
9.	The Phantom Number 14 Bus	20/06/1999	8:00p.m.	180	AJW135
10.	Ironing Day	27/06/1999	8:00p.m.	181	AJW136

MILLENIUM SPECIAL 2000
Filmed in 1999 Producer/Director Alan J.W. Bell
Starring, Bill Owen, Peter Sallis, Frank Thornton and Thora Hird
All-film Super16 widescreen programme transmitted in 16x9
(No end credits as a tribute to Bill Owen's death)

Last Post And Pigeon (50mins) 2/01/2000 6:00p.m. 182 AJW137

(Bill Owen died during the filming of this special and the series)

TWENTY-FIRST SERIES – V- 2000
Filmed in 1999 Producer/Director Alan J.W. Bell
Starring Peter Sallis, Frank Thornton, Thora Hird and Bill Owen (first three episodes only)
All-film Super16 widescreen programmes transmitted in 16x9
(* marks programmes restructured to use some of Bill Owen's scenes after he died)

1.	Lipstick And Other Problems*	2/04/2000	6:00p.m.	183	AJW138
2.	Under The Rug*	9/04/2000	6:00p.m.	184	AJW139
3.	Magic And The Morris Minor*	16/04/2000	6:00p.m.	185	AJW140
4.	Elegy To Fallen Wellies	23/04/2000	6:00p.m.	186	AJW141
5.	Surprise At Throstlenest (with Liz Fraser)	30/04/2000	6:00p.m.	187	AJW142
6.	Just A Small Funeral (with Liz Fraser)	7/05/2000	6:00p.m.	188	AJW43
7.	From Here To Paternity (Introducing Tom Owen)	14/05/2000	6:00p.m.	189	AJW144
8.	Some Vans Can Make You Deaf	21/05/2000	6:00p.m.	190	AJW145
9.	Waggoners Roll	28/05/2000	6:00p.m.	191	AJW146
10.	I Didn't Know Barry Could Play	4/06/2000	6:00p.m.	192	AJW147

TWENTY SECOND SERIES – W – 2001
Filmed in 2000 Producer/Director Alan J.W. Bell
Starring, Peter Sallis, Frank Thornton and Thora Hird
All-film Super16 widescreen programmes transmitted in 16x9

1. Getting Barry's Goat	1/04/2001	7:00p.m.	193	AJW148
2. The Art of the Shorts Story	8/04/2001	6:00p.m.	194	AJW149
3. The Missing Bus of Mrs. Avery	15/04/2001	6:00p.m.	195	AJW150
4. Hey, Big Vendor	22/04/2001	6:00p.m.	196	AJW151
5. Enter The Hawk	29/04/2001	7:00p.m.	197	AJW152
6. Gnome and Away	6/05/2001	7:00p.m.	198	AJW153
7. A Hair of the Blonde that Bit You	13/05/2001	7:00p.m.	199	AJW154
8. A White Sweater and a Solicitors Letter	20/05/2001	7:00p.m.	200	AJW155
9. Why Is Barry At An Angle?			201	AJW156
10. The Coming of the Beast (with Norman Wisdom)	3/06/2001	7:00p.m.	202	AJW157

SPECIAL 2001
Filmed in 2001 Producer/Director Alan J.W. Bell
Starring, Bill Owen, Peter Sallis, Frank Thornton, Thora Hird, June Whitfield and Warren Mitchell
All-film Super16 widescreen programme transmitted in 16x9

Potts In Pole Position(30mins)	30/12/2001	6:00p.m.	203	AJW158

TWENTY THIRD SERIES – X – 2002
Filmed in 2001 Producer/Director Alan J.W. Bell
StarringPeter Sallis, Frank Thornton and Thora Hird
All-film Super16 widescreen programmes transmitted in 16x9

1. A Brief Excursion Into The Fast Lane (Final appearance of Danny O'Dea)	6/01/2002	6:00p.m.	204	AJW159
2. The Mystical Squeak of Howard's Bicycle	13/01/2002	6:00p.m.	205	AJW160
3. Mervyn Would Be Proud	20/01/2002	6:00p.m.	206	AJW161
4. The Incredible Ordeal of Norman Clegg	27/01/2002	6:00p.m.	207	AJW162
5. Beware of the Hot Dog	3/02/2002	6:00p.m.	208	AJW163
6. In Search Of Childlike Joy and the Farthest Reaches of the Lotus Position	10/02/2002	6:00p.m.	209	AJW164
7. A Chaise Longue Too Far	17/02/2002	6:00p.m.	210	AJW165
8. Exercising Father's Bicycle	24/02/2002	6:00p.m.	211	AJW166
9. Sadly, Madly, Bradley	3/03/2002	6:00p.m.	212	AJW167
10. It All Began With An Old Volvo Headlamp (Featuring Hywell Bennett – Final appearance of Gordon Wharmby)	10/03/2002	6:00p.m.	213	AJW168

SPECIAL 2002
Filmed in 2002 Producer/Director Alan J.W. Bell
StarringPeter Sallis, Frank Thornton, Thora Hird and Norman Wisdom
All-film Super16 widescreen programme transmitted in 16x9

A Musical Passing for a Miserable Muscroft (30m) (First appearance of Burt Kwouk)	29/12/2002	5.45p.m.	214	AJW169

TWENTY-FOURTH SERIES – Y – 2003
Filmed in 2002 Producer/Director Alan J.W. Bell
StarringPeter Sallis, Frank Thornton and Thora Hird
All-film Super16 widescreen programmes transmitted in 16x9

1.	The Lair of the Cat Creature (with Brian Murphy)	5/01/2003	6.15p.m.	215	AJW170
2.	Ancient Eastern Wisdom -An Introduction. (introducing Burt Kwouk)				
		12/01/2003	6.15p.m.	216	AJW171
3.	A Pick-Up of the Later Ming Dynasty	19/01/2003	6.15p.m.	217	AJW172
4.	The Secret Birthday of Norman Clegg	26/01/2003	5.45p.m.	218	AJW173
5.	In Which Gavin Hinchcliffe Loses The GulfStream (with Bernard Cribbins and Josephine Tewson)				
		2/02/2003	6.15p.m.	219	AJW174
6.	The Miraculous Curing of Old Goff Helliwell				
	(with Henry McGee)	9/02/2003	6.15p.m.	220	AJW175
7.	The Frenchies Are Coming	16/02/2003		221	AJW176
8.	The Man Who Invented Yorkshire Funny Stuff	23/02/2003		222	AJW177
9.	The Second Husband and the Showgirls (with William Lucas)				
		2/03/2003		223	AJW178
10.	All Of A Florrie	9/03/2003		224	AJW179

CHRISTMAS SPECIAL 2003
Filmed in 2003 Producer/Director Alan J.W. Bell
StarringPeter Sallis, Frank Thornton, Brian Murphy, and Keith Clifford
All-film Super16 widescreen programme transmitted in 16x9

A Short Blast of Fred Astaire (30m) (Lionel Blair)	21/12/2003	6.15p.m.	225	AJW180

TWENTY-FIFTH SERIES – Z – 2003/4
Filmed in 2003 Producer/Director Alan J.W. Bell
StarringPeter Sallis, Frank Thornton and Keith Clifford
All-film Super16 widescreen programmes transmitted in 16x9
Brian Murphy and Josephine Tewson now regulars.

1.	Jurassic No Parking		8/2/20046.15p.m.	226	AJW181
2.	The General's Greatest Battle	15/2/2004	6.15p.m.	233	AJW182
3.	Spores (Guest Roy Hudd)	29/2/2004	5.45p.m.	231	AJW183
4.	Happy Birthday Robin Hood	7/2/2004	6.30 p.m.	232	AJW184
5.	Who's That with Barry and Glenda – That's not Barry and Glenda				
		14/03/2004	6:30p.m.	227	AJW185
6.	An Apple a Day	21/03/2004	6:30p.m.	228	AJW186
7.	Barry Becomes a Psychopathic Killer	28/03/2004	6:00p.m.	229	AJW187
8.	Things To Do When Your Wife Runs Away with a Turkish Waiter				
		04/04/2004	6:00p.m	230	AJW188
9.	Beware of Laughing at Nora's Hats	11/04/2004	6:00p.m	234	AJW189
10.	Yours Truly – if You're Not Careful	18/04/2004	6:00p.m	235	AJW190

CHRISTMAS SPECIAL 2004

Filmed in 2004 Producer/Director Alan J.W. Bell
Starring Peter Sallis, Frank Thornton, Brian Murphy, and Keith Clifford
Guest Norman Wisdom
All-film Super16 widescreen programme transmitted in 16x9

Variations on an Theme of the Widow Winstanley (30m)	19/12/2004	6.15p.m.	236	AJW191

TWENTY- SIXTH SERIES – AA – 2005

Filmed in 2004 Producer/Director Alan J.W. Bell
Starring Peter Sallis, Frank Thornton and Keith Clifford
All-film Super16 widescreen programmes transmitted in 16x9

1.	The Swan Man of Ilkley (Guest Bobby Ball)	13/03/2005	6.15p.m	237	AJW192
2.	Watching the Clock	20/03/2005	6.15p.m	238	AJW193
3.	Has Anyone Seen a Peruvian Wart?	27/03/2005	6.15p.m	239	AJW194
4.	Hermione (the short course)	10/04/2005	6.15p.m	240	AJW195
5.	Who's That Mouse at the Poetry Group?	17/04/2005	6.15p.m	241	AJW196
6.	Available for Weddings	24/04/2005	6.15p.m	242	AJW197
7.	The McDonaghs of Jamieson Street	01/05/2005	6:25p.m	243	AJW198
8.	The Afterthoughts of a Co-op Manager	08/05/2005	6:05p.m	244	AJW199
9.	Lot Number Eight	15/05/2005	6:20p.m	245	AJW200
10.	Little Orphan Howard	29/05/2005	6:15p.m	246	AJW201

CHRISTMAS SPECIAL 2005

Made in 2005 as part of AB series. Producer/Director Alan J.W. Bell
Captured in High Definition 16x9 with Sony HD 75 camera

Merry Entwistle and Jackson Day	18/12/2005	20.00p.m	247	AJW202

TWENTY-SEVENTHSERIES-AB – 200/6

Filmed in 2005 Producer/Director Alan J.W. Bell
Starring Peter Sallis, Frank Thornton, Keith Clifford, Brian Murphy and Kathy Staff
Shot in High Definition 16X9 with Sony HD 75 camera

1.	Follow That Bottle	05/03/2006		248	AJW203
2.	How to Remove a Cousin	12/03/2006	6:15p.m	249	AJW204
3.	Has Anyone Seen Barry's Midlife Crisis?	19/03/2006	6:15p.m	250	AJW205
4.	The Genuine Outdoors Robin Hood Barbi	26/03/2006	6:20p.m	251	AJW206
5.	Barry in Danger from Reading and Aunt Jessie	02/04/2006	6:20p.m	252	AJW207
6.	Who's That Merry Man with Billy, Then? (Guest Valerie Leon)	09/04/2006	6:20p.m	253	AJW208
7.	Who's That Talking to Lennie? (Guest Bobby Ball)	16/04/2006	6.25p.m.	254	AJW209
8.	Oh, Look! Mitzi's Found Her Mummy.	23/04/2006	6:20p.m	255	AJW210
9.	Plenty of Room in the Back	07/05/2006	6:05p.m	256	AJW211

CHRISTMAS SPECIAL 2006
Filmed in Aug/Oct 2006 with VIPER HD Camera
Starring Peter Sallis, Peter Sallis, Frank Thornton, Brian Murphy and Kathy Staff

A Tale of Two Sweaters (30min)	28/12/06	6:30p.m	257	AJW212
Music Nigel Hess				

TWENTY-EIGHTH SERIES – AC – 2007
Filmed in 2006 – with VIPER HD Camera
Starring Peter Sallis, Frank Thornton, Brian Murphy and Kathy Staff

1. The Second Stag Night of Doggie Wilkinson (Guest Eric Sykes)
       15/07/2007   6:20p.m   258   AJW213
2. What Happened to the Horse?   29/07/2007   6:05p.m   259   AJW214
3. Variations on a Theme of Road Rage   05/08/2007   7:05p.m   260   AJW215
4. In Which Howard gets Double Booked   12/08/2007   6:30p.m   261   AJW216
5. Will the Nearest Alien Please Come In.   19/08/2007   6:30p.m   262   AJW217
6. Elegy to Small Creature and Track Bike**   26/08/2007   6:30p.m   263   AJW218
7. The Crowcroft Challenge**   02/09/2007   6:30p.m   264   AJW219
8. Must be Good Dancer**   09/09/2007   7:10p.m   265   AJW220
9. In Which Howard Remembers Where He Left his Bicycle Pump**
       16/09/2007   6:05p.m   266   AJW221
10. Sinclair and the Wormley Witches**   23/09/2007   6:30p.m   267   AJW222

** Music by NIGEL HESS

CHRISTMAS SPECIAL 2007
Filmed in June/|Aug/Oct 2007 with VIPER HD Camera
Starring Peter Sallis, Frank Thornton, Brian Murphy and Kathy Staff
Cannon and Ball

Get Out Of That! (29min)				
Additional Music by JIM PARKER	31/08/2008	7:05p.m	268	AJW223

TWENTY-NINTH SERIES – AD – 2006/7
Filmed in 2007– with VIPER HD Camera
Starring Peter Sallis, Frank Thornton, Brian Murphy and Kathy Staff

1. Enter The Finger (Guest Brian Conley)   22/06/2008   6:35p.m   269   AJW224
2. Would the Genuine Racer Please Come In   29/06/2008   6.00p.m.   270   AJW225
3. A Short Introduction to Cooper's Rules   06/07/2008   7:00p.m   271   AJW226
4. Will Jeremy Be Quite Safe?(Guest John Challis)   13/07/2008   5:05p.m   272   AJW227
5. All That Glitters Is Not Elvis (Guests Kenneth Cope Maggie Ollerenshaw)
       20/07/2008   7:10p.m   273   AJW228
6. Eva's Back In Town (Guest ShirleyAnne Field)   27/07/2008   6:40p.m   274   AJW229
7. In Which Love Isn't Dead – JustIncompetent (Guest Tyler Butterworth)
       03/08/2008   6:05p.m   275   AJW230
8. The Mischievous Tinkle In Howard's Eyes   10/08/2008   5:30p.m   276   AJW231
9. Of Passion and Pizza (Guest Philip Fox)   17/08/2008   6:00p.m   277   AJW232
10. It's Never Ten Years   24/08/2008   7:10p.m   278   AJW233

CHRISTMAS SPECIAL 2008
Filmed in June/|Aug/Oct 2008 with VIPER HD Camera
Starring Russ Abbot, Brian Murphy, Burt Kwouk, Peter Sallis and Frank Thornton

I was a Hitman for Primrose Dairies (29min)	31/12/08	279	AJW234

THIRTIETH SERIES – AE – 2008/9
Filmed in 2008– with VIPER HD Camera
Starring Russ Abbot, Brian Murphy, Burt Kwouk, Peter Sallis and Frank Thornton

1.	Some Adventures of the Inventor of the Mother Stitch	19/04/2009	280	AJW235
2.	The Mother of All Mistakes – Or is it?	26/04/2009	281	AJW236
3.	Will Howard Cross the Atlantic Single-Handed?	03/05/2009	282	AJW237
4.	Who's That Looking Sideways at Nelly?	10/05/2009	283	AJW238
5.	Nobody Messes with Tony the Throat	17/05/2009	284	AJW239
6.	Will Stella Find True Love with Norris Fairburn?	24/05/2009	285	AJW240
7.	Will Randolph Make a Good Impression?	31/05/2009	286	AJW241
8.	In Which Romance Springs a Leak	07/06/2009	287	AJW242
9.	Variations on a Theme of Fathers Day	14/06/2009	288	AJW243
10.	Goodnight Sweet Ferret Guest (Peter Baldwin)	21/06/2009	289	AJW244

THIRTY-FIRST SERIES – AF 2009 – 2010
Filmed 17th August – 5th October 2009 with VIPER HD Camera

1.	Behind Every Bush There Is Not Necessarily a Howard	25/07/10	290	AJW245
2.	Happy Camping	01/08/10	291	AJW246
3.	The Rights of Man (Except for Howard)	08/08/10	292	AJW247
4.	Howard and the Great Outdoors	15/08/10	293	AJW248
5.	Look Who's Wheel's Come Off	22/08/10	294	AJW249
6.	How Not to Cry At Weddings	28/08/10	295	AJW250

Statistics:

James Gilbert 7 Episodes
Bernard Thompson 7 Episodes
Sydney Lotterby 31 Episodes
Alan J.W. Bell 250 Episodes
Ronnie Hazlehurst 262 Episodes
Nigel Hess 6 Episodes
Roy Clarke 295 Episodes
Peter Sallis 296 Episodes
Bill Owen 185 Episodes
Michael Bates 14 Episodes
Brian Wilde 117 Episodes
Michael Aldridge 30 Episodes
Frank Thornton 135 Episodes
Russ Abbot 16 Episodes
Kathy Staff 255 Episodes
Jane Freeman 263 Episodes
Thora Hird 159 Episodes

Jean Alexander 177 Episodes
Mike Grady 179 Episodes
Sarah Thomas 216 Episodes
Robert Fyfe 219 Episodes
Juliette Kaplan 219 Episodes
Jean Fergusson 217 Episodes
Keith Clifford 55 Episodes
Trevor Bannister 25 Episodes

Film+Multicamera 105 Episodes
All Film 127 Episodes
All Film TV Movies 3
High Definition 46
Series (inc. pilot) 31
Christmas Specials 22
TV Movies (all film) 3

THANKS

Alan J W Bell would like to thank Charis Bacheller and Clive Eardley for their help and enthusiasm. Thanks to my publisher, Bruce Sachs at Tomahawk Press and also Steve Kirkham who designed the book and Kenneth Bishton for proof reading the manuscript.

And special thanks to Roy Clarke for his permission to use the title *Last of the Summer Wine* and extracts from his scripts, and for giving me something worthwhile to write about.

ABOUT THE AUTHOR

It was the whir of film running through a camera that attracted Alan J W Bell to the business of film-making: He had a disrupted education due, initially to the war, and then the early loss of his father, which resulted in the family moving from London to Scotland. Aware of the advanced standard of Scottish education, and conscious of his inadequacy at bridging the gap, he found himself seeking solace around the attractive coastline of Fife. Drawn to the wonders of film-making through a friendship with a local headmaster's son (Ernest Mackie, who had a cine camera), together, they turned out epics which invariably, featured people falling over cliffs and meeting sudden, gory deaths.

Alan's interest in film was to be encouraged by the BBC who advertised for people with a strong interest in film to join its burgeoning film department at the very bottom as a Film Assistants Class 2. Within two years, he was making short films to replace the over-used and monotonous 'Windmill' and 'Potters Wheel' interlude films. It wasn't long before Alan became a Film Editor, working on drama and entertainment programmes. It was when he became a Light Entertainment Production Assistant in 1968 that he found his true calling. Directing inserts for Morecambe and Wise, and taking over as producer and director of the renowned *Crackerjack* series, gave him the foundations to direct Michael Palin's *Ripping Yarns*, and the television version of *The HitchHiker's Guide to the Galaxy*, which he also produced. It was obvious to the then Light Entertainment hierarchy that there was one programme that would fit Alan's talents down to the ground – and that was *Last of the Summer Wine*. And they were right.